ENLIGHTENED EMPIRICISM

A far cry, this, from old epistemology. Yet it is no gratuitous change of subject matter, but an enlightened persistence rather in the original epistemological problem. It is enlightened in recognizing that the skeptical challenge springs from science itself, and that in coping with it we are free to use scientific knowledge. The old epistemologist failed to recognize the strength of his position.

—W. V. Quine, *The Roots of Reference*

Roger F. Gibson, Jr.

ENLIGHTENED EMPIRICISM

An Examination of W. V. Quine's
Theory of Knowledge

UNIVERSITY PRESSES OF FLORIDA
University of South Florida Press / Tampa

Library of Congress Cataloging in Publication Data
Gibson, Roger F., Jr.
  Enlightened empiricism.

  Bibliography: p.
  Includes index.
  1. Quine, W. V. (Willard Van Orman)—Contributions
in theory of knowledge. 2. Knowledge, Theory of—
History—20th century. I. Title.
B945.Q54G49 1988   121'.092'4   87-21585
ISBN 0-8130-0886-7 (alk. paper)

University Presses of Florida is the central agency for scholarly publishing of the State of Florida's university system. Its offices are located at 15 NW 15th Street, Gainesville, FL 32603. Works published by University Presses of Florida are evaluated and selected for publication by a faculty editorial committee at any one of Florida's nine public universities: Florida A&M University (Tallahassee), Florida Atlantic University (Boca Raton), Florida International University (Miami), Florida State University (Tallahassee), University of Central Florida (Orlando), University of Florida (Gainesville), University of North Florida (Jacksonville), University of South Florida (Tampa), University of West Florida (Pensacola).

A list of publishers who have granted permission to reproduce copyrighted material in this volume appears on page 192.

Copyright © 1988 by the Board of Regents of the State of Florida

Printed in U.S.A on acid-free paper

To Sharon, Pyewacket, and Widget

CONTENTS

Foreword by Dagfinn Føllesdal	ix
List of Abbreviations	xi
Preface	xv
Introduction	xvii
1. Quine's Philosophy: A Systematic Overview	1
2. Holism, Realism, and Naturalized Epistemology	23
3. Naturalized Epistemology Reconsidered	53
4. Analyticity Reconsidered	85
5. Indeterminacy, Underdetermination, and Facts of the Matter	102
6. Ontological Relativity	132
7. Quine on Ethics	155
Afterword	177
Notes	179
References	181
Index	187

FOREWORD

by Dagfinn Føllesdal

As lucid and lively a writer as Quine might seem to need no expositors. And yet the many failures by critics to grasp what he is up to cry out for presentations that adopt new perspectives and emphasize points that get overlooked. Roger Gibson's *The Philosophy of W. V. Quine* did this admirably, and the present volume succeeds even better at closing in upon the core of Quine's thought.

This core is Quine's naturalism: philosophy is natural science trained upon itself; there is no first philosophy, no external vantage point. In particular, this holds for epistemology: epistemology is contained in natural science, as a chapter of empirical psychology, and yet it is epistemology that provides an account of the evidential bases of natural science, including empirical psychology itself. As Gibson expresses it (using "ontology" for "natural science"): epistemology and ontology contain one another.

This governing idea of Gibson's book helps to provide a proper understanding of many other intricate and often misunderstood points in Quine—notably, the difference between the indeterminacy of translation and the underdetermination of our theory of nature, ontological relativity, and Quine's special kind of realism.

Briefly, our theory of nature aims at "full coverage." It settles, for the present, what are the facts of the matter. If two translation manuals are compatible with all these facts, the choice between these manuals does not concern matters of fact. Ontological relativity, too, turns on differences between natural science and other enterprises; such relativity becomes apparent when we do translation and epistemology, but not when we do ontology—that is, natural science. Reality, or factuality, and truth are internal to our theory of nature. As Quine puts it in "Things and Their Place in Theories": " . . . it is within science itself, and not in some prior philosophy, that reality is to be identified and described."

We could press further and ask why our theory of nature has this factual character. One reason may be that our theory of nature is an outgrowth of our everyday conception of the world around us. Unlike Stroud, as quoted by Gibson, I do not think that "I know what all my beliefs about the world are." Our conception of the world is like an iceberg: largely submerged and invisible. It is a web of "beliefs" that we rarely think about and have not acquired in any conscious or willful way. So, these beliefs did not arise through a decision to believe. Our beliefs are about a world that we cannot help believing in. Science's connection with these beliefs—its umbilical cord—gives it its "ontological" character and makes it deal with truth and reality. No more ultimate tribunal exists and none is needed.

Oslo, January 1988

LIST OF ABBREVIATIONS

Works by W. V. Quine

EC   "Empirical Content." In *Theories and Things*, 24–30. Cambridge: Harvard University Press, 1981.

EN   "Epistemology Naturalized." In *Ontological Relativity and Other Essays*, 69–90. New York: Columbia University Press, 1969.

FME   "Five Milestones of Empiricism." In *Theories and Things*, 67–72. Cambridge: Harvard University Press, 1981.

GT   "Grades of Theoreticity." In *Experience and Theory*, edited by L. Foster and J. Swanson, 1–17. Amherst: University of Massachusetts Press, 1970.

IR   "Intensions Revisited." In *Theories and Things*, 113–23. Cambridge: Harvard University Press, 1981.

LPG   "Letter to Professor Grunbaum." In *Can Theories Be Refuted? Essays on the Duhem-Quine Thesis*, edited by S. Harding, 132. Dordrecht, Holland: D. Reidel Publishing Company, 1976.

NK   "Natural Kinds." In *Ontological Relativity and Other Essays*, 114–38. New York: Columbia University Press, 1969.

NMV   "On the Nature of Moral Values." In *Theories and Things*, 55–66. Cambridge: Harvard University Press, 1981.

NNK "The Nature of Natural Knowledge." In *Mind and Language,* edited by S. Guttenplan, 67–81. Oxford: Clarendon Press, 1975.

OEES "On Empirically Equivalent Systems of the World." *Erkenntnis* 9 (1975): 313–28.

OIR "Ontology and Ideology Revisited." *Journal of Philosophy* 80 (1983): 499–502.

OR "Ontological Relativity." In *Ontological Relativity and Other Essays,* 26–68. New York: Columbia University Press, 1969.

OWTI "On What There Is." In *From a Logical Point of View,* 1–19. 2d ed. rev., paperback. Cambridge: Harvard University Press, 1980.

PPE "The Pragmatists' Place in Empiricism." In *Pragmatism: Its Sources and Prospects,* edited by R. Mulvaney and P. Zeltner, 21–39. Columbia: University of South Carolina Press, 1981.

PPLT "Philosophical Progress in Language Theory." *Metaphilosophy* 1 (1970): 2–19.

R "Responses." In *Theories and Things,* 173–86. Cambridge: Harvard University Press, 1981.

RA "Relativism and Absolutism." *The Monist* 67 (1984): 293–96.

RC "Reply to Chomsky." In *Words and Objections: Essays on the Work of W. V. Quine,* edited by D. Davidson and J. Hintikka, 302–11. Dordrecht, Holland: D. Reidel Publishing Company, 1969.

RCP "Reply to Charles D. Parsons." In *The Philosophy of W. V. Quine,* edited by L. Hahn and P. Schilpp, 396–403. La Salle, Ill.: Open Court, 1986.

REE "Replies to the Eleven Essays." *Philosophical Topics* 12 (1981): 227–43.

RG "Reply to Roger F. Gibson, Jr." In *The Philosophy of W. V. Quine,* edited by L. Hahn and P. Schilpp, 155–57. La Salle, Ill.: Open Court, 1986.

RH "Reply to Geoffrey Hellman." In *The Philosophy of W. V. Quine,* edited by L. Hahn and P. Schilpp, 206–8. La Salle, Ill.: Open Court, 1986.

RIT "On the Reasons for Indeterminacy of Translation." *Journal of Philosophy* 67 (1970): 179–83.

RL	"Reply to Harold N. Lee." In *The Philosophy of W. V. Quine,* edited by L. Hahn and P. Schilpp, 315–18. La Salle, Ill.: Open Court, 1986.
RM	"Reference and Modality." In *From a Logical Point of View,* 139–59. 2d ed. rev., paperback. Cambridge: Harvard University Press, 1980.
RN	"Reply to Robert Nozick." In *The Philosophy of W. V. Quine,* edited by L. Hahn and P. Schilpp, 364–67. La Salle, Ill.: Open Court, 1986.
ROD	"Russell's Ontological Development." In *Theories and Things,* 73–85. Cambridge: Harvard University Press, 1981.
RP	"Reply to Hilary Putnam." In *The Philosophy of W. V. Quine,* edited by L. Hahn and P. Schilpp, 427–31. La Salle, Ill.: Open Court, 1986.
RPR	"Reply to Paul A. Roth." In *The Philosophy of W. V. Quine,* edited by L. Hahn and P. Schilpp, 459–61. La Salle, Ill.: Open Court, 1986.
RR	*The Roots of Reference.* La Salle, Ill.: Open Court, 1974.
RS	"Reply to Smart." In *Words and Objections: Essays on the Work of W. V. Quine,* edited by D. Davidson and J. Hintikka, 292–94. Dordrecht, Holland: D. Reidel Publishing Company, 1969.
RTS	"Reply to Stroud." *Midwest Studies in Philosophy* 6 (1981): 473–75.
RV	"Reply to Jules Vuillemin." In *The Philosophy of W. V. Quine,* edited by L. Hahn and P. Schilpp, 619–22. La Salle, Ill.: Open Court, 1986.
RW	"Reply to Morton White." In *The Philosophy of W. V. Quine,* edited by L. Hahn and P. Schilpp, 663–65. La Salle, Ill.: Open Court, 1986.
SS	"Sticks and Stones; Or the Ins and Outs of Existence." In *On Nature,* edited by L. Rouner, 13–26. Notre Dame, Ind.: University of Notre Dame Press, 1984.
SSS	"The Sensory Support of Science." Typescript read at Washington University, St. Louis, Mo., April 22, 1986.
TDE	"Two Dogmas of Empiricism." In *From a Logical Point of View,* 20–46. 2d ed. rev., paperback. Cambridge: Harvard University Press, 1980.

TL *The Time of My Life: An Autobiography.* Cambridge: M.I.T. Press, 1985.
TPT "Things and Their Place in Theories." In *Theories and Things,* 1–23. Cambridge: Harvard University Press, 1981.
UPM "Use and Its Place in Meaning." In *Theories and Things,* 43–54. Cambridge: Harvard University Press, 1981.
VITD "On the Very Idea of a Third Dogma." In *Theories and Things,* 38–42. Cambridge: Harvard University Press, 1981.
WB (with J. S. Ullian). *The Web of Belief.* 2d ed. New York: Random House, 1978.
WIB "What I Believe." In *What I Believe,* edited by M. Booth, 69–75. London: Waterstone, 1984.
WO *Word and Object.* 1960. Reprint. Cambridge: M.I.T. Press, 1970.

PREFACE

A premise of this book, and a justification for its existence, is that Quine's philosophy is not well understood by most philosophers, not even by some of those who have spent considerable time studying Quine's writings. This contentious fact is somewhat surprising since Quine has been publishing philosophy for over fifty years, and his writings are neither mystical nor cryptic. This is not to say that his ideas are always clearly expressed and simple. But whatever unclarity or complexity occurs in his thinking is insufficient to explain the fact that his philosophy is so ill understood by most philosophers. How, then, is this to be accounted for? Alas, one reason is that in the present climate of the world of academic philosophers success sometimes depends more than it should upon amassing publications. And, as failure to comprehend begets criticism, so criticism begets publications. (Thus are the journals full of uncomprehending essays on Quine.) Another reason is that only lately have students of Quine's philosophy come to the realization that Quine-the-paradigmatic-analytic-philosopher is also Quine-the-paradigmatic-systematic-philosopher; a piecemeal treatment of Quine's thought therefore will not do. Finally, but very importantly, students of Quine's thought have failed to appreciate just how thoroughly naturalistic his philosophy is. Thus, again, have they been led into misunderstandings of his views. Quine himself seems to concur with this assessment of the matter: "Gibson has plausibly surmised that the major obstacle to understanding my position is a failure to take my commitment to naturalism seriously" (RN, 367).

As desirable as it might be, altering the philosophical community's method of measuring success is beyond my powers. However, in the following pages, I shall strive to alleviate the other two sources of misinterpretation of Quine's thought: failure to perceive Quine as a systematic philosopher, and failure to appreciate the scope of Quine's commitment to naturalism.

Acknowledgments

This book is parasitic upon my earlier book (Gibson 1982, 1986), as readers of that book will soon see. Thus, I acknowledge again the help and support of all those persons who were named in its acknowledgments. In addition, I would like to thank my anthropologist friend, Ray Scupin, for many valuable hours spent discussing Quine's philosophy, and the students and colleagues who attended my graduate seminar on Quine at Washington University in the spring of 1986; they helped me immensely to get my thoughts straight on Quine's philosophy. Also, I want to thank Professor Quine for coming to St. Louis to attend my seminar, answer questions, and present a paper. His generosity knows no bounds! Finally, I would like to thank the National Endowment for the Humanities, which supported this project for a year through a Fellowship for College Teachers, and Washington University, which supported the project for a summer through a Faculty Research Grant.

INTRODUCTION

In a previous book (Gibson 1982), I presented Quine's philosophy as a systematic attempt to answer, from a uniquely empiricistic point of view, what Quine takes to be the central question of epistemology, viz., 'How do we acquire our theory of the world and why does it work so well?'. The picture of Quine that emerged from that undertaking—Quine the systematic epistemologist—is, I believe, both surprising and accurate. It is surprising because it contrasts markedly with the theretofore predominant picture of Quine the logician and sometime essayist. Its accuracy may be less obvious because many philosophers who call themselves epistemologists do something quite different from what my picture of Quine paints him as doing. The epistemologists I have in mind are those who concern themselves with providing a set of necessary and sufficient conditions for knowledge, such as, for example, S knows that p if and only if (1) p is true, (2) S believes that p, (3) S is justified in believing that p, and (4) S's justification for believing that p is indefeasible.

It certainly must be granted that Quine is not attempting to ascertain the set of necessary and sufficient conditions for the truth of such claims as 'S knows that p':

> Knowledge, nearly enough, is true belief on strong evidence. How strong? There is no significant cut off point. 'Know' is

like 'big': useful and unobjectionable in the vernacular where we acquiesce in vagueness, but unsuited to technical use because of lacking a precise boundary. Epistemology, or the theory of knowledge, blushes for its name. (RA, 295)

Even so, there is no good reason for concluding that because Quine offers no theory of the necessary and sufficient conditions for '*S* knows that *p*' he therefore has no theory of knowledge.

At worst, the issue is predicated on the fallacy of persuasive definition; at best, the issue is a mere quibble. Thus, it is resolvable either by pointing out the fallacy or by giving the necessary-and-sufficient theorists the terms 'theory of knowledge' and 'epistemology' in their *strict* sense and giving people like Quine the terms 'theory of knowledge' and 'epistemology' in their *broad* sense. In the interests of both logic and the nonproliferation of technical philosophical terms, I prefer the former resolution of the issue.

Moreover, I believe that there is a fruitful connection between epistemology in the *strict* sense and epistemology in the *broad* sense. The majority of recent attempts at providing necessary and sufficient conditions for knowledge have hypostatized a fourth condition for knowledge. And analyses of these proffered fourth conditions have regularly relied upon current scientific theories of human perceptual mechanisms and psychological processes. In this way, epistemology in the *strict* sense has opened the door for epistemology in the *broad* (naturalistic) sense.

There remains, however, a substantial question concerning what to count as epistemology. The substantive dispute is over the question of whether *naturalized* epistemology is *really* epistemology. This substantive dispute arises in two ways. First, it arises from the fact that *real* epistemology (i.e., traditional epistemology) is normative, whereas naturalized epistemology is purely descriptive. It also arises from the fact that traditional epistemology attempts to answer the question 'How is knowledge possible?', whereas naturalized epistemology either does not attempt to answer this question or attempts to do so but must fail. Both sources of this dispute are examined in these pages.

The general plan of the book is as follows:

Chapter 1 is a revised version of "A New Perspective on Quine" (Gibson 1983). Also, it borrows liberally from the first three chapters of *The Philosophy of W. V. Quine: An Expository Essay* (Gibson 1982). It provides a systematic overview of the major features of Quine's philosophy, highlighting its epistemological motivation. Many of the doctrines and theses to be discussed in later chapters are introduced in this chapter.

Chapter 2 shows how Quine argues for naturalized epistemology, assesses his argument, and examines his contention that epistemology and ontology reciprocally contain one another. Parts of this chapter are taken from "Quine on Naturalism and Epistemology" (Gibson 1987) and "Translation, Physics, and Facts of the Matter" (Gibson 1986b).

Chapter 3 examines the two sources of the substantive dispute over whether naturalized epistemology really is epistemology, viz., the assertion that naturalized epistemology is descriptive (while traditional epistemology is normative) and the argument that naturalized epistemology either cannot or does not answer the question of how knowledge is possible (while traditional epistemology can and does answer the question). Parts of this chapter are taken from "Stroud and Naturalized Epistemology" (Gibson, forthcoming b).

Chapter 4 offers yet another analysis of Quine's argument against analyticity and of Strawson and Grice's defense of the notion.

Chapter 5 attempts to make clear Quine's distinction between indeterminacy of translation and underdetermination of physical theory, and why there is a fact of the matter to the latter but not to the former. It also attempts to determine whether Quine's indeterminacy thesis is logically independent of his commitment to behaviorism. Parts of this chapter are taken from "Quine's Dilemma" (Gibson 1986a) and "Translation, Physics, and Facts of the Matter" (Gibson 1986b).

Chapter 6 aims at clarifying and defending Quine's doctrine of ontological relativity. The first few paragraphs of this chapter are borrowed from *The Philosophy of W. V. Quine: An Expository Essay* (Gibson 1982).

Chapter 7 examines Quine's views on the nature and origin of moral values. It focuses on his claims that ethics is epistemologically infirm as compared to science, and it defends this claim against some philosophers who have had their doubts about it. This chapter incorporates material from "Flanagan on Quinean Ethics" (Gibson, forthcoming a).

Quine's Philosophy:
A Systematic Overview

CHAPTER 1

§1.1 *Introduction*

Willard Van Orman Quine (b. 1908) has rarely been characterized either by his critics or by his commentators as a *systematic* philosopher. I shall not speculate on the reasons why this is so, but I do believe it is unfortunate, because Quine *is* a systematic philosopher, and failure to recognize this fact can lead to misunderstandings and misinterpretations of his views.

In this chapter I shall sketch a reading of Quine that highlights the systematic character of his philosophy. My thesis is that his philosophy is best understood as a systematic attempt to answer, from a uniquely empiricistic point of view, what he regards as the central question of epistemology, namely, 'How do we acquire our theory of the world and why does it work so well?'.

§1.2 *The naturalistic-behavioristic thesis*

The reading of Quine that I am advocating focuses on what I have elsewhere (Gibson 1980 and 1982) dubbed the naturalistic-behavioristic thesis (NB thesis) of language. The thesis is naturalistic in that it makes the study of language accessible to empirical investigation, and it is behavioristic in that it relies upon behavior as the substance of observable data. This thesis is expressed in countless places in Quine's writings; here are four instances:

> (1) "Language is a social art. In acquiring it we have to depend entirely on intersubjectively available cues as to what to say and when" (WO, ix).
>
> (2) "Language is a social art which we all acquire on the evidence solely of other people's overt behavior under publicly recognizable circumstances" (OR, 26).
>
> (3) "A language is mastered through social emulation and social feedback, and these controls ignore any idiosyncrasy in an individual's imagery or associations that is not discovered in his behavior" (PPLT, 4).
>
> (4) "Language is socially inculcated and controlled; the inculcation and control turn strictly on the keying of sentences to shared stimulation. Internal factors may vary *ad libitum* without prejudice to communication as long as the keying of language to external stimuli is undisturbed" (EN, 81).

The NB thesis may be construed both substantively and heuristically. It is *substantive* insofar as it makes a factual claim about the (behavioral) parameters of the language-learning context: language is learned by emulating the verbal behavior of members of the linguistic community. It is *heuristic* insofar as it proscribes the development of mentalistic theories of language learning and linguistic meaning: any underlying psychological mechanisms of language learning and any "meaning" not discoverable behaviorally may be safely ignored.

The new perspective on Quine that I am sketching establishes the NB thesis as the central axiom of his entire systematic philosophy.[1] On the basis of the NB thesis, Quine develops his NB conception of language, which consists of his theory of language learning and his theory of linguistic meaning. Furthermore, Quine's NB conception of language provides him with the constraints, or framework, within which he articulates his response to the central question of epistemology: 'How do we acquire our theory of the world and why does it work so well?'. It is imperative, therefore, that we examine the NB conception of language.

§1.2.1 *Language learning*

Quine's behavioral *theory of language learning* consists of a number of substantive claims about the methods and psychological mechanisms involved in language learning. These claims are best viewed as empirical hypotheses, some of which are of an idealized and highly speculative sort. There are, according to Quine, two general methods of language learning (ignoring the method of giving definitions) employed by a child learning his first language: ostension and analogic synthesis. Ostension is the initial method of his learning and is generally known among psychologists as direct conditioning. The child begins by observing and imitating the behavior of other language users as it occurs amid publicly recognizable circumstances. In such circumstances the child learns to associate sentences *as unstructured wholes* with appropriate verbal stimulations. In short, the child learns (by induction) the ranges of stimulus conditions (similarity bases) that in some sense determine the correct use of various expressions. Such learning, Quine claims, approximates the classical process of reinforcement and extinction of responses. Moreover, he claims that the dimensions of the innate structure presupposed by the process of conditioning can, in principle, be ascertained through techniques of operant conditioning (i.e., conditioned response, stimulus generalization, experimental extinction, and so on).

Unfortunately, however, the method of ostension (direct conditioning) does not carry the child very far in his learning, since most sentences he learns are not tied, even derivatively, to any fixed ranges of nonverbal stimulation. How, then, does the child learn to formulate and appropriately respond to such sentences? Quine's answer to this question is that the greater part of language is learned by way of analogic synthesis. Parts of sentences already learned are linked together to build new sentences, the function and placement of those parts being determined by analogy with their function and placement in previous sentences. These previous sentences themselves may have been learned by ostension or by earlier analogic synthesis. However, the important thing about analogic synthesis is that it involves irreducible leaps of analogy which, if traced backward, will not reveal a smooth derivation of theoretical language (i.e., referential language) from observational language (i.e., unstructured sentences directly conditioned to nonverbal stimulation). While psycholinguists do have some understanding of the mechanisms at work in the ostensive method of sentence learning, virtually nothing is known about the psychological mechanisms underlying analogic synthesis. Nevertheless, as part of his commitment to the NB thesis Quine maintains that "[w]hatever the best eventual theory regarding the inner mechanism of language may turn out to be, it is bound to conform to the behavioral character of language learning: the dependence of verbal behavior on observation of verbal behavior" (PPLT, 4).

§1.2.2 *Scientific semantics*

Quine develops the other component of his NB conception of language, a *theory of meaning,* or scientific semantics, by marrying a behavioristic classification of sentences to a behavioristic conception of meaning: stimulus meaning. Quine's classification of sentences is subservient to his epistemological quest for an adequate account of how we acquire our theory of the world; consequently, it pertains only to those sentences that are either true or false. He divides such sentences into two classes: occasion sentences and standing sentences. Occasion sentences are further divided into observation and nonobservation (occasion) sentences; standing sentences are further divided into eternal and noneternal (standing) sentences. Quine draws these distinctions among sentences in a clearly behavioristic manner. For example, an *occasion sentence* is a sentence that would elicit an affirmative or negative response only if some prompting (usually nonverbal) stimulus were present, e.g., 'This is my father'. An occasion sentence to which everyone in the speech community would respond affirmatively (or negatively) under like stimulation Quine calls an *observation sentence,* e.g., 'The cat is on the mat'. A *standing sentence* is a sentence that would elicit affirmation or negation each time it is presented, without further prompting by some (usually nonverbal) stimulus, e.g., 'Today is Friday'. A standing sentence that remains true or false for all time Quine calls an *eternal sentence,* e.g., 'Copper conducts electricity'.

The *stimulus meaning* of a sentence for a speaker at a time also is defined behavioristically by Quine. A stimulation *a* is said to belong to what Quine calls the *affirmative stimulus meaning* of a sentence *S* for a given speaker if and only if there is a stimulation *a'* such that if the speaker were given *a'*, and were asked *S*, then were given *a* and were asked *S* again, he would dissent the first time and assent the second. *Negative stimulus meaning* can be defined similarly, interchanging 'assent' and 'dissent'. Stimulus meaning of a sentence for a speaker at a time is the ordered pair of the two.

We shall not pause to recount the myriad details of Quine's scientific semantics, since my aim here is merely to indicate that Quine's NB conception of language is conditioned by the NB thesis.[2] (We will call up the details when needed.) My present point is not that the details of Quine's theories of language learning and linguistic meaning are wholly dictated by the NB thesis, but only that the general behavioristic orientation of these theories is in accord with the NB thesis. Assuming that this has been established, we must now show that Quine's conception of language provides a *framework for appreciating* the systematic unity of his discursive philosophy.

§1.3 *The genetic approach*

I claimed earlier that Quine's philosophy is best understood as an attempt to answer, in an empirically responsible way, the central question of epistemology, namely, 'How do we acquire our theory of the world and why does it work so well?'. Since, in Quine's view, scientific conceptualization is inseparable from language, the various theories comprising our overall theory of the world could be regarded as systems of sentences. Consequently, the central problem of epistemology is one of giving an account of the relationship between our theoretical *talk* and our observations.

But how are we to construe our observations? Being sensory, they are subjective; yet when observations must be taken into account in the contexts of language learning and assessing evidence, it is crucial that those observations be accessible to the relevant linguistic community. On the other hand, nothing is gained if we construe observations simply as shared environmental circumstances, for in this latter case we cannot presume intersubjective agreement about the environing situation. This is because two people will assess the environing situation differently if they notice different features and/or hold different theories. Quine suggests a solution to this difficulty by recommending that observations be handled as follows:

> It consists in talking neither of sensation nor of environing situation, but of language: talking of language at the observational end no less than at the theoretical end. I do not suggest that observations themselves are something verbal, but I propose that we drop the talk of observation and talk instead of observation sentences, the sentences that are said to report observations: sentences like 'This is red', 'This is a rabbit'. No matter that sensations are private, and no matter that men may take radically different views of the environing situation; the observation *sentence* serves nicely to pick out what witnesses can agree on. (RR, 39)

In light of the above, the central problem of epistemology becomes one of giving an account of the relation between our theoretical *talk* and our observational *talk*, i.e., between the sentences learned by analogic synthesis and the sentences learned by ostension. This relation has two aspects, an evidential one and a semantical one. According to Quine, the two are isomorphic: "The channels by which, having learned observation sentences, we acquire theoretical language, are the very channels by which observation lends evidence to scientific theory" (NNK, 74).

Thus, the central epistemological problem of accounting for the link between theory and observation has two aspects, expressed by the following two questions: (1) how is it that one sentence can serve as evidence for another? and (2) how do sentences acquire whatever meanings they can be said to have? The answers to both of these questions begin with the roles that observation sentences play in providing both evidential support and meaning for the other kinds of sentences in theories. Observation sentences play an *evidential role* in theories because they are the kind of sentences that (by definition) enjoy virtually unanimous acceptance among the members of a particular speech community. Two theorists may disagree about the truth of some theoretical sentence, but they can descend to the level of observation sentences and find a common ground for assessing relevant evidence. (". . . whatever evidence there *is* for science *is* sensory evidence" [EN, 75].)[3] Observation sentences also play a *semantical role* in theories, for although most of language consists of interverbal associations, somewhere there have to be nonverbal reference points, nonverbal circumstances that can be intersubjectively appreciated and associated with appropriate utterances—otherwise language could not be learned along the behavioristic lines that Quine claims. (". . . all inculcation of meanings of words must rest ultimately on sensory evidence" [EN, 75].)[4] Observation sentences are therefore the gateway to language and hence to science—insofar as scientific theories are conceived of as systems of sentences. Moreover, observation sentences are the gateway to Quine's *naturalized epistemology:*

> We see, then, a strategy for investigating the relation of evidential support, between observation and scientific theory. We can adopt a *genetic approach,* studying how theoretical language is learned. For the evidential relation is virtually enacted, it would seem, in the learning. This genetic strategy is attractive because the learning of language goes on in the world and is open to scientific study. It is a strategy for the scientific study of scientific method and evidence. *We have here a good reason to regard the theory of language as vital to the theory of knowledge.* (NNK, 74–75; my italics)

Thus, we may conclude, Quine's NB conception of language, *his* theory of language, is vital to *his* theory of knowledge. It is the framework within which Quine develops his entire systematic philosophy—*his* answer to the central question of epistemology. It is my contention that the NB conception of language *prescribes* the content of almost all of Quine's more important doctrines and theses, by restricting what are to count as acceptable answers to a multitude of philosophical questions. Let us now turn to an examination of the doctrines and theses that comprise Quine's systematic philosophical response to the central question of epistemology.

§1.4 *The Quinian system*

In the early pages of his Dewey Lectures, together entitled "Ontological Relativity," Quine clearly indicates the fundamental importance of the NB conception of language to his philosophy:

8 *Enlightened Empiricism*

> Philosophically I am bound to Dewey by the naturalism that dominated his last three decades. With Dewey I hold that knowledge, mind, and meaning are part of the same world that they had to do with, and that they are to be studied in the same empirical spirit that animates natural science. There is no place for a prior philosophy.
>
> When a naturalistic philosopher addresses himself to the philosophy of mind, he is apt to talk of language. Meanings are, first and foremost, meanings of language. Language is a social art which we all acquire on the evidence solely of other people's overt behavior under publicly recognizable circumstances. Meanings, therefore, those very models of mental entities, end up as grist for the behaviorist's mill. Dewey was explicit on the point: "Meaning . . . is not psychic existence; it is primarily a property of behavior." (OR, 26–27; note omitted)

Once language is understood in this naturalistic way, as a social art to be studied empirically (i.e., behavioristically), it is immediately obvious that there cannot be any validity to the claims that language is private or that meaning is private. Nor can one acquiesce any longer in an uncritical semantics:

> Uncritical semantics is the myth of a museum in which the exhibits are meanings and the words are labels. To switch languages is to change the labels. Now the naturalist's primary objection to this view is not an objection to meanings on account of their being mental entities, though that could be objection enough. The primary objection persists even if we take the labeled exhibits not as mental ideas but as Platonic ideas or even as the denoted concrete objects. Semantics is vitiated by a pernicious mentalism as long as we regard a man's semantics as somehow determinate in his mind beyond what might be implicit in his dispositions to overt behavior. (OR, 27)

Quine argues, in sympathy with Dewey, that when we turn toward a naturalistic view of language and a behavioral view of meaning we (1) give up the museum figure of speech, (2) give up assurance of determinacy with respect to meaning and reference, and (3) recognize that there are no meanings, likenesses, or distinctions of meaning beyond those implicit in people's dispositions to overt behavior.

It is my contention that, fully expanded, these three claims can be shown to amount to the following Quinian doctrines and theses: (a) indeterminacy of translation, (b) inscrutability of reference, (c) ontological relativity, (d) underdetermination of physical theory, (e) revisibility or holism thesis (Duhem-Quine thesis), (f) rejection of intensional objects, including meanings, propositions, attributes, and relations, (g) rejection of synonymy, (h) rejection of the analytic-synthetic distinction, (i) rejection of epistemological reductionism, (j) rejection of quantified modal logic, (k) acceptance of a pragmatic philosophy of science, (l) acceptance of a holistic account of the truth of logic and mathematics, and finally, (m) acceptance of a naturalistic account of morality. (See Gibson 1982 for a more detailed defense of this claim.) We now turn to the task of sketching each of these doctrines and theses.

§1.4.1 *Indeterminacy of translation*

The indeterminacy of translation thesis asserts that "manuals for translating one language into another can be set up in divergent ways, all compatible with the totality of speech dispositions, yet incompatible with one another" (WO, 27); *and* that there is no sense to the question of any one translation being the uniquely correct one. For example, two field linguists, working independently of each other, might set up manuals for translating a foreign language such that the foreign sentence 'S' is translated as 'Cats are divine' by one linguist and as 'Cats are human' by the other. Quine's indeterminacy thesis claims that where both translations are consistent with the speech dispositions of all parties concerned, both are equally justified *and* there is no answer (and therefore no sense) to the question of which of the two translations is uniquely correct. The crucial point is that according to the NB conception of language the linguists have only the behavioral dispositions of the foreigner upon which to base their translations, and if no possible behavioral disposition can settle the question 'What did the foreigner *really* mean by "S"?' then the question is senseless. Quine's way of putting the point is to say that there is *no fact of the matter* to the question of which translation is uniquely correct.

§1.4.2 *Inscrutability of reference*

The doctrine of inscrutability of reference refers to indeterminacy as it applies specifically to the question of reference. For example, a foreigner might assent to (and dissent from) a linguist's query of the foreigner's one-word sentence 'Gavagai' under just those conditions where the (English-speaking) linguist would do likewise to the query of the one-word sentence 'Rabbit'. In other words, the foreigner's stimulus meaning for 'Gavagai' correlates with the linguist's stimulus meaning for 'Rabbit'. But this correlation of behavioral dispositions is insufficient evidence for the linguist to conclude *absolutely* that the foreigner's 'Gavagai' *refers* to rabbits. Perhaps 'Gavagai', if it refers at all, refers to undetached rabbit parts or to rabbithood, and so on. The only way for the linguist to settle such questions is by fixing upon the foreigner's equivalents of English "plural endings, pronouns, numerals, the 'is' of identity, and its adaptations 'same' and 'other'" (OR, 32). These, according to Quine, constitute the cluster of interrelated grammatical particles and constructions with which the individuating of terms of divided reference in English is connected. Unfortunately, however, this very same cluster of grammatical particles and constructions is itself susceptible to the indeterminacy of translation. In short, all the possible behavioral evidence is insufficient for settling absolutely the reference of the foreigner's terms, *and* there is no evidence beyond the behavioral evidence to which the linguist can appeal. This, of course, is just what the NB thesis asserts. Indeterminacy of translation and inscrutability of reference are what Quine has in mind when he says, in his Dewey Lectures, that when we adopt the NB conception of language we give up assurances of determinacy, both of meaning and of reference.

§1.4.3 *Ontological relativity*

The doctrine of ontological relativity claims that it makes no sense to say what the objects of a theory are, beyond saying how to interpret or reinterpret that theory in another; there is no saying *absolutely* what the objects of a theory are. Putting the matter this way suggests that Quine tends to equate ontological relativity with a generalized doctrine of inscrutability of reference. Quine confirms as much when he says: "I do not see what difference there is between the two" (RPR, 459). Recently, however, Quine has chosen to argue for ontological relativity on the basis of what he calls a proxy function, viz., "a rule whereby a unique object of the supposedly new sort is assigned to each of the old objects" (TPT, 19). The argument proceeds as follows:

> [For example,] instead of predicating a general term 'P' of an old object x, saying that x is a P, we reinterpret x as a new object and say that it is the f of a P, where 'f' expresses the proxy function. Instead of saying that x is a dog, we say that x is the lifelong filament of space-time taken up by a dog. Or, really, we just adhere to the old term 'P', 'dog', and reinterpret it as 'f of a P', 'place-time of a dog'. (TPT, 19)

The doctrine of ontological relativity seemingly has the shocking consequence of virtually trivializing ontology; thus:

> It is occasion sentences that report the observations on which science rests. The scientific output is likewise sentential: true sentences, we hope, truths about nature. The objects, or values of variables, serve merely as indices along the way, and we may permute or supplant them as we please as long as the sentence-to-sentence structure is preserved. The scientific system, ontology and all, is a conceptual bridge of our own making, linking sensory stimulation to sensory stimulation. (TPT, 20)

However, ontology is spared trivialization, according to Quine, because of his commitment to naturalism. Questions of existence are to be raised and settled *within* one's scientific theory of the world; there is no higher tribunal.

§1.4.4 *Underdetermination*

The doctrine of underdetermination of theory claims that theories about the world transcend all possible observations of the world, and, further, that different, competing theories can be developed on the same observational basis. In a word, theories can be shown to be logically incompatible with one another, yet empirically equivalent. "This is a point on which I expect wide agreement," says Quine, "if only because the observational criteria of theoretical terms are commonly so flexible and fragmentary" (RIT, 179). The explanation of why the criteria of theoretical terms are as Quine describes them can be found within his account of the way theoretical language is learned, namely, by a series of irreducible, short leaps of analogy taken on bits and pieces of fragmentary evidence (see NNK, 79–80). Thus, the doctrine of underdetermination, too, is shown to be connected with Quine's NB conception of language.

§1.4.5 *Holism*

The holism thesis claims that sentences of a theory are not separately vulnerable to adverse observations, because it is only jointly as a theory that such sentences imply their observable consequences. In other words, the individual sentences of a theory do not usually— observation sentences are exceptions—have unique ranges of confirming and infirming observations associated with them.[5] Thus, we can adhere to any one of the sentences of the theory in the face of adverse observations by revising truth values of other sentences in the theory. For example, a given theory might entail (or predict) that under certain conditions water boils at 212 degrees Fahrenheit. Now suppose we set up an experiment designed to test this claim only to find that our water boiled at 214 degrees Fahrenheit. Have we refuted the hypothesis? Not necessarily, not if we are willing to revise truth values of other sentences in the theory. Perhaps our water is not pure, or some other condition was violated, or our thermometer is faulty, or we simply misread the thermometer. There are any number of ways of saving the hypothesis, for despite appearances it is not the single hypothesis that is being tested, but the theory as a whole.

As was the case with underdetermination of theories, the explanation for why holism occurs is to be sought within Quine's theory of language learning. The child learns the observational part of his language in well-understood ways (i.e., by ostension); and then, by means of analogic synthesis, he must go on to acquire the theoretical part of language. To repeat an earlier point, such learning "is not a continuous derivation, which, followed backward, would en-able us to reduce scientific theory to sheer observation. It is a progress by short leaps of analogy" (NNK, 77–78). No wonder any one of the hypotheses of a theory can be adhered to come what may, for empirical evidence simply cannot be allocated to the individual sentences of a theory in any unique way.

§1.4.6 *Intensions*

Quine's rejection of intensional objects, including meanings, propositions, attributes, and relations, is not a reaction to their being abstract objects. Rather, his concern is, for the most part, that we have no *behavioristic* identity criteria for such objects. How do we know when we have one proposition and when we have two? How do we know when one attribute or relation is different from, or identical with, some other attribute or relation? But at a deeper level, Quine's claim is stronger, for it asserts that because these idioms are *behaviorally indeterminate* there are no answers to such questions. Here, again, it is Quine's commitment to the NB conception of language that shapes his position.

§1.4.7 *Synonymy and analyticity*

Quine's rejections of synonymy and the analytic-synthetic distinction are, in the end, based on the same considerations as his rejection of intensional objects. Again, Quine sees the problem as a lack of behavioristic identity criteria for synonymy and analyticity. In responding to the charge that he demands unreasonably high standards of clarity for any proposed accounts of synonymy and analyticity, Quine replies that he seeks "no more, after all, than a rough characterization in terms of dispositions to verbal behavior" (WO, 207). This remark perhaps better than any other clearly brings to the fore the connection between Quine's rejection of both synonymy and analyticity and his commitment to the NB conception of language. There is also, however, a more tortuous connection via the holism thesis. If the holism thesis is true, i.e., if evidence cannot be allocated to individual (nonobservation) sentences in any unique fashion, then there is no hope of singling out a unique class of such sentences as analytic, i.e., as true come what may. And, as we have noted, the fact that scientific theories are holistic is intimately (if obscurely) connected with the way theoretical language is learned. The connection is obscure because so little is known about the psychological mechanisms of analogic synthesis underlying such learning. Nevertheless, Quine maintains that such learning takes place by innumerable, irreducible leaps of analogy and, as a result, allocating evidence to theoretical sentences in any unique way is rendered impossible (see RN, 364, for speculations on non-Duhemian languages.)

§1.4.8 *Radical reductionism*

According to Quine, radical reductionism, the view that every meaningful statement can be reduced to statements about immediate experience, has been universally abandoned by modern empiricists. Nevertheless, their thought continues to be influenced by a subtler form of epistemological reductionism: "The notion lingers that to each statement, or each synthetic statement, there is associated a unique range of possible sensory events such that the occurrence of any of them would add to the likelihood of truth of the statement, and that there is associated also another unique range of possible sensory events whose occurrence would detract from that likelihood" (TDE, 40–41). However, the plausibility of this form of epistemological reductionism has been scotched by the doctrine of holism. (Recall our water-boiling example.) Quine's holism thesis is an outright denial of this form of reductionism, and, as we noted, Quine's holism thesis is connected with the NB conception of language. Thus, we may conclude that Quine's rejection of epistemological reductionism results from his allegiance to the NB conception of language.

§1.4.9 *Quantified modal logic*

Quine's chief reason for rejecting quantified modal logic is that in order to accept it, one must also accept an untenable doctrine of metaphysical essentialism. In order to grasp the connection between modal logic and essentialism, consider the following modal statement: 'Necessarily x is greater than 7'. Now, suppose the value of *x* is the number 9, then 'Necessarily 9 is greater than 7' appears to be a true instance of the above schema. But now suppose that we choose to designate the number 9 by 'the number of major planets' instead of by '9', then we would produce the following apparently false modal statement: 'Necessarily the number of major planets is greater than 7'. In other words, the same number, 9, is being designated by '9' and 'the number of major planets' in the two statements, and yet they have opposite truth values. But how can this be, for 9 *is* the number of major planets? Here is where essentialism enters the picture. Essentialism is the view that "[a]n object, of itself and by whatever name or none, must be seen as having some of its traits necessarily and others contingently, despite the fact that the latter traits follow just as analytically from some ways of specifying the object as the former traits do from other ways of specifying it" (RM, 155). Are we to conclude, then, that the number 9 has the essential property *designated by* '9' and the contingent property *designated by 'the number of major planets'*? Such a doctrine seems absurd. Consider another example in the same vein given by Quine,

> Perhaps I can evoke the appropriate sense of bewilderment as follows. Mathematicians may conceivably be said to be necessarily rational and not necessarily two-legged; and cyclists necessarily two-legged and not necessarily rational. But what of an individual who counts among his eccentricities both mathematics and cycling? Is this concrete individual necessarily rational and contingently two-legged or vice versa? Just insofar as we are talking referentially of the object, with no special bias toward a background grouping of mathematicians as against cyclists or vice versa, there is no semblance of sense in rating some of his attributes as necessary and others as contingent. Some of his attributes count as important and others as unimportant, yes; some as enduring and others as fleeting; but none as necessary or contingent. (WO, 199)

So accepting quantified modal logic, according to Quine, depends upon also accepting a metaphysical doctrine of essentialism according to which objects possess some of their properties necessarily and others merely contingently. But, such a doctrine of essentialism is not something Quine can accept, given his commitment to the NB conception of language. That conception of language has led him to the view that what objects there are, together with their properties, is a question to be settled only relative to some theoretical framework that itself is underdetermined by experience; moreover, it is a question to be settled only relative to some translation of that theory into the *purely extensional* canonical notation. "Relative to a particular inquiry, some predicates may play a more basic role than others, or may apply more fixedly; and these may be treated as essential" (IR, 121). But the notion of objects having essential or contingent properties in some absolute sense is, for Quine, an unintelligible metaphysical view.

§1.4.10 *Philosophy of science*

The next aspect of Quine's philosophy with which we shall here concern ourselves is his pragmatic philosophy of science. As we noted earlier, Quine regards scientific theories as networks of sentences that are both underdetermined by and holistically related to experience. These features of Quine's philosophy, underdetermination and holism, give rise to a decidedly pragmatic view of science. Furthermore, Quine's pragmatic philosophy of science is rather provocative. It is so because it contains both a radical tendency as well as a conservative tendency. The radical tendency results from Quine's *instrumentalism:* "As an empiricist," Quine says, "I continue to think of the conceptual scheme of science as a tool, ultimately, for predicting future experience in the light of past experience. Physical objects are conceptually imported into the situation as convenient intermediaries—not by definition in terms of experience, but simply as irreducible posits comparable, epistemologically, to the gods of Homer" (TDE, 44, note omitted). The conservative tendency issues from Quine's commitment to *realism:*

> For my part I do, qua lay physicist, believe in physical objects and not in Homer's gods; and I consider it a scientific error to believe otherwise. But in point of epistemological footing the physical objects and the gods differ only in degree and not in kind. Both sorts of entities enter our conception only as cultural posits. The myth of physical objects is epistemologically superior to most in that it has proved more efficacious than

other myths as a device for working a manageable structure into the flux of experience. (TDE, 44)

These apparently contrary forces at work in Quine's view of science prompted J. J. C. Smart to remark that Quine's view of science *vacillates* between instrumentalism and realism (see Smart, 8–9). This apparent vacillation evinces a deep subtlety in Quine's philosophy, a subtlety associated with his attempt to accommodate both realism and instrumentalism within a consistent naturalism.

> To call a posit a posit is not to patronize it. . . . Everything to which we concede existence is a posit from the standpoint of a description of the theory-building process, and simultaneously real from the standpoint of the theory that is being built. Nor let us look down on the standpoint of the theory as make-believe; for we can never do better than occupy the standpoint of some theory or other, the best we can muster at the time. (WO, 22)

The explanation of this subtle aspect of Quine's thought will be undertaken in the next chapter. For now we must content ourselves with completing our sketch of his philosophy of science.

Quine has written very little about the so-called scientific method, but he has isolated six virtues of plausible hypotheses: conservation, modesty, simplicity, generality, refutability, and precision.

When Quine says that a hypothesis should be *conservative,* he means that it should be consistent with as many of our presently held beliefs as possible. In the context of revising a theory, Quine sometimes calls this desideratum the *maxim of minimum mutilation.* Suppose, for example, that a theory (or a part thereof) implies some sentence predicting a future observation that later proves to be false. If we choose not to discount this failure as a mistake in measurement, or as an illusion, or the like, then we must recognize that the part of the theory that implies this false sentence is itself false—but the mere failure does not tell us *where* the theory is false. The ideal of conservatism is to fasten on the minimum amount of theory for revision—divide and conquer, as Quine says in *The Web of Belief.* A graphic instance of this sort of thing would be the case where we attempt to salt our food but, despite our best efforts, no salt comes out of the shaker. We could explain this by hypothesizing that the shaker is empty, or that the salt inside it is wet, or that salt is lighter than air, or that salt doesn't conform to the law of falling bodies, and so on. Surely, though, the maxim of minimum mutilation dictates that once we have thus divided our hypotheses, the ones to conquer (i.e., to reject) are the latter two hypotheses, rather than either of the former. Conservatism dictates that we adopt the minimum revision of our beliefs in the face of change, and the first two hypotheses meet this requirement better than the latter two hypotheses. Moreover, "[c]onservatism is rather effortless on the whole, having inertia in its favor. But it is sound strategy too, since at each step it sacrifices as little as possible of the evidential support, whatever that may have been, that our overall system of beliefs has hitherto been enjoying" (WB, 67).

Modesty is a virtue of hypotheses that is closely akin to conservatism. Quine distinguishes two varieties of modesty, the logical and the humdrum: "One hypothesis is more modest than another if it is weaker in a logical sense: if it is implied by the other, without implying it. . . . Also, one hypothesis is more modest than another if it is more humdrum: that is, if the events that it assumes to have happened are of a more usual and familiar sort, hence more to be expected" (WB, 68). The idea here is to bring in a big myth only if a small myth will not do the job. For example, suppose that while hiking in the mountains we narrowly escape a terrible avalanche. Upon regaining our composure, we might hypothesize that the avalanche was merely a fortuitous (if untimely) act of nature or we might hypothesize that some malicious person set the avalanche in motion. If avalanches are common in the area, but people (or malicious people) aren't, then modesty favors the former hypothesis.

Quine emphasizes that there is no need to draw a sharp line between conservatism and modesty—the one can grade off into the other. Nevertheless, there remain grades of modesty still to choose among even though conservatism—compatibility with previous beliefs—is achieved to perfection; for a modest and an immodest hypothesis might both be compatible with all of a person's previous beliefs.

Modesty can also grade off into *simplicity*. Simplicity is another virtue of plausible hypotheses, but simplicity is even more valued as a virtue of scientific *theories*: "There is a premium on simplicity in any hypothesis, but the highest premium is on simplicity in the giant joint hypothesis that is science, or the particular science, as a whole. We cheerfully sacrifice simplicity of a part for greater simplicity of the whole when we see a way of doing so" (WB, 69). Exactly what simplicity is, Quine is not sure. He thinks it is closely linked to our innate standards of perceptual similarity but, nevertheless, subjective. Whatever it is, it has survival value for the species, for it plays a major role in the formation of our expectations about the course of future experience.

The plausibility of a hypothesis also depends on its degree of *generality*. Requiring a hypothesis to be general is a way of guarding against ad hoc hypotheses, a way of ensuring that hypotheses will not be confirmed by mere coincidences. Also, generality is required of a hypothesis if it is to lend itself to being tested repeatedly, at different times and places, under slightly different conditions.

Simplicity and generality are wanted together in a hypothesis. One without the other would render a hypothesis rather useless. A simple hypothesis without generality would lack applicability; a general hypothesis without simplicity would be unwieldy. Nevertheless, there is a certain give and take between simplicity and generality: "When a way is seen of gaining great generality with little loss of simplicity, or great simplicity with no loss of generality, then conservatism and modesty give way to scientific revolution" (WB, 75).

The fifth virtue of plausible hypotheses is *refutability*. There must be some conceivable event (or events) that would suffice to refute the hypothesis. If this requirement is not met, then the hypothesis implies nothing and is, therefore, confirmed by nothing; it is vacuous. However, Quine cannot lean very heavily on this virtue of plausible hypotheses, for his holism also claims that *any* theoretical hypothesis can be retained, come what may.

The final virtue of plausible hypotheses is *precision*. The more precise a hypothesis is, the more strongly it is confirmed by each of its successful predictions. Precision comes mainly with the utilization of quantitative measurement. However, explication of terms can also be a means for introducing precision into hypotheses.

§1.4.11 *Logic and mathematics*

Over the centuries, logic and mathematics have stood out as *the* problem confronting empiricists: how can the empiricists' claim that all knowledge of the world is based upon experience be made consistent with the apparent necessity of the knowledge of logic and mathematics?

The empiricist John Stuart Mill met the challenge by denying the apparent necessity of logic and mathematics. He explained that the so-called logical laws of thought, far from being necessary, are not even true, and he explained that while we come to believe that necessarily 7 and 5 are 12 this belief is actually the product of mere habit of mind, an empirical generalization of our experiences with aggregates.

The empiricist A. J. Ayer took a different line. Ayer accepted the apparent necessity of logic and mathematics as real, but he denied that logic or mathematics provides knowledge about the world. The assertions of logic and mathematics are necessary because analytic.

Quine, of course, rejects the doctrine of analyticity and therewith Ayer's account of logic and mathematics. Rather, Quine agrees with Mill that the apparent necessity of logic and mathematics is just that, apparent (see RCP, 396–97). But he rejects Mill's view that such truths are mere empirical generalizations. His view is a more sophisticated one. He sees the justification of logic and mathematics on a par with the justification of theoretical physics. All three are needed in the construction of our overall best theory of the world, and all three are justified to the extent that they make that theory come out right, i.e., maximize true predictions.

§1.4.12 *Ethics*

Only recently has Quine written an essay devoted entirely to the nature and origin of moral values. The essay, "On the Nature of Moral Values" (NMV), is a contribution to meta-ethics, but to meta-ethics of a distinctively scientific kind.

Descriptive ethics is usually conceived as a discipline whose task is to describe the actual ethical beliefs, attitudes, and practices of a group or a society. This is certainly a scientific task, and one which has lately been left to social scientists (i.e., sociologists, anthropologists, and psychologists) to carry out. Normative ethics is usually conceived as the attempt to establish or discover the norms or standards of ethical behavior (including actions and character, or virtue). Meta-ethics is usually conceived as the attempt to provide semantical and logical analyses and to provide justifications of the findings of normative ethics.

Under the sway of the logical positivists' analytic-synthetic distinction, many philosophers of the thirties, forties, and fifties abandoned normative ethics, claiming its pronouncements to be cognitively meaningless. According to this view, descriptive ethics utilizes empirical (synthetic) claims and, therefore, belongs to the domain of the (social) scientist; meta-ethics utilizes analytic claims and, therefore, belongs to the domain of the philosopher; normative ethics utilizes noncognitive utterances and, therefore, belongs neither to science nor to philosophy. One way to characterize the situation is to say that the positivists' analytic-synthetic distinction separated philosophy from science, and their principle of verifiability separated meta-ethics and descriptive ethics from normative ethics.

As we have noted, however, Quine rejects the positivists' analytic-synthetic distinction. All cognitively meaningful claims are, for Quine, empirical (synthetic). Thus, he bursts the positivists' supposed barrier between science and philosophy and, therefore, their barrier between descriptive ethics and meta-ethics. As a result, as we shall see in chapter 7, Quine's meta-ethics relies heavily on the findings of the sciences of psychology and biology. He offers neither analytic definitions of ethical terms nor analytic justifications of ethical precepts. Instead, he offers a naturalistic etiology of moral values based on evolution and moral training. Contrary to popular opinion, Quine retains the positivists' criterion of verifiability. Nevertheless, he does not accept the positivists' conclusion that this principle renders all ethical pronouncements cognitively meaningless. Even so, as we shall see in chapter 7, he regards ethics to be methodologically infirm as compared to science.

§1.5 Conclusions

I have tried to sketch the systematic character of Quine's philosophy by emphasizing its naturalistic-behavioristic basis. In particular, I have tried to do this by explaining how the NB conception of language (i.e., a naturalistic view of language and a behavioral view of meaning), once adopted and seriously adhered to, provides a heuristical framework within which the bulk of Quine's system develops. My view is that, given Quine's genetic strategy (i.e., his method of looking at how theoretical language is learned) together with his NB conception of language and the view that scientific theories are essentially linguistic structures, he is naturally led to conclude that science must be underdetermined by experience to some extent in that theoretical language goes beyond the simple reiteration of observation sentences. Further, the theories of science will be viewed as holistically related to experience. In other words, it is not the case that every sentence of a scientific theory will possess its own unique empirical evidence or meaning. And, if scientific theories are both underdetermined and holistic, then one must encounter indeterminacy of translation and inscrutability of reference as one moves from one account of experience to another. Furthermore, the NB conception of language leads to the doctrine of ontological relativity, for all of the sentence-to-sentence relations of a theory can be fully maintained even though all of its objects are supplanted. Quinian holism also entails the rejection of the traditional analytic-synthetic distinction and, similarly, classic attempts at epistemological reductionism. As one might expect, synonymy goes by the board too, and with it go meanings, propositions, attributes, and relations. From a behavioristic point of view, they all lack identity criteria. In addition, quantified modal logic must be given up along with the metaphysical essentialism it presupposes. Underdetermination and holism lead to Quine's pragmatic philosophy of science as well as to his views on the nature of logic and mathematics. Finally, rounding out this naturalistic tour de force, Quine offers a postpositivist, naturalistic account of the origin and nature of moral values.

Consequently, in Quine's fully developed philosophy one finds, not a mere collection of doctrines and theses on a multiplicity of apparently disparate philosophical topics, but rather a *systematic*, naturalistic response to the epistemological question of how we acquire our theory of the world.

Holism, Realism, and Naturalized Epistemology

CHAPTER 2

§2.1 *Introduction*

Behaviorism, physicalism, holism, realism, fallibilism, gradualism, and naturalism are all important aspects of Quine's philosophy, but of all these '-isms' none plays a larger role in Quine's thought than naturalism. In short, Quine's philosophy is nothing if not naturalistic! But what, precisely, does Quine mean by 'naturalism'? Here are some samples of his usage:

> (1) ". . . naturalism: the recognition that it is within science itself, and not in some prior philosophy, that reality is to be identified and described" (TPT, 21).
>
> (2) ". . . naturalism: abandonment of the goal of a first philosophy prior to natural science" (FME, 67).
>
> (3) ". . . naturalism: abandonment of the goal of a first philosophy. It sees natural science as an inquiry into reality, fallible and corrigible but not answerable to any supra-scientific tribunal, and not in need of any justification beyond observation and the hypothetico-deductive method" (FME, 72).
>
> (4) ". . . naturalism, . . . [a] readiness to see philosophy as natural science trained upon itself and permitted free use of scientific findings" (ROD, 85).

(5) "... my position is a naturalistic one; I see philosophy not as an *a priori* propaedeutic or groundwork for science, but as continuous with science. I see philosophy and science as in the same boat—a boat which, to revert to Neurath's figure as I so often do, we can rebuild only at sea while staying afloat in it. There is no external vantage point, no first philosophy" (NK, 126–27).

This selection of quotations gives some indication of the sense Quine assigns to his use of 'naturalism'. In his negative usage, it amounts to the denial of first philosophy; in his affirmative usage, it amounts to scientism. But if this is the *sense* of Quine's naturalism, what is its *source*? He is explicit on the matter:

> Naturalism has two sources, both negative. One of them is despair of being able to define theoretical terms generally in terms of phenomena, even by contextual definition. A holistic or system-centered attitude should suffice to induce this despair. The other negative source of naturalism is unregenerate realism, the robust state of mind of the natural scientist who has never felt any qualms beyond the negotiable uncertainties internal to science. (FME, 72)

In short, *holism* and *unregenerate realism* are Quine's principal grounds for embracing naturalism. The holism argument serves to refute traditional epistemology (first philosophy), rationalistic and empiricistic. However, it also has the consequence of lending plausibility to the realism argument, which serves to establish scientism. Thus do holism and unregenerate realism clear the way for *naturalized epistemology*, i.e., for the scientific investigation of the acquisition of scientific knowledge.

In the remainder of this chapter, I pursue answers to the following questions: how does Quine argue for naturalizing epistemology? (2.2); is Quine's argument for naturalizing epistemology sound? (2.3); what does Quine mean by his claim that epistemology and ontology are reciprocally contained? (2.4).

§2.2 How does Quine argue for naturalizing epistemology?

As traditionally practiced, epistemology is a normative undertaking. It inquires after the norms, or standards, if any, which might be used to justify beliefs, judgments, and so on. Over the years, epistemologists have sought these norms in the apparently antithetical realms of reason and sense experience. Rationalists (e.g., Descartes) have typically claimed that reason is the sole source of unconditionally accepted truths which supply the norms for justifying all other knowledge claims, while empiricists (e.g., Locke) have typically claimed that sense experience is the sole source of such truths and norms. Despite disagreeing on the source of such norms, traditional rationalists and empiricists do agree that it would be illicit to seek such norms *within* natural science, for it is the institution of natural science itself that they are seeking to justify! Thus, for traditional epistemologists, using natural science to justify natural science would be viciously circular. By their lights, justifying science requires norms whose source lies outside of science itself. As we shall see, however, Quine argues that the common quest of rationalists and empiricists for some privileged class of unconditionally accepted, nonscientific truths is a wild-goose chase and, therefore, ought to be abandoned.

§2.2.1 Holism and Quine's argument against traditional epistemology

Practitioners of traditional epistemology can be classified not only as rationalists and empiricists, but also as idealists and realists. Presumably these two pairs of categorical opposites yield four possible classifications of traditional epistemologists: rationalistic idealists (Hegel?), rationalistic realists (Descartes?), empiricistic idealists (Berkeley?), and empiricistic realists (Locke?).

So far as I know, Quine offers no specific argument against rationalistic idealists, probably because very few, if any, contemporary Anglo-American philosophers take this view seriously. On the other hand, Quine does argue against empiricistic idealism (viz., Berkeley's), but he does so only because it is a peculiar form of empiricism and not because it is a form of idealism. Even Quine's attack on the "Idea idea" is not directed specifically toward any form of idealism. Rather, it is directed toward *any* theory of linguistic meaning that construes "a man's semantics as somehow determinate in his mind beyond what might be implicit in his dispositions to overt behavior" (OR, 27). In short, Quine's attitude toward idealism seems to be that it deserves to be ignored rather than refuted. Thus is Quine's attack on traditional epistemology focused on rationalistic realism and empiricistic realism. Let us agree therefore, for the purposes of this discussion, to construe rationalism and empiricism in their realistic forms.

Traditional rationalists contend that reason reveals to them certain *a priori*, synthetic, nonscientific truths and norms (e.g., Descartes' *cogito* and its "mark" of clarity and distinctness) sufficient for deducing all other truths. Quine's argument against rationalism consists first in denying the *a priori* character of any such alleged truths and norms, and second in denying that even if there were such, they would be sufficient for deducing all other truths.

Quine's argument against the rationalists' claim that there are *a priori* truths is virtually identical with his argument against the empiricists' claim that there are analytic truths, which will be explained below in discussing traditional empiricism. His argument against the rationalists' claim that all other truths are deducible from *a priori* truths (supposing there were such truths) is simply to point out that "even the truths of elementary number theory are presumably not in general derivable . . . by self-evident steps from self-evident truths. We owe this insight to Godel's theorem, which was not known to the old-time philosophers" (WB, 65). So much for traditional rationalists.

Traditional empiricists contend that sense experience reveals to them certain *a posteriori*, synthetic, nonscientific truths and norms from which they can deduce or rationally reconstruct all of the truths of nature. Quine's argument against this form of empiricism, which he calls *radical empiricism*, consists in showing that the truths of nature can neither be deduced from nor rationally reconstructed from such a basis, and, further, that there simply are no analytic truths of the sort envisioned by these empiricists.

In "Epistemology Naturalized," Quine identifies two central ambitions of radical empiricism. The first is to *deduce* the truths of nature from sensory evidence, the second is to *translate* (or *define*) those truths in terms of observation and logico-mathematical auxiliaries. Using studies in the foundation of mathematics as his model, Quine labels the former ambition the *doctrinal* side of (empiricistic) epistemology, the latter he labels the *conceptual* side of (empiricistic) epistemology. The primary concern on the doctrinal side is with justifying our knowledge of the truths of nature in sensory terms; the primary concern on the conceptual side is with explaining the notion of *body* in sensory terms.

However, these two central ambitions of radical empiricism remain unfulfilled: there is no successful first philosophy. On the doctrinal side of epistemology, the radical empiricists' ambition of deducing all of the truths of nature from sensory evidence has not gotten beyond the position of Hume. Bodies, understood as bundles of sensory qualities, can be known immediately and indubitably, but no statement about *absent matters of fact* can be deduced from statements about such bodies. And, as Quine laconically puts the point, "The Humean predicament is the human predicament" (EN, 72). Thus, the ambition of deducing all of the truths of nature from immediate, sensory experience, and the Cartesian-like motivation behind this ambition—the desire to establish all the truths of nature with a certitude comparable to the certitude attaching to the truths of immediate, sensory experience—must be abandoned. Fallibilism fills the void. What of the conceptual side of radical empiricism? Here, even though the most profound radical empiricist, Rudolf Carnap, readily acknowledged the impossibility of deducing science from immediate experience, he nevertheless kept pursuing the other primary aim of radical empiricism, namely, the defining of the concepts of science in sensory and logico-mathematical terms.

However, according to Quine, Carnap's heroic attempt at *rationally reconstructing* scientific discourse in observation terms and logico-mathematical auxiliaries was doomed to fail because not every sentence of scientific theories has a fund of experiential implications it can call its own. When this observation is coupled with the verificationist theory of meaning, the result is that not every sentence of scientific theories has a *meaning* it can call its own. And, if this is so, then it is clear that Carnap's program of rationally reconstructing theoretical discourse on the basis of observation terms and logico-mathematical auxiliaries is hopeless. Thus, just as the central ambition of the doctrinal side of radical empiricism must be abandoned, so must the central ambition of the conceptual side be abandoned.

This same holism—not every sentence of scientific theories has its own unique empirical content—also serves to refute the radical empiricists' claim of analyticity (and the rationalists' claim of *a priority*). Analytic (and other kinds of *a priori*) statements were said to be just those that a theorist could hold true in the face of *all* experiences. But, if holism is true, then

> it is misleading to speak of the empirical content of an individual statement—especially if it is a statement at all remote from the experiential periphery of the field. Furthermore it becomes folly to seek a boundary between synthetic statements, which hold contingently on experience, and analytic statements, which hold come what may. Any statement can be held true come what may, if we make drastic enough adjustments elsewhere in the system. (TDE, 43)

Thus, not only is it impossible to deduce the truths of nature from truths of immediate experience, it is also impossible to translate (or define) the former, individually, in terms of the latter. Furthermore, it is impossible to segregate the sentences of scientific theories into those that are analytic and those that are synthetic, in any *absolute* (as opposed to arbitrary) manner.

Such is the fate of the two dogmas of empiricism, radical reductionism and the analytic-synthetic distinction: they must go. More generally, we may say that the traditional epistemological program, empiricistic or rationalistic, must be abandoned, for it has foundered on the rock of holism. Such is Quine's argument against traditional epistemology. What now of his argument for scientism?

§2.2.2 *Robust realism and Quine's argument for scientism*

As we have seen, radical empiricism fails on both its doctrinal and conceptual sides. Nevertheless, there are still two cardinal tenets of empiricism that Quine believes remain unscathed: "One is that whatever evidence there *is* for science *is* sensory evidence. The other . . . is that all inculcation of meanings of words must rest ultimately on sensory evidence" (EN, 75). I suggest that these two tenets are, respectively, the *doctrinal* and *conceptual* sides of the new empiricism that Quine is forging.

According to this new empiricism, epistemology is to remain a legitimate enterprise, except that now its goal is to provide a *factual account* of the link between observation and theory, "between the meager input and the torrential output" (EN, 83). The chief difference between the old and the new empiricistic epistemology is just that this factual account is to be pursued naturalistically, *within the framework of natural science itself*. Nevertheless:

> Such a study could still include, even, something like the old rational reconstruction, to whatever degree such reconstruction is practicable; for imaginative constructions can afford hints of actual psychological processes, in much the way that mechanical simulations can. But a conspicuous difference between old epistemology and the epistemological enterprise in this new psychological setting is that we can now make free use of empirical psychology. (EN, 83)

But how does Quine propose to justify taking this scientistic turn in epistemology? How can the new epistemologist legitimately use the findings of science to justify science? Would this not be viciously circular? The answers to these questions are to be found in an examination of Quine's attitude of unregenerate realism, "the robust state of mind of the natural scientist who has never felt any qualms beyond the negotiable uncertainties internal to science" (FME, 72).

Quine's response to the question of how the new epistemologist can legitimately use the findings of science to justify science has, I believe, two parts. First, he argues that skepticism about science presupposes science. Second, he argues that science needs no justification beyond measuring up to the demands of observation and the hypothetico-deductive method.

Traditionally, skeptics launched their assaults on science by means of illusions. Purported physical objects were shown not to be physical objects, after all. However, illusions are known as illusions only because they are known to be other than they appear—they appear to be material objects, but they are not. The idea here is that illusions are recognizable as illusions only relative to a prior acceptance of genuine bodies with which to contrast them. "Rudimentary physical science, that is, common sense about bodies, is thus needed as a springboard for skepticism" (NNK, 67–68).

A more up-to-date version of the skeptic's challenge to science might be put as follows:

> Science itself teaches that there is no clairvoyance; that the only information that can reach our sensory surfaces from external objects must be limited to two-dimensional optical projections and various impacts of air waves on the eardrums and some gaseous reactions in the nasal passages and a few kindred odds and ends. How, the challenge proceeds, could one hope to find out about the external world from such meager traces? (RR, 2)

Here, as before, the skeptic's challenge turns science upon itself.

Quine does not make the mistake of arguing that the skeptic's use of science against itself is illegitimate. Rather, his point is that because the skeptic makes essential use of scientific claims in his assault upon science, the defender of science is therefore free to use scientific claims in his defense of science. Moreover, the defender of science will have made his case if he can show that his science measures up to observation and the hypothetico-deductive method. "Our overall scientific theory demands of the world only that it be so structured as to assure the sequences of stimulation that our theory gives us to expect. More concrete demands are empty" (TPT, 22). Thus, the naturalized epistemologist's "problem is that of finding ways, in keeping with natural science, whereby the human animal can have projected this same science from the sensory information that could reach him according to this science" (RR, 2). "A far cry, this, from old epistemology. Yet it is no gratuitous change of subject matter, but an enlightened persistence rather in the original epistemological problem" (RR, 3). The new epistemologist's undertaking is *enlightened* because he recognizes that the skeptical challenge to science springs from within science itself and, therefore, that in coping with this challenge the epistemologist is free to use whatever scientific knowledge is available. Thus the charge of vicious circularity is deflected: "The crucial logical point is that the [new] epistemologist is confronting a challenge to natural science that arises from within natural science" (RR, 2). Thus does Quine justify his scientism.

So, we have seen how Quine uses holism and realism to support his naturalism and his naturalizing of epistemology. *Holism* ushers out first philosophy: theoretical terms can neither be defined nor translated into terms of immediate experience, and neither the analytic nor the *a priori* (in general) can be isolated in any absolute manner—*any* sentence can be held true come what may. *Unregenerate realism* ushers in naturalized epistemology: skeptical doubts about science are themselves scientific doubts; fear of circularity is misplaced, once hope for a first philosophy is abandoned.

Another noteworthy source of Quine's naturalism that is closely related to his attitude of unregenerate realism is what might be called his *epistemic priority argument*. Traditional epistemologists disagree over how to construe the epistemological given, over whether sensory atoms or, say, Gestalten are to be accorded epistemic priority in a proper account of knowledge of the external world. However, once we recognize that the positions of both sensory atomists and Gestalt psychologists presuppose the scientific finding "that all our information about the external world reaches us through the impact of external forces on our sensory surfaces" (SSS, 2), we ought thereby to recognize as well a way out of this quandary. "Obscurity about the nature of the given, or epistemic priority, is dissipated by talking frankly of the triggering of nerve endings. We then find ourselves engaged in an internal question within the framework of natural science" (SSS, 2); that is, we find ourselves doing epistemology naturalistically.

Having thus explained Quine's argument for naturalizing epistemology as grounded principally on holism and unregenerate realism, we must now inquire whether his argument is sound.

§2.3 *Is Quine's argument for naturalizing epistemology sound?*

The question of whether Quine's argument for naturalizing epistemology is sound divides into three others (I shall ignore Quine's *epistemic priority argument*): Is Quine's argument for holism sound? Is Quine's argument for unregenerate realism sound? Is naturalized epistemology *really* epistemology? In this chapter, I shall respond only to the first two of these three questions—leaving the third question as a topic for chapter 3.

§2.3.1 *Is Quine's holism argument sound?*

Before inquiring into the soundness of Quine's argument for holism, we might first get clear about exactly what Quine's holism is: "It is holism that has rightly been called the Duhem thesis and also, rather generously, the Duhem-Quine thesis. It says that scientific statements are not separately vulnerable to adverse observations, because it is only jointly as a theory that they imply their observable consequences" (OEES, 313). However, this thesis is one that must be accepted with reservations:

> One reservation has to do with the fact that some statements are closely linked to observation, by the process of language learning. These statements are indeed separately susceptible to the test of observation; and at the same time they do not stand free of theory, for they share much of the vocabulary of the more remotely theoretical statements. They are what link theory to observation, affording theory its empirical content. Now the Duhem thesis still holds, in a somewhat literalistic way, even for these observation statements. For the scientist does occasionally revoke even an observation statement, when it conflicts with a well attested body of theory and when he has tried in vain to reproduce the experiment. But the Duhem thesis would be wrong if understood as imposing an equal status on all the statements in a scientific theory and thus denying the strong presumption in favor of the observation statements. It is this bias that makes science empirical.
>
> Another reservation regarding the Duhem thesis has to do with breadth. If it is only jointly as a theory that the scientific sentences imply their observable consequences, how inclusive does that theory have to be? Does it have to be the whole of science, taken as a comprehensive theory of the world?

. . .

Science is neither discontinuous nor monolithic. It is variously jointed, and loose in the joints in varying degrees. In the face of a recalcitrant observation we are free to choose what statements to revise and what ones to hold fast, and these alternatives will disrupt various stretches of scientific theory in various ways, varying in severity. Little is gained by saying that the unit is in principle the whole of science, however defensible this claim may be in a legalistic way. (OEES, 314–15; cf. also RP and RV)

So, the two important "reservations" to keep in mind regarding Quine's version of Duhemian holism are: (1) some sentences are separately susceptible to the test of observation, namely, observation sentences—indeed, a sentence's susceptibility to observation is a matter of degree for Quine; and (2) while science is neither discontinuous nor monolithic, it is more accurate of current scientific practice (legalisms aside) to think of significant stretches of science, rather than the whole of science, as having observable consequences.

What are Quine's arguments in favor of holism? I believe there are three: the scientific practices argument; the language learning argument; and the *reductio* argument. The *scientific practices argument* is simply the claim that, as a matter of empirical fact, a scientist involved in the testing of some hypothesis, H, must assume the truth of a set of auxiliary assumptions, A, and the hypothesis can always be saved by making drastic enough adjustments in A. The *language learning argument* claims that the bulk of scientific, or referential, language is learned via irreducible leaps of analogy (viz., analogic synthesis). These analogical links are so tenuous as to allow the kind of gerrymandering of truth values of sentences, or empirical slack, that holism evinces. The *reductio argument* goes as follows: If every sentence of a theory had its own unique sets of confirming and infirming experiential conditions, then we ought to be able to arrive at an acceptable theory of the confirmation of *individual* sentences, and we ought to be able to draw an absolute analytic-synthetic distinction. However, we have not been able to do either of these two things. Therefore, not every sentence of a theory has its own unique sets of confirming and infirming experiential conditions (i.e., therefore holism). Conversely, if holism is true, then epistemological reductionism is impossible and the quest for an absolute analytic-synthetic distinction is folly (see TDE, 41–42). Let us examine each of these three arguments for holism.

§2.3.1.1 *The scientific practices argument*

Not everyone has been convinced by Quine's arguments. Adolf Grunbaum has been among the leading critics of the Duhem-Quine thesis. With respect to the scientific practices argument, Grunbaum has argued that when Quine's formulation of Duhem's thesis (hereafter called the D-thesis) is construed as a *restricted* claim, disallowing revisions of a theory that alter the meaning of any of the theory's terms, then it is both a non sequitur and *false*; and when the D-thesis is construed as an *unrestricted* claim, allowing revisions of a theory that alter the meanings of some of a theory's terms, then it is *true but trivial*.

Suppose, for example, that we have a theory composed of some hypothesis, H, and a set of auxiliary assumptions, A, and that this theory has certain observational consequences, O. Now, according to the substantive, restricted version of the D-thesis, the failure of O, say, O′, is not sufficient to refute H, for *there always exists* some alternative set of auxiliary assumptions, A′, such that the conjunction of H and A′ entails O′. In other words, without changing the meanings of any terms in the theory, any hypothesis, H, can always be saved because A′ always exists. This argument is a non sequitur because, as Grunbaum points out,

> there is no logical guarantee at all of the existence of the *required kind* of revised set A′ of auxiliary assumptions such that
>
> $$(H \cdot A') \longrightarrow O'$$
>
> for any one component hypothesis H and any O′. Instead of being guaranteed logically, the existence of the required set A′ needs *separate* and *concrete* demonstration for each particular context. In the absence of the latter kind of *empirical* support for Quine's unrestricted Duhemian claim, that claim is an unempirical dogma or article of faith. (19)

Furthermore, Grunbaum suggests a case drawn from the history of physics where no such A′ does exist, and he concludes from this counterexample that the restricted D-thesis is false (see Grunbaum, 19).

On the other hand, so far as the unrestricted D-thesis is concerned,

> unless Quine restricts in very specific ways what he understands by "drastic enough adjustments elsewhere in the (theoretical) system" the D-thesis is a thoroughly unenlightening truism. For if someone were to put forward the false empirical hypothesis H that "Ordinary buttermilk is highly toxic to humans," this hypothesis could be saved from refutation in the face of the observed wholesomeness of ordinary buttermilk by making the following "drastic enough" adjustment in our system: changing the rules of English usage so that the intension of the term "ordinary buttermilk" is that of the term "arsenic" in its customary usage. (Grunbaum, 20)

In short, Grunbaum argues that the D-thesis is either *substantive but false*, or *true but trivial*.

And how does all this affect Quine? Like water off a duck's back! In a 1962 letter to Grunbaum, Quine says:

> Your claim that the Duhem-Quine thesis, as you call it, is untenable if taken nontrivially, strikes me as persuasive. Certainly it is carefully argued.
>
> For my own part I would say that the thesis as I have used it *is* probably trivial. I haven't advanced it as an interesting thesis as such. I bring it in only in the course of arguing against such notions as that the empirical content of sentences can in general be sorted out distributively, sentence by sentence, or that the understanding of a term can be segregated from collateral information regarding the object. For such purposes I am not concerned even to avoid the trivial extreme of sustaining a law by changing a meaning; for the cleavage between meaning and fact is part of what, in such contexts, I am questioning. (LPG, 131)

It is fairly obvious from these remarks that as late as 1962 Quine's primary interest in the D-thesis lay in its service in the cause of ushering out traditional epistemology, and not in the D-thesis itself as, say, a substantive claim about scientific theories. Nevertheless, it seems to me that Quine has subsequently come to regard the D-thesis as a substantive (and true) claim about scientific theories.

§2.3.1.2 *The language learning argument*

But what kind of claim is the D-thesis, that is, what is its cognitive status? I want to urge that Quine regards the D-thesis as an *empirical* claim not only about the actual practice of scientists but about the language of theory. In particular, I want to urge that the D-thesis does *not* enjoy some special *a priori*, transcendental, or quasi-empirical status in Quine's philosophical system, as some of his commentators have suggested (see Roth, 434, and Siegel 1984, 667ff.).

The following quotation from Quine's "Reply to Robert Nozick" indicates pretty clearly that Quine does *not* regard the D-thesis as, for example, some kind of Kantian precondition for the possibility of any human language:

> Turning to holism, he [Nozick] asks whether a non-Duhemian language would be impossible for us. Let me say that the observation sentences, in my behaviorally defined sense, constitute already a rudimentary language of the kind. It admits of non-Duhemian enlargement, moreover, without clear limits. The tight-fitting sort of science that I speculated on at one point in my paper "On Empirically Equivalent Systems of the World" would be non-Duhemian. But I see no hope of a science comparable in power to our own that would not be subject to holism, at least of my moderate sort. Holism sets in when simple induction develops into the full hypothetico-deductive method. (RN, 364)

The last sentence of the above quotation is extremely important for understanding Quine's advocacy of holism, for it helps to *explain* why holism occurs. How is this so? The answer lies with Quine's theory of language learning. As we noted in chapter 1, he believes that some elementary parts of language (e.g., observation sentences) can be learned by extrapolating along the lines of observed similarities. However, most of language—and certainly most of scientific theory—goes beyond the realm of observable things and their similarities. Such language is mastered, Quine claims, by means of analogic synthesis, i.e., by means of analogies. This "ponderous linguistic structure [viz., scientific theory], fabricated of theoretical terms linked by fabricated hypotheses, and keyed to observable events here and there" (NNK, 71), stands as a remarkable improvement over simple induction as a means for anticipating experience. But there is a price to be paid for this advance. In acquiring habits by simple induction over instances, if some anticipated experience fails to materialize, that very habit (i.e., expectation) will wither. But now, with the hypothetico-deductive method in full force, when some expected or predicted event implied by some part of a theory fails to materialize, there is a *choice* to be made as to how to revise the theory (i.e., holism occurs) so that such false predictions will not be made in the future. That there is a choice as to what to revise (i.e., holism) in the face of a falsified prediction is a consequence of the fact that the language of theory goes beyond occasion sentences to include sentences that are not directly linked to observation and that can be learned only by dint of irreducible leaps of analogy, leaps that if traced backwards would not yield a smooth derivation of theoretical language on the basis of observational language (see NNK, 77–78). Such is Quine's naturalistic *explanation* of why holism occurs.

So, the D-thesis is a *scientific* claim about scientific theories, and it is explained scientifically within the science of linguistics. It is not some *a priori* or transcendental or quasi-empirical claim. On the contrary, it is merely another naturalistic plank in Neurath's boat. However, if in time Quine's theory of language learning proves to be radically wrong, then this plank may very well give way.

§2.3.1.3 *The* reductio *argument*

We have said that Quine argues that if the holism thesis (H) were false, then one ought to be able to arrive at an acceptable theory of confirmation for *individual* sentences of theories (C), and one ought to be able to distinguish *absolutely* the analytic sentences of theories from the synthetic sentences of theories (D). However,

Quine claims we are unable to do either and that the holism thesis (H) is therefore true. Schematically (and condensed), his *reductio* is as follows:

$$\sim H \longrightarrow (C \cdot D)$$
$$\sim C \cdot \sim D \: / \therefore H$$

However, and conversely, Quine also claims that if the holism thesis is true (H), then epistemological reductionism is but an impossible dream ($\sim$C) and the seeking of an *absolute* (as opposed to arbitrary) analytic-synthetic distinction is but folly ($\sim$D); schematically:

$$H \longrightarrow (\sim C \cdot \sim D)$$
$$H \: / \therefore \sim C \cdot \sim D$$

Thus inextricably intertwined are Quine's *reductio* argument in favor of holism and his argument against analyticity and reductionism. Indeed, it would *appear* that Quine is guilty of arguing in a vicious circle: he seems to use the rejection of the analytic-synthetic distinction ($\sim$D) to establish the holism thesis (H) (re: first schema given above); and he uses the holism thesis (H) to establish the rejection of the analytic-synthetic distinction ($\sim$D) (re: second schema given above).

In the remainder of this section, our task will be to uncover the details of Quine's *reductio* argument and to answer the question of whether Quine is guilty of arguing in a vicious circle, as suggested above. Our task requires, then, that we examine, in general, Quine's argument against analyticity and reductionism.

In *Word and Object*, Quine says:

> My misgivings over the notion [of an analytic-synthetic dichotomy] came out in a limited way in "Truth by convention" (1936), and figured increasingly in my lectures at Harvard. Tarski and I long argued the point with Carnap there in 1939–40. Soon White was pursuing the matter with Goodman and me in triangular correspondence. Essays questioning the distinction issued from a number of pens, sometimes independently of the Harvard discussions. . . . Carnap and White mentioned my position in their 1950 papers, but my pub-

lished allusions to it were slight . . . until in 1950 I was invited to address the American Philosophical Association on the issue, and so wrote "Two dogmas." (WO, 67–68, n. 7)

"Two Dogmas of Empiricism" is not the only place where Quine argues against the analytic-synthetic distinction, but it is the main place. Furthermore, while Quine has "poured out the full content . . . of . . . brief metaphors of the last pages of 'Two Dogmas' into utterest prose" (R, 180) in *Word and Object* and *The Roots of Reference,* and while he now claims that the holism adumbrated in "Two Dogmas" exceeds what is required in controversion of the dogmas of reductionism and analyticity (see RV, 619), still he has not abandoned any of the arguments of "Two Dogmas" (cf. RV).

In short, "Two Dogmas" remains the *locus classicus* of Quine's attack on the analytic-synthetic distinction. In that essay, his attack against the analytic-synthetic distinction is two-pronged. One prong is the argument claiming that no one has ever succeeded in making clear precisely what the analytic-synthetic distinction comes to, and that any further attempt along the same general lines is likewise doomed to fail. I shall postpone consideration of this argument until we discuss the objections of P. F. Strawson and H. P. Grice in chapter 4. The other prong is the argument claiming that empiricists' attempts at segregating the sentences of theories into those that are analytic and those that are synthetic is predicated upon a fundamental misconception (viz., a nonholistic conception) of the way that sentences of scientific theories relate to the world. In connection with this point, Quine says:

> If this view [i.e., holism] is right, it is misleading to speak of the empirical content of an individual statement—especially if it is a statement at all remote from the experiential periphery of the field [dogma of reductionism]. Furthermore it becomes folly to seek a boundary between synthetic statements, which hold contingently on experience, and analytic statements, which hold come what may [dogma of analytic-synthetic distinction]. Any statement can be held true come what may, if we make drastic enough adjustments elsewhere in the system [holism]. (TDE, 43)

This is the argument briefly schematized above thusly:

H ⟶ (~C · ~D)
H / ∴ ~C · ~D

Clearly, the above argument against the analytic-synthetic distinction begins with, and presupposes the truth of, the holism thesis. Is there an argument in "Two Dogmas" for the truth of the holism thesis? I believe that there is, but it is scant. Furthermore, what argument is there is embedded in this broader *reductio* of Quine's:[1]

P1: The truth/falsity of each statement of a theory is analyzable into a linguistic component and a factual component.
P2: As empiricists, we construe the factual component of each statement as confirmed/infirmed by experience.
∴ C1: Each statement of a theory, considered separately, has associated with it a unique range of confirming experiences and a unique range of infirming experiences (dogma of reductionism).
∴ C2: Those statements of a theory whose truth depends solely upon the linguistic component (i.e., that are true in the face of all possible experiences) are analytic (dogma of analytic-synthetic distinction).
P3: There is no acceptable theory of empirical confirmation for individual synthetic statements.
∴ C3: C1 is false.
P4: There is no acceptable analytic-synthetic distinction.
∴ C4: C2 is false.
∴ C5: P1 is false.

Within this general argument is Quine's argument for holism. It occurs at P3, which is intended as a refutation of C1, the dogma of reductionism. C1 tells us that each individual synthetic statement of a theory has its own unique ranges of confirming and infirming experiences associated with it. But if this is so, then we ought to be able to work out an acceptable theory of the confirmation of *individual* statements of theories. However, P3 asserts that this has not occurred. (Quine's actual words are: "I am impressed also, apart from prefabricated examples of black and white balls in an urn, with how baffling the problem has always been of arriving at any explicit theory of the empirical confirmation of a synthetic statement" (TDE, 41–42).) Therefore, Quine concludes, C1 is false, i.e., the holism thesis is true (C3). The relevant portion of this broader *reductio* (P1–C5) was schematized above thusly:

$\sim H \longrightarrow (C \cdot D)$
$\sim C \cdot \sim D / \therefore H$

Now, what are we to make of the apparent vicious circularity that arises from taking Quine's two arguments in tandem? Apparently, Quine argues in favor of rejecting the analytic-synthetic distinction ($\sim D$) on the basis of the holism thesis (H) and, simultaneously, he argues in favor of the holism thesis (H) on the basis of the rejection of the analytic-synthetic distinction ($\sim D$). Now if the *only* evidence that Quine can muster for $\sim D$ is H and vice versa, then surely he is guilty of arguing in a vicious circle.

In responding to this charge of vicious circularity, we should note first that Quine argues for the truth of $\sim D$ in the early pages of "Two Dogmas" *without* recourse to holism, i.e., he argues that no one has ever succeeded in making clear what the analytic-synthetic distinction comes to, and that any further attempt along the same general lines is likewise doomed to fail—this is the prong of his attack whose consideration we have postponed until chapter 4. However, if this argument is successful, then Quine's *overall* argument is not open to the charge of vicious circularity; for while he may be understood as arguing for $\sim D$ on the basis of the holism thesis (H), he also argues for it on grounds logically independent of that thesis. So, even if he used $\sim D$ to support H, which I shall deny momentarily, such a maneuver would not be vicious.

Similarly, as we have already seen, Quine has arguments for the holism thesis in addition to his *reductio* argument—arguments that do not presuppose the rejection of the analytic-synthetic distinction ($\sim D$). So, even if Quine used $\sim D$ to establish H, he again would be acquitted of vicious circularity. Furthermore, even if Quine's arguments for $\sim D$ that are logically independent of H were to fail, and even if his aforementioned arguments for H that are logically independent of $\sim D$ were to fail, still he would *not* be guilty of arguing in a vicious circle. The reason for this is that his *reductio* argument for holism *does not*, appearances to the contrary notwithstanding, rely upon $\sim D$: it is a simple matter to derive H from $\sim H \longrightarrow (C \cdot D)$, given *only* $\sim C$; $\sim D$ of the second premise of the *reductio* is superfluous. This is only to say again what was said earlier: Quine's argument (in "Two Dogmas") for the holism thesis is P3. ~D plays no role in the argument. So, even though Quine *does* argue for ~D on the basis of H (but not only on that basis), he *does not* argue for H on the basis of ~D. Rather, he argues for H on the basis of ~C (P3). So, while this argument for H is a rather weak one (weaker than either the scientific practices argument or the language learning argument), and while it is the *only* argument that Quine provides for H in all of "Two Dogmas," still, it does not render his overall argument viciously circular.[2]

Let us now return to the question posed earlier regarding the soundness of Quine's argument for realism.

§2.3.2 *Is Quine's realism argument sound?*

Quine's "unregenerate realism, the robust state of mind of the natural scientist who has never felt any qualms beyond the negotiable uncertainties internal to science" (FME, 72) is, as we have seen, logically grounded on the recognition that the skeptical challenge to science presupposes science. Quine's point here is not that the skeptic is begging the question:

> I am not accusing the sceptic of begging the question. He is quite within his rights in assuming science in order to refute science; this, if carried out, would be a straightforward argument by *reductio ad absurdum*. I am only making the point that sceptical doubts are scientific doubts. (NNK, 68)

In short, Quine plausibly insists that the epistemologist and the skeptic be armed equally before the battle: if the skeptic is free to use the findings of science in his attack upon science, then the epistemologist is free to use the findings of science in his defense of science. Add to this the two points noted earlier, namely, that the holism argument lends plausibility to the realism argument by way of eliminating first philosophy as a valid approach to epistemology, and that the quandary over the epistemic priority of sense data versus Gestalten is dissolved by talking instead of nerve endings; and then it can be seen that Quine has some fairly solid grounds for his unregenerate realism. However, let this be our tentative conclusion about the soundness of Quine's argument for unregenerate realism, for in the next chapter we shall examine a formidable challenge to this argument.

It would seem, then, that the two negative sources of naturalism—holism and unregenerate realism—are fairly well grounded, if not conclusively confirmed. From this perspective:

> Epistemology is best looked upon, then, as an enterprise within natural science. Cartesian doubt is not the way to begin. Retaining our present beliefs about nature, we can still ask how we can have arrived at them. Science tells us that our only source of information about the external world is through the impact of light rays and molecules upon our sensory surfaces. Stimulated in these ways, we somehow evolve an elaborate and useful science. How do we do this, and why does the resulting science work so well? These are genuine questions, and no feigning of doubt is needed to appreciate them. They are scientific questions about a species of primates, and they are open to investigation in natural science, the very science whose acquisition is being investigated. (NNK, 68)

As the above quotation makes abundantly clear, according to Quine's program of naturalized epistemology *epistemological* questions regarding the relation of evidence to theory are to become *scientific* questions about the acquisition of science.

But if epistemological questions are to become scientific questions, and if epistemology is normative and science is descriptive, then is *naturalized* epistemology *really* epistemology? Does the holism argument, then, *really* lend plausibility to the realism argument? Why does the rejected, traditional epistemology need to be supplanted by some successor subject (viz., naturalized epistemology)? Why not just regard the rock of holism as having scuttled *all* epistemic ships, including Neurath's and Quine's? Attempting satisfactory answers to these questions must await chapter 3.

§2.4 On the reciprocal containment of epistemology and ontology

As we have seen, Quine abandons traditional epistemology (first philosophy) but he does not abandon epistemology itself. Rather, he advocates "an enlightened persistence . . . in the original epistemological problem" (RR, 3). Unburdened of the impossible task of propounding a first philosophy (i.e., a class of unconditionally accepted, nonscientific truths upon which to justify science), the enlightened epistemologist turns to psychology and allied sciences for an answer to the central question of epistemology, namely, 'How do we acquire our overall theory of the world and why does it work so well?' (see NNK, 68). Thus, for Quine:

> Naturalism does not repudiate epistemology, but assimilates it to empirical psychology. Science itself tells us that our information about the world is limited to irritations of our surfaces, and then the epistemological question is in turn a question within science: the question how we human animals can have managed to arrive at science from such limited information. Our scientific epistemologist pursues this inquiry and comes out with an account that has a good deal to do with the learning of language and with the neurology of perception. He talks of how men posit bodies and hypothetical particles, but he does not mean to suggest that the things thus posited do not exist. Evolution and natural selection will doubtless figure in this account, and he will feel free to apply physics if he sees a way.
>
> The naturalistic philosopher begins his reasoning within the inherited world theory as a going concern. He tentatively believes all of it, but believes also that some unidentified portions are wrong. He tries to improve, clarify, and understand the system from within. He is the busy sailor adrift on Neurath's boat. (FME, 72)

Let us investigate further the nature of the relationship, implicit in these remarks, between ontology and epistemology in the context of naturalized epistemology. Ontology and epistemology are concerned with different issues. Ontology focuses on the issue of what there is; and what there is is a question of *truth*. Epistemology focuses on the issue of how we know what there is; and how we know what there is is a question of *method* and *evidence*. Evidence is, for Quine, sensory evidence, so epistemology is, for Quine, empiricism. It follows that empiricism is not a theory of truth but a theory of evidence (i.e., of warranted belief) (see VITD, 39). It does not purport to tell us what there is, but only what evidence there is for what there is. It is in this sense that Quine suggests that empiricism is the epistemology of ontology (see OIR, 500).

Despite the fact that ontology and epistemology focus on different issues, ontology and epistemology are, for Quine, intimately related to each other. *And Quine's philosophy cannot be properly understood without grasping the nature of this intimate relationship.* The relationship is complex and subtle, and it is best characterized, in Quine's own words, as "reciprocal containment" (EN, 83).

When Quine says that ontology and epistemology are related to each other by way of reciprocal containment, what he means is that epistemology (empiricism) is contained in ontology (natural science) as a chapter of empirical psychology, and yet it is epistemology (empiricism) that provides an account of the methodological and evidential bases of ontology (natural science), including empirical psychology itself. As we have seen, the circularity that this reciprocal containment evinces is something that Quine fully owns up to. At the cost of enduring some repetition, let us investigate more closely this business of the reciprocal containment of epistemology and ontology.

§2.4.1 *How epistemology is contained in ontology*

Quine's epistemology—his empiricistic theory of method and evidence—is contained in his ontology (natural science) on at least three grounds: his epistemology assumes the existence of the external world; the two cardinal tenets of his epistemology (noted earlier) are implications of his ontology; and epistemology's contact points with the world, sensory receptors, are physical objects—objects belonging to the ontology of physiology. Let us examine each of these three grounds, in turn.

§2.4.1.1 *The external world*

As we have noted, traditional epistemology, rationalistic or empiricistic, attempted to deduce or to rationally reconstruct ontological claims concerning the external world from a conceptual foundation that, itself, was not to be a part of that body of ontological claims, and yet was to be absolutely indubitable. Three central assumptions of such epistemology are: that if there is an external world, then its existence needs proving; that any such proof would be viciously circular should it depend essentially on any existential claim about the external world; and that knowledge, by its very nature, must be indubitable.

Quine rejects all three of these central assumptions of traditional epistemology. From a Quinian perspective, the three hundred years from Descartes to Carnap (Idealism aside) were dominated by a forlorn squabble revolving around the comparative foundationalist merits of innate ideas and sense data—a squabble that could only end up just where it did, namely, in a repudiation of traditional (Realist) epistemology. Both the *deduction of* and the *reconstruction of* knowledge of the external world on the basis of some epistemologically prior footing are impossible dreams (see EN, 74). The moral to be drawn is, simply, that there is no such prior footing to be had: three hundred years of meditating on first philosophy have only culminated in repudiating first philosophy! But, to repudiate first philosophy is not to repudiate epistemology *in toto*: there is still *naturalized* epistemology, an epistemology that presupposes ontology—the ontology of natural science.

Such an epistemology is, of course, circular but not, as we saw, viciously so (see EC, 24). The keys to understanding this point are the following: First, skepticism about the external world presupposes the existence of the external world. Once this point is grasped, it is clear that the defender of the belief in the existence of the external world is also free to use scientific knowledge in his defense (see RR, 3, and FME, 72). Second, naturalized epistemology, unlike traditional empiricistic epistemology, does not attempt to *rationally reconstruct* the ontology of natural science from some kind of pristine, unadulterated sensory experience, nor does it attempt to *deduce* the ontology of natural science from sensory experience, unadulterated or otherwise. These traditional goals of empiricism must be abandoned, according to Quine, for the very notion of pristine, unadulterated sensory experience is rather dubious, and anyway there are no unique evidential relations to be found between sensory evidence and the theories it supports. Finally, this same holism opens the way for Quine's fallibilism, enabling him to reject the traditional characterization of knowledge as indubitable (see R, 180). Thus Quine's program of naturalized epistemology is circular (because it presupposes ontology), but it is not viciously so (because it renounces the affectations—and afflictions—of first philosophy).

§2.4.1.2 *Two cardinal tenets of (empiricistic) epistemology*

We have already noted that epistemology is concerned with the theory of method and evidence, and evidence is, for Quine, sensory evidence. Thus is Quine's epistemology empiricistic. We have also noted the two cardinal tenets of such epistemology: (1) "... whatever evidence there *is* for science *is* sensory evidence" (EN, 75); and (2) "... all inculcation of meanings of words must rest ultimately on sensory evidence" (EN, 75).

Now, what is the *source* of these two tenets? In a word, science. "Science itself teaches that there is no clairvoyance; that the only information that can reach our sensory surfaces from external objects must be limited to two-dimensional optical projections and various impacts of air waves on the eardrums and some gaseous reactions in the nasal passages and a few kindred odds and ends" (RR, 2; also see RS, 293–94). Note the *normative* force of this claim: if the only information about the external world comes to us via the senses, then one *ought not* to seek such information via some other channel. As we shall see, Quine conceives of naturalized epistemology as a partly normative inquiry (see RW, 664–65). Nevertheless, it should be emphasized that Quine does not regard the norms of present-day science to be immutable (see R, 181). Even if unlikely, it is possible, for example, that sensory stimulation might cease to be the chief source of our expectations regarding future events in the world, being replaced, say, by prophetic dreams. "At that point we might reasonably doubt our theory of nature in even fairly broad outlines. But our doubts would still be immanent, and of a piece with the scientific endeavor" (TPT, 22). So, even though Quine insists that our ontology (natural science) tells us that our epistemology is *true*, and our epistemology tells us that our ontology is *warranted*, still both of these claims are *part of science itself* and are therefore mutable and fallible. I take this to be a very important point when it comes to understanding Quine's philosophy.

§2.4.1.3 *Epistemology's contact points with the world*

We have just noted that ontology (natural science) tells us that its only evidence is sensory evidence. But what is sensory evidence? It is the activation of (physical) nerve endings by physical objects. But the very idea of nerve endings, epistemology's contact points with the world, belong to that part of ontology called physiology; in other words, epistemology presupposes an ontology of nerve endings. And thus it is that the two cardinal tenets of Quine's empiricistic epistemology presuppose an ontology of nerve endings and their physical stimulators, external objects. And thus it is, too, that empiricism remains in contact with the external world, making "scientific method partly empirical rather than solely a quest for internal coherence" (VITD, 39).

So much for how epistemology is contained in ontology. We now turn to a consideration of the second aspect of the reciprocal containment of ontology and epistemology.

§2.4.2 *How ontology is contained in epistemology*

> The old epistemology aspired to contain, in a sense, natural science; it would construct it somehow from sense data. Epistemology in its new setting, conversely, is contained in natural science, as a chapter of psychology [as we have just seen]. But the old containment remains valid too, in its way. We are studying how the human subject of our study posits bodies and projects his physics from his data, and we appreciate that our position in the world is just like his. Our very epistemological enterprise, therefore, and the psychology wherein it is a component chapter, and the whole of natural science wherein psychology is a component book—all this is our own construction or projection from stimulations like those we were meting out to our epistemological subject. There is thus reciprocal containment, though containment in different senses: epistemology in natural science and natural science in epistemology. (EN, 83)

In short, ontology is contained in epistemology in the sense that the ontology of natural science, which the new epistemologist relies upon in providing his account of natural science, is itself a projection from the very same kinds of stimulations attributed to the human subject of his study. Another way of putting this same point is to say that scientific epistemologists are themselves prohibited from making appeals to any alleged *a priori* (or otherwise transcendental) sources of knowledge—after all, they deny same to the human subjects of their inquiry.

It should be obvious from these remarks that Quine is no Kantian. However, some of Quine's commentators have insisted on interpreting him as a Kantian. This interpretation comes in two varieties: the ontological and the epistemological.

Quine the alleged ontological Kantian is supposedly arguing for the view that there are alternative systems of concepts (alternative conceptual frameworks) which can be used to order the raw data of experience into various theories of what there is (alternative ontologies). But, if what has been said regarding the reciprocal containment of ontology and epistemology is true, then this reading of Quine must be rejected, for there are simply no "raw data of experience" to be conceptualized. Instead, Quine talks of activated sensory receptors. And such talk is not transcendental, for sensory receptors are already part of the ontology of natural science, namely, of physiology and anatomy (see TPT, 21). To read Quine as an ontological Kantian is, therefore, to read him as doing first philosophy. And that would certainly be mistaken: we have already seen that Quine's epistemology *presupposes* ontology, namely, the ontology of natural science. (Furthermore, Quine denies that conceptual frameworks are separable from language, but that is another story [see VITD, 41].)

Quine the alleged epistemological Kantian is supposedly arguing for the view that there are certain *a priori* (i.e., immutable) constraints on theory construction. But, again, if what we have said regarding reciprocal containment is true, then this reading of Quine also must be rejected; for, as we have seen, the constraints on theory construction are as tentative and mutable as science itself. To repeat an earlier important claim: our ontology (natural science) tells us that our epistemology is *true*, and our epistemology (empiricism) tells us that our ontology is *warranted*, but still *both of these claims are part of science itself* and are therefore fallible and mutable.

50 *Enlightened Empiricism*

§2.5 *Instrumentalism, realism, and naturalism*

We are now in a position to address the subtle matter, touched upon in chapter 1, of how Quine attempts to accommodate the contrary forces of instrumentalism and realism within a consistent, pragmatic philosophy of science.

Quine has said that the criterion for settling what objects a theory *says* there are is a matter of determining the range of values of the bound variables of the theory: "To be assumed as an entity is, purely and simply, to be reckoned as the value of a variable" (OWTI, 13). But this criterion is neutral on the issue of instrumentalism versus realism. Once the theory is formalized and interpreted, the question of the reality of its objects remains.

Regarding Quine's instrumentalism, we can say that he sees science as an instrument for predicting future experiences and for explaining past experiences. Beyond conforming to experience, however, the hypotheses of science must measure up to the six virtues of plausibility surveyed in chapter 1. Even within these constraints, however, science is underdetermined by experience. Different systems of science (with different ontologies) could, Quine insists, be built on the same observational base. This view suggests that the ontology of a science is a mere instrument facilitating the making of predictions.

Regarding Quine's realism, we can say that he regards the objects (including the so-called theoretical and abstract objects) that are posited in the best current scientific theory as real. How are these two positions to be reconciled? Quine's response is:

> The reconciliation lies in my naturalism. Disavowing as I do a first philosophy outside science, I can attribute reality and truth only within the terms and standards of the scientific system of the world that I now accept: only immanently. But also, within this system, I can study man at work and appreciate how his theory—mine—is underdetermined. (RL, 316)

Quine's position is that, even though we occasionally condescend to mock our forefathers for believing in, say, phlogiston and the ether, and even though we know that our theory of the world is (no less than our forefathers' was) underdetermined by experience, and even though we can be confident that our progeny will someday ridicule us for having ascribed reality to some objects they think laughable—despite all this, we, like our forefathers and our progeny, can never do better than to occupy the perspective of some historical theory or other. *There is no first philosophy, no cosmic exile from which to pontificate on reality.*

This thoroughgoing naturalism is not only the key to a proper understanding of how Quine attempts the reconciliation of his instrumentalism and his realism; it is, I believe, the key to a proper understanding of his entire systematic philosophy. However, when we delve further into Quine's doctrine of underdetermination of physical theory in chapter 5, we shall find that Quine's attempted reconciliation of instrumentalism and realism may not be entirely successful.

§2.6 *Conclusions*

In this chapter, we have investigated the nature of, the scope of, and Quine's arguments for naturalized epistemology. In Quine's negative usage, 'naturalism' amounts to the denial of first philosophy, "abandonment of the goal of a first philosophy prior to natural science" (FME, 67). In his affirmative usage, 'naturalism' amounts to scientism, "the recognition that it is within science itself . . . that reality is to be identified and described" (TPT, 21).

The two negative bases of Quine's naturalism are holism and unregenerate realism. The former ushers out traditional epistemology; the latter ushers in naturalized epistemology. Quine bases his holism on observations about the actual practices of scientists, on his theory of language learning, and on a *reductio* of epistemological reductionism. In short, holism is an empirical hypothesis about sufficiently rich languages—languages rich enough for the purposes of science. Quine bases his unregenerate realism (scientism) on the recognition that skepticism presupposes scientific knowledge and on his confidence that the defenders of science, accorded access to the same, can successfully fend off the skeptics' attacks. Beyond these negative bases for naturalism, Quine claims that naturalism is desirable on the grounds that it renders the question of epistemic priority moot. Furthermore, Quine successfully slips Grunbaum's criticisms of holism, and it only seems fair that the defenders of science should be availed of the same caliber of ammunition as their attacking skeptics.

Within the context of naturalized epistemology Quine envisions a mutual containment of epistemology and ontology. Epistemology is contained in ontology (i.e., empiricism is contained in natural science) on at least three grounds: (1) epistemology assumes the existence of the external world; (2) the two cardinal tenets of (empiricistic) epistemology that Quine isolates are implications of ontology; (3) sensory receptors, epistemology's contact points with the world, are physical objects—objects belonging to the ontology of anatomy-physiology. Ontology, on the other hand, is contained in epistemology in the sense that in giving their account of the acquisition of science naturalized epistemologists are themselves limited to just the same data they accord to the human subjects of their study. If the two tenets of empiricism circumscribe the data of their subjects, then the same two tenets circumscribe their own data.

This analysis of Quine"s "reciprocal containment" metaphor reveals the incorrectness of interpreting him as a sort of Kantian. Quine is arguing neither for the view that there are alternative conceptual frameworks with which to conceptualize the raw data of experience (ontological Kantianism) nor for the view that there are *a priori* constraints on theory construction (epistemological Kantianism). Neither "the raw data of experience" nor "the *a priori*" are notions acceptable to Quine. Only their naturalistic analogues, "stimulation" and "the last sentences to be relinquished," make the grade.

Finally Quine attempts to reconcile the instrumentalist and realist tendencies in his philosophy of science by appealing to naturalism. Our currently best scientific theory of what there is informs us that this theory itself is underdetermined by experience. Thus, the entities posited by the theory go beyond anything that is humanly possible to experience. However, this instrumentalist conclusion is mitigated by Quine's naturalism, the view that, because there is no first philosophy, science is the measure of reality. At any given time, the objects posited by the best scientific theory answer the question of what is real. Whether Quine's attempted reconciliation is entirely successful remains to be seen.

Naturalized Epistemology Reconsidered

CHAPTER 3

§3.1 *Introduction*

As we saw toward the end of chapter 2, according to Quine's program of naturalized epistemology *epistemological* questions regarding the relation of evidence to theory are to become *scientific* questions about science; questions like: 'How is science acquired solely on the basis of sensory stimulations?' and 'Why does the resulting science work so well?'.

Philosophers there are, however, who believe that Quine's program for epistemology is misconceived. Some of these philosophers regard Quine's proposal as constituting too radical a break with traditional epistemology. They believe that epistemology simply cannot be naturalized; thus, they deny that Quine's naturalized epistemology is *really* epistemology. They argue for this conclusion either on the grounds that Quine's naturalized epistemology is incoherent or on the grounds that psychology is a descriptive discipline, epistemology is a normative discipline, and the former therefore cannot do the job of the latter—the job of providing an analysis of *justified* true belief. Other philosophers, however, regard Quine's proposal as constituting an insufficiently radical break with traditional epistemological practices. These philosophers applaud Quine's rejection of traditional epistemology, but they disagree with Quine that this rejection should be followed by the installation of any successor subject at all. They argue that the quest for epistemology in the traditional sense is predicated upon grave misunderstandings regarding man's nature and the nature of the human mind, while at the same time (ironically) agreeing with Quine's more traditionally minded critics that psychology cannot do the work that traditional epistemology was intended to do. Thus is Quine's proposal for naturalizing epistemology caught in a crossfire between an unlikely coalition of traditionally minded epistemologists and philosophers of a more radical bent of mind. The traditionalists' attack is motivated by their fear that Quine has gone too far; the radicals' attack is motivated by their disappointment that Quine has not gone far enough.

In this chapter, we shall examine the arguments of some of these critics of Quine's proposal for naturalizing epistemology. However, before going on to this task, it will be helpful to have in mind Quine's *strategy* for carrying out the program of naturalized epistemology.

§3.2 *Externalizing empiricism: a genetic approach*

Quine believes that the most fruitful approach toward answering the questions 'How is science acquired solely on the basis of sensory stimulations?' and 'Why does the resulting science work so well?' is to *externalize* them. This means that in seeking an understanding of the relation between evidence and theory the naturalized epistemologist will not talk of the relation between, say, sensations and reflection, impressions and ideas, or sense data and theory. Instead, he will talk of the relation between observation *sentences* and theoretical *sentences*, and of the relation between observation *sentences* and stimuli. Sentences, or their utterances, and stimuli are out in the open, accessible to the intersubjective techniques of study characteristic of natural science generally. Thus, *naturalizing epistemology calls for the externalization of empiricism*.

Answering the central questions of epistemology now becomes a matter of providing an account of the relation between observational *talk* and stimuli, and observational *talk* and theoretical *talk*. These relations have two aspects, an epistemological (evidential) aspect and a semantical (meaning) aspect. The stimuli related via conditioning to the observation sentences constitute their evidence and their (stimulus) meanings. In turn, the multifarious relations between observation sentences and theoretical sentences constitute the evidence for, and the "meanings" of, the latter. We have already dwelled on the holistic nature of these relations. (Also see Gibson 1982, 30.)

Correlatively, the central problem of accounting for the link between evidence and theory has two aspects, expressed by the following two questions: 'How does one sentence serve as evidence for another?' and 'How do sentences acquire their meanings?'. The answers to these questions begin with the roles that observation sentences play in providing both evidential support and meaning for the other kinds of sentences in theories. Observation sentences play an *evidential role* in theories because they are the kind of sentences that enjoy virtually unanimous acceptance among the members of the speech community. Two theorists may disagree about the truth of some theoretical sentence, but at the level of observation sentences they will find a common ground for assessing relevant evidence. Observation sentences also play a *semantical role* in theories, for although most of language consists of interverbal associations, somewhere there have to be nonverbal reference points, nonverbal circumstances that can be intersubjectively appreciated and associated with appropriate utterances—this follows from the empirical claim that we learn our language from other people amid intersubjectively appreciable stimulus conditions. Observation sentences are therefore the gateway to language *and* to science; and *language is the gateway to naturalized epistemology:* "We see, then, a strategy for investigating the relation of evidential support, between observation and scientific theory. We can adopt a *genetic approach*, studying how theoretical language is learned" (NNK, 74; my italics).

Quine's externalization of empiricism and his genetic approach toward answering the central questions of such a naturalized epistemology are, I believe, methodological measures of tremendous historical moment for empiricism. For if Quine's program is sound, then *much* (but not all) of what is central to traditional empiricism, the very empiricism that Quine has done so much to undermine, can be salvaged—naturalistic analogues of a good many notions of traditional empiricism can be forged. This is the meaning of Quine's claim that "[n]aturalism does not repudiate epistemology, but assimilates it to empirical psychology" (FME, 72). However, as we have noted, Quine's proposal is not without its critics, and it is their criticisms to which we now turn.

§3.3 *The Conservative Wing*

Among the philosophers who fear that Quine has gone too far is Barry Stroud. In his recent book, *The Significance of Philosophical Scepticism*, Stroud includes a long chapter entitled "Naturalized Epistemology" (Stroud 1984, 209–54), dealing exclusively with Quine's version of naturalized epistemology. The first part of the chapter (209–28) provides an excellent overview of Quine's conception of naturalized epistemology. Nevertheless, it is not without its flaws, two of which are: (1) Stroud provides no account of Quine's doctrine of the reciprocal containment of ontology and epistemology, and (2) he takes no note of the genetic strategy Quine uses in answering the central epistemological question.

In the remainder of the chapter (229–54), Stroud focuses on Quine's claim that, compared to traditional epistemology, naturalized epistemology "is no gratuitous change of subject matter, but an enlightened persistence rather in the original epistemological problem" (RR, 3). Stroud construes "the original epistemological problem" to be one of explaining how knowledge is possible, in the face of the skeptical challenge. He argues that insofar as Quine's naturalized epistemology purports to be "an enlightened persistence . . . in the original epistemological problem," it is a failure, for it *does not* answer the skeptic (228–43). Furthermore, he argues that naturalized epistemology *cannot* answer the skeptic (243–54).

Stroud has a pretty good grasp of Quine's epistemology, and Stroud himself is a pretty good philosopher. Thus, his criticisms of Quine's position ought to be taken seriously. Nevertheless, I believe his arguments are flawed, as I shall try to show.

As we noted in the previous chapter, Quine points out that skepticism presupposes science. The philosophical significance of this observation is just that it frees the epistemologist of the impossible burden of propounding a first philosophy upon which to base scientific knowledge. Quine appropriately refers to such a naturalized epistemology as *enlightened empiricism*; it is enlightened because the new epistemologist is now free to use the findings of science in constructing his defense of scientific knowledge:

> A far cry, this, from old epistemology. Yet it is no gratuitous change of subject matter, but an enlightened persistence rather in the original epistemological problem. It is enlightened in recognizing that the skeptical challenge springs from science itself, and that in coping with it we are free to use scientific knowledge. The old epistemologist failed to recognize the strength of his position. (RR, 3)

Stroud does not deny Quine's logico-historical point that skepticism is prompted by knowledge, but he argues that if naturalized epistemology is to be understood as Quine suggests, as "an enlightened persistence . . . in the original epistemological problem," as attempting to answer the skeptic, then it must be seen as having failed to do so. His argument turns on Quine's admission that the skeptical challenge to science is a legitimate enterprise, which, if carried out, would be a straightforward argument by *reductio ad absurdum*:

> I am not accusing the sceptic of begging the question. He is quite within his rights in assuming science in order to refute science; this, if carried out, would be a straightforward argument by *reductio ad absurdum*. I am only making the point that sceptical doubts are scientific doubts. (NNK, 68)

According to Stroud, this admission by Quine

> is an important concession, and amounts to a very powerful point in the traditional philosopher's defence. If there is nothing logically peculiar or self-defeating in starting with some scientific knowledge and ending up by rejecting or doubting it all, what becomes of 'the crucial logical point' that the traditional epistemologist is said to have missed? If the 'only' point Quine is making is that 'sceptical doubts are scientific doubts', does it follow that epistemology, 'then', is part of natural science, and that 'clearly' the epistemologist may make free use

of all scientific theory? Once it is granted that the sceptic might be arguing by *reductio ad absurdum,* I think it does not follow. (228)

Stroud concludes:

> If I am right, the fact that 'sceptical doubts are scientific doubts' does not put the epistemologist who raises such doubts in the stronger position of being free to use scientific knowledge of the world in his effort to answer those doubts and explain how knowledge is possible. (229)

The putative issue between Stroud and Quine can be summarized as follows: Quine argues that epistemological skepticism presupposes scientific knowledge about the world. Once this fact is recognized, it is clear that the defender of science is free to use scientific knowledge in defending science against the skeptical challenge. Furthermore, the skeptic's challenge is not illegitimate: the skeptic may argue by *reductio* that scientific knowledge (so-called) is false. This being conceded, Stroud concludes that the naturalized epistemologist has not answered the skeptic, for the epistemologist cannot use the now discredited science in constructing his defense of science.

As Stroud reports, in reaction to this apparent problem, Quine emphasizes his naturalism:

> . . . in keeping with my naturalism, I am reasoning within the overall scientific system rather than somehow above or beyond it. The same applies to my statement, quoted by Stroud, that "I am not accusing the sceptic of begging the question; he is quite within his rights in assuming science in order to refute science." The skeptic repudiates science because it is vulnerable to illusion on its own showing; *and my only criticism of the skeptic is that he is overreacting.* (RTS, 475; note omitted, my italics)

But what does Quine mean here by "the skeptic is . . . overreacting"? Stroud understands Quine to mean "that the sceptical 'theory' is not yet as well-confirmed as some other views. Perhaps it will become so, but for the moment it lacks sufficient justification"

(Stroud 984, 232). And, as Stroud rightly protests, this "is a far cry from the position reached at the end of Descartes's *First Meditation*" (232). It certainly does seem ludicrous that Cartesian skepticism could be shown to be correct or incorrect by making further observations and experiments! Unmoved by Quine's appeal to naturalism, Stroud reasserts his conclusion that "if the sceptic can be seen as arguing by *reductio* to the conclusion that all of that science nevertheless provides no knowledge of the world, the consolations of naturalism alone will not be enough" (233–34).

Is Stroud correct? Is Quine's appeal to naturalism beside the point? I do not believe that Stroud is correct. I believe he misunderstands what Quine has in mind when he accuses the skeptic of overreacting. Furthermore, I believe this misunderstanding is the consequence of Stroud's failure to appreciate how epistemology and ontology reciprocally contain one another, in Quine's thoroughgoing naturalism.

Stroud understands very well the sense in which ontology is contained in epistemology, i.e., how our theory of the world, our ontology, is a projection, or a posit, that goes beyond our sensory evidence. As we shall see, this is the ground for Stroud's saying that naturalized epistemology *cannot* answer the skeptic. However, Stroud completely misses the other aspect of the reciprocal containment of epistemology and ontology, i.e., how ontology contains epistemology. Recall that ontology contains epistemology in at least three ways: (1) epistemology presupposes the existence of the external world; (2) epistemology's contact points with the external world are (physical) nerve endings; and (3) the two cardinal tenets of empiricism regarding evidence and meaning are derived from science. Because Stroud overlooks this aspect of the reciprocal containment of epistemology and ontology, he arrives at his mistaken interpretation of what Quine means by accusing the skeptic of overreacting.

The relevant point about the containment (of epistemology by ontology) is that transcendental epistemology is incoherent. The skeptic may indeed use a portion of science to bring doubt to bear upon science, but only by presupposing the truth of other portions of science. For example, the skeptic might show that some scientific posits are epistemologically unwarranted, but his epistemological deliverances presuppose his *interim* acceptance of other scientific posits, namely, those presupposed by his own theory of evidence:

"our questioning of objects can coherently begin only in relation to a system of theory which is itself predicated on our interim acceptances of objects. We are limited in how we can start even if not in where we may end up" (WO, 4).

Now, how does all this relate to Quine's remark about the skeptic overreacting? Just so: the skeptic who "repudiates science because it is vulnerable to illusion on its own showing" is overreacting in the sense that his position is a transcendental one and thus an incoherent one. Skepticism, like epistemology, presupposes some further ontology: ". . . we might reasonably doubt our theory of nature in even its broadest outlines. But our doubts would still be immanent, and of a piece with the scientific endeavor" (RTS, 475). Never can all ontological commitments be coherently doubted simultaneously; one would be overreacting if one thought that all ontological commitments could be simultaneously doubted.

To sum up: I have argued that Stroud is mistaken in his claim that naturalized epistemology *does not* answer the skeptic because Quine acknowledges that the skeptic's *reductio* is a legitimate undertaking. Because he overlooks or ignores Quine's "reciprocal containment" metaphor, Stroud focuses only on how epistemology contains ontology, thereby failing to notice that ontology also contains epistemology. Thus is he led into his misinterpretation of what Quine means by saying that the skeptic is overreacting. Contrary to Stroud's interpretation, Quine *is not* claiming "that the sceptical 'theory' is not yet as well-confirmed as some other views. Perhaps it will become so, but for the moment it lacks sufficient justification." Rather, Quine is pointing out that epistemology does not occur in an ontological vacuum (i.e., transcendentally), that the skeptic's "doubts would still be immanent, and of a piece with the scientific endeavor," and to think otherwise is overreacting. What now of Stroud's second criticism?

We have been examining Stroud's argument that naturalized epistemology, construed as "an enlightened persistence . . . in the original epistemological problem," does *not* answer the skeptical challenge, because it does not answer the skeptic's *reductio;* and we have found Stroud's argument wanting. But Stroud has an even stronger claim to make against naturalized epistemology, namely, that it *cannot* answer the skeptic, regardless of the outcome of the skeptic's *reductio*:

Quine's naturalistic study of knowledge proceeds in terms of a general distinction between what we get through the senses and everything we believe about the physical world on the basis of those data. I would now like to argue that that conception of knowledge and of the epistemological task not only tolerates scepticism, as I have just been suggesting, but is actually committed to it. It would make it impossible for us to understand, even on its own terms, how our knowledge of the external world in general is possible. (234)

Before we can understand Stroud's argument for the above position we must first come to understand his view of what knowledge amounts to within the Quinian problematic:

In the kind of experimental situation Quine is imagining, then, I can explain the subject's knowledge in the right way only if I know that the world around him is as he says it is, and that its being that way is partly responsible for his saying or believing it to be that way. Only then would I be doing more than explaining the origin of a belief that happens to be true. (238)

Stroud's view is that, as a Quinian epistemologist, I can witness a human subject's nerve endings being stimulated (input) and I can observe his subsequent behavior, including his verbal behavior (output). And, if I know that his beliefs "are true, and I can explain how they come to stand in the proper relation to the facts they are about, I can understand how the person knows what he does. If they are not true, I can see that he lacks knowledge" (1984, 239). It is doubtful that Quine would accept this characterization of knowledge as it stands, without further elaboration, for Quine does not see knowledge as a matter of individual beliefs (or sentences) "corresponding" to worldly facts. Thus, a certain amount of talking past one another is to be expected in this exchange between Stroud and Quine.

The next step in Stroud's argument is to show that this view of knowledge (possessed by the human subject of our epistemological study) cannot be applied to one's self:

> The position we find another human subject in, on Quine's view, is that of 'positing' bodies or 'projecting' all of physics from the 'meager' sensory data to which he is restricted in his contact with the world he believes to exist. If each of us, in thinking of himself, must 'appreciate that our position in the world is just like his', each of us will have to appreciate that we too are restricted to 'meager' sensory data, and that all of our beliefs about the physical world around us go far beyond, or are grossly underdetermined by, those data. (242)

However, Stroud does not believe that we can actually perform this act of "appreciation": "we cannot see all our own beliefs about the world as 'construction or projection from stimulations'—while still explaining how our own, or anyone else's, knowledge of the world is possible" (242). But why is this? Why can't we perform the Quinian act of "appreciation"? Stroud explains further:

> What happens when I try to take up the view that all my beliefs about the external physical world amount to a 'construction or projection' from 'meager' sensory 'data'? I know what all my beliefs about the world are, but I do not have any independent access to the world those beliefs are about on the basis of which I could determine whether or not they are true. In the normal case in which I am studying another person in interaction with the world, I can do that. I know what his beliefs are, and I can know, independently of the fact that he has those beliefs, what is the case in the world those beliefs are about. That is what enables me to explain how his knowledge is possible in that situation. In my own case, if I regard all my beliefs about the world as 'posits' or 'projections' from sensory data, I would not be in that position.
>
> . . .
>
> My . . . point is that I could not check my beliefs about the physical world against the facts of the world . . . *if* I at the same time regarded *all* my beliefs about the physical world as nothing more than a 'construction or projection from stimulations' in the way Quine intends. I would have no independent information about that world that I could use as a test or a check. (243–44)

I think we must grant Stroud his claim that "we cannot perform *that* act of 'appreciation'—we cannot see all our own beliefs about the world as a 'construction or projection from stimulations'—*while* still explaining how our own, or anyone else's, knowledge of the world is possible." However, as a criticism of Quine's position this point misfires, for "*that* act" described by Stroud is not Quine's:

> Stroud finds difficulty in reconciling my naturalistic stance with my concern with how we gain our knowledge of the world. We may stimulate a psychological subject and compare his resulting beliefs with the facts as we know them; this much Stroud grants, but he demurs at our projecting ourselves into the subject's place, since we no longer have the independent facts to compare with. My answer is that this projection must be seen not transcendentally but as a routine matter of analogies and causal hypotheses *within our scientific theory*. True, we must hedge the perhaps too stringent connotations of the verb 'know'; but such is fallibilism. (RTS, 474; my italics)

Quine's chief point is that the act of "appreciation" takes place *within science,* not transcendentally. Contrary to Stroud's belief, the recognition that one's beliefs are projections from one's data does not force one "to repudiate the ontology in terms of which the recognition took place" (TPT, 21). Of course, one could repudiate that ontology, but only by relying on some other ontology (see TPT, 21–22, and RA, 24–26).

Why does Stroud fail to accept this answer? The obstacle appears to be the same old difficulty: failure to appreciate that for Quine epistemology is contained in ontology, that epistemology does not exist in an ontological vacuum.

> Transcendental argument, or what purports to be first philosophy, tends generally to take on rather this status of immanent epistemology insofar as I succeed in making sense of it. What evaporates is the transcendental question of the reality of the external world—the question whether or in how far our science measures up to the *Ding an sich*. (TPT, 22)

64   *Enlightened Empiricism*

On this point, I believe—in Richard Rorty's terms—that we have a classic confrontation between a philosopher who has given up the idea that the mind is a mirror of nature and a philosopher who has not. The former acquiesces in "the robust state of mind of the natural scientist who has never felt any qualms beyond the negotiable uncertainties internal to science" (FME, 72), while the latter takes philosophical skepticism far more seriously.

However, Stroud is not through; he concludes:

> What I have meant to deny, with Kant, is that we can regard all our beliefs about the world as 'projections' or as 'theoretical' relative to some 'data' or bits of 'evidence' epistemically prior to them, while at the same time explaining how our knowledge of the world is possible. . . . Quine's project of naturalized epistemology has the interest and the apparent connection with traditional epistemology that it has only because it contains and depends on just such a bi-partite conception of human knowledge of the world. That is what I have argued cannot succeed in explaining how knowledge is possible. But without that conception, 'naturalized epistemology' as Quine describes it would be nothing but the causal explanation of various physiological events. (253)

In short, Stroud argues that naturalized epistemology either fails *as* epistemology or it fails *to be* epistemology.

Relative to the first of these points, I have argued that Stroud really has not proven that naturalized epistemology fails *as* epistemology; for his argument that naturalized epistemology *does not* answer the skeptic's *reductio*, and his argument that naturalized epistemology *cannot* answer the skeptic because the Quinian account of knowledge cannot be applied to one's self, are both flawed insofar as they both overlook the fact that for Quine epistemology is contained in ontology, the ontology of natural science. Transcendental skeptical doubts, like transcendental epistemology, are incoherent.

The second of Stroud's points, that naturalized epistemology fails *to be* epistemology, is something new. Quine has claimed that "[t]he relation between the meager input [viz., stimulations] and the torrential output [viz., theory of nature] is a relation that we are prompted to study for somewhat the same reasons that always prompted epistemology; namely, in order to see how evidence relates to theory, and in what ways one's theory of nature transcends any available evidence" (EN, 83). However, Quine has also claimed that by appealing to stimulations rather than, say, to sense data or to Gestalten we avoid debates about awareness and epistemic priority. Now, Stroud's claim is that Quine cannot have it both ways. Here is his argument:

> Something happens at a sensory surface, and then a coming-to-believe-something-about-the-world occurs. The relation between those two events is simply that the former causes the latter (along with the help of those in between). But 'underdetermination' speaks of a relation between something that is 'meager' relative to something else that is 'torrential'; the latter 'transcends' the former. If we think only about the events involved—the events at the sensory surface and the events closer to 'our cognitive mechanism' that result in our believing what we do—and we drop all talk of 'meagerness', 'underdetermination', 'torrential output', and so on, what becomes of Quine's question about our knowledge of the world around us? We are left with questions about a series of physical events, and perhaps with questions about how those events bring it about that we believe what we do about the world around us. But in trying to answer those questions we will not be pursuing in an 'enlightened' scientific way a study of the relation between 'observation' and 'scientific theory', or of the 'ways one's theory of nature transcends any available evidence', or of 'the domain within which [man] can revise theory while saving the data'. We will be studying the connection between one kind of event and another. (251–52)

What are we to make of this claim that naturalized epistemology fails *to be* epistemology, that nerve hits cannot be evidence? I believe Stroud is led to perceive a difficulty where there is none because he has ignored or overlooked Quine's genetic approach toward resolving the epistemological problem. Quine's *genetic approach* amounts to reconstruing the epistemological problem—the problem of explaining the evidential relation between observation and theory—as the problem of explaining the evidential relation between *observation sentences* and *theoretical sentences*. And, surely, there is no difficulty with saying that observation sentences can be true or false and therefore can serve as repositories of evidence for theoretical sentences: 'It's green' may be evidence for 'It contains copper'. There is, however, another relation that needs explaining, and that is the relation between observation sentences and stimulus conditions. And Quine's account of this relation is well known: observation sentences are learnable by the method of ostension; they are linked to their stimulus conditions by the psychological mechanism of conditioned response. Why can't nerve hits serve (sometimes unconsciously) as evidence for holophrastically acquired observation sentences? The stimulus conditions under which a child, say, would assent to a queried observation sentence are just the conditions under which the sentence is true. By Quine's lights, "[a]ny realistic theory of evidence must be inseparable from the psychology of stimulus and response, applied to sentences" (WO, 17).

I have argued that Stroud's claim that Quine's version of naturalized epistemology *does not* answer the skeptic and his claim that it *cannot* answer the skeptic are unjustified. In both cases, Stroud has failed to see that for Quine epistemology (empiricism) is contained in ontology (natural science). This failure is indicative of a deeper disagreement between Stroud and Quine, having to do with the nature of epistemology and the philosophical importance of skepticism. Quine has rejected first philosophy, the quest for a non-scientific basis upon which to justify science. He believes that science requires no justification beyond measuring up to observation and the hypothetico-deductive method. Furthermore, he is a fallibilist, making no claim that knowledge entails certainty or incorrigibility. Thus, unlike Stroud, he is not much moved by the skeptic's doubts about science.

I have also argued that Stroud's claim that naturalized epistemology is rightly considered as merely the physiology of belief formation is mistaken because it overlooks Quine's genetic approach toward dealing with the epistemological problem. On Quine's approach the question of the relation between the "meager input" and the "torrential output" becomes two questions: 'How are observation *sentences* acquired on the basis of sensory stimulation?' and 'How do observation *sentences* serve as evidence for theoretical *sentences?*' Indeed, I believe that this *externalizing* of empiricism that

Quine's genetic approach requires is one of Quine's major philosophical contributions. (See Gibson 1982, 30.)

Hilary Putnam is another of Quine's conservative-minded critics. In "Why Reason Can't Be Naturalized," Putnam maintains that Quine's program of naturalized epistemology contains incompatible elements which Putnam can see no way of reconciling. According to Putnam, the Quine of "Epistemology Naturalized" (1969) rules out normative epistemology, while the Quine of "On Empirically Equivalent Systems of the World" (1975) advocates it. On the one hand, Quine emphasizes the *descriptive* nature of his program; on the other hand, he emphasizes the *normative* nature of his program. Regarding the normative, Putnam says, "I believe that . . . this is what the 'normative' becomes for Quine: the search for methods that yield verdicts that one oneself would accept" (20). In Putnam's hands, Quine's view of the normative becomes something like psychological self-description, so perhaps Putnam has inadvertently reconciled the two Quines after all! However, as I explain further below, I do not think that this is Quine's way of construing the normative.

Another writer who shares Putnam's uneasiness with Quine's program is Harvey Siegel. In his "Justification, Discovery and the Naturalizing of Epistemology," Siegel charges Quine with having fallen victim to a gross equivocation:

> . . . the notion of "understanding the link between observation and science" is equivocal. It equivocates between two distinct senses of "understanding the link": (a) understanding the psychological mechanisms by which scientific theories are produced, and (b) understanding the criteria by which we select one link over and against other links, one theory over and against other theories. This latter sense, of course, demands the evaluation of competing theories; the former does not. It is the former sense, though, that is amenable to empirical psychological research; the latter is not. (1980, 318–19)

In sum, "Quine's appeal to psychology can only help in accounting for the psychological mechanisms and processes of theory development—not in the rational evaluation of theory" (319).

Putnam and Siegel are harmonizing on a single theme: Quine's naturalized epistemology is sheepish psychology in wolf's clothing; it is descriptive, whereas *real*, wolfish epistemology is normative; therefore, since sheep aren't wolves, naturalized epistemologists aren't *real* epistemologists!

Is it true, though, that psychological explanation is descriptive and not normative? That is, cannot the psychologist who is studying the psychological mechanisms of belief formation and change say: "Now here are two causal mechanisms of belief formation. Mechanism *a* provides the means for making reliable predictions about future experience, while mechanism *b* does not"? So far the psychologist is merely describing the mechanisms and their differing utilities. But suppose he continues: "Therefore, one *ought* to utilize mechanism *a* rather than mechanism *b*." Now this is clearly a normative claim, as the word 'ought' indicates. Should the naturalized epistemologist-cum-psychologist be prohibited from making such normative claims? Certainly Quine does not think so:

> Naturalization of epistemology does not jettison the normative and settle for the indiscriminate description of ongoing procedures. For me normative epistemology is a branch of engineering. It is the technology of truth-seeking, or, in a more cautiously epistemological term, prediction. Like any technology, it makes free use of whatever scientific findings may suit its purpose. It draws upon mathematics in computing standard deviation and probable error and in scouting the gambler's fallacy. It draws upon experimental psychology in exposing perceptual illusions, and upon cognitive psychology in scouting wishful thinking. It draws upon neurology and physics, in a general way, in discounting testimony from occult or parapsychological sources. There is no question here of ultimate value, as in morals; it is a matter of efficacy for an ulterior end, truth or prediction. The normative here, as elsewhere in engineering, becomes descriptive when the terminal parameter is expressed. [E.g.: Anyone interested in making highly reliable predictions *ought* to utilize mechanism *a*.] We could say the same of morality if we could view it as aimed at reward in heaven. (RW, 664–65)

This does not sound like a Quine who has succumbed to a gross equivocation approaching the genetic fallacy (Siegel) nor a Quine who construes the normative to be mere psychological self-description (Putnam). The point that needs noticing and emphasizing is that science itself, including psychology, is normative. The norms involved are, of course, hypothetical, not categorical: 'One ought to do x, *if* one wants y', not 'One ought to do x'. (This is an issue we shall take up again in chapter 7, when discussing Quine's views on ethical values.) My suspicion is that Quine's conservative-minded critics assume without much argument that *true* epistemic norms are somehow grounded transcendentally. Siegel hints at this when he writes that "understanding the criteria by which we select one link over and against other links . . . is [not] amenable to empirical research." If this is not amenable to *empirical* research, then is it amenable to *a priori* "research"? That suggestion does not sound very promising to the ears of another of Quine's critics, Richard Rorty.

§3.4 *The Radical Wing*

Richard Rorty is foremost among those writers who have expressed disappointment that Quine has not gone further in distancing himself from traditional epistemology. As Rorty sees it, traditional epistemology is a misguided endeavor that emerged in the seventeenth and eighteenth centuries as a result of widespread misconceptions among philosophers regarding man's nature (viz., as an apprehender of essences) and the human mind (viz., as a mirror of nature's essences), a pathological preoccupation with skepticism and certainty, and a tendency of philosophers to mistake the *explanation* of belief (formation and change) for the *justification* of belief (see Rorty 1979, 10). He credits Quine, among others, with having exposed the folly of it all, but he suggests that, ironically, Quine has not understood the full consequences of his own (holistic-based) critique of traditional epistemology, since Quine persists in conflating explanation and justification, and since Quine succumbs to "*the* philosophical urge" to talk of "'correspondence'" (Rorty 1979, 179, 195; also see 229). Thus, while Rorty applauds (10) Quine's holistic-based attack on traditional epistemology, he criticizes Quine for misguidedly offering up empirical psychology as a successor subject to traditional epistemology when, so Rorty contends, none is either required or possible: ". . . such a 'new epistemology' can offer nothing relevant to issues of justification, and . . . consequently it has no relevance to the cultural demands which led to the emergence of epistemology in the seventeenth and eighteenth centuries" (220).

In sum, Rorty's argument can be put as follows:

> P1: Epistemology is concerned with justification.
> P2: Justification is public (i.e., social).
> P3: Empirical psychology is concerned with explanation.
> P4: Psychological explanation is private (i.e., it is concerned with internal mechanisms and processes).
> P5: Private psychological mechanisms and processes have no epistemological relevance to public (i.e., social) practices of justification.
> P6: Naturalized epistemology is limited to giving private, psychological explanations.
> C1: Naturalized epistemology has no relevance to public (i.e., social) practices of justification, that is, naturalized epistemology is in no legitimate sense epistemology.

The form of this argument is very similar to those of Putnam and Siegel, except that whereas they focus on the normative-descriptive distinction, Rorty focuses on the justification-explanation and public-private distinctions: justification is public, psychological explanation is private. However, unlike the criticisms of Putnam and Siegel, Rorty's criticisms of Quine's program should not be construed as a defense of traditional epistemology against Quine's onslaught. Rorty is not *merely* saying that Quine's naturalized epistemology cannot answer traditional philosophical questions concerning knowledge, he is also saying that such questions are themselves ill-conceived:

> Can we find any relevance to traditional philosophical problems concerning *knowledge* in actual or expected results of empirical psychological research? Since I wish to say that these "philosophical problems" should be dissolved rather than solved, it is predictable that I should give a negative answer. (219–20)

In sum, Rorty would have philosophy make a clean sweep of epistemology, old and new:

> The thing to do with epistemology is to "cure philosophers of the delusion that there were epistemological problems." Such therapy does not separate philosophy from science: it takes philosophy to be just common sense or science mobilized to provide "reminders for a particular purpose." (229–30; note omitted)

Thus, while the Conservative Wing and the Radical Wing agree in their attacks on Quine, they offer one another cold comfort indeed.

Let us thread our way through some of the specifics of Rorty's critique of Quine's position so that we may understand and evaluate Rorty's rejection of Quine's version of naturalized epistemology.

As we have seen, Quine understands naturalized epistemology to be a scientific (i.e., psychological) study of

> a physical human subject. This human subject is accorded a certain experimentally controlled input—certain patterns of irradiation in assorted frequencies, for instance—and in the fullness of time the subject delivers as output a description of the three-dimensional external world and its history. The relation between the meager input and the torrential output is a relation that we are prompted to study for somewhat the same reasons that always prompted epistemology; namely, in order to see how evidence relates to theory, and in what ways one's theory of nature transcends any available evidence. (EN, 82–83)

Rorty wants "to show how very remote any psychological discovery of the sort . . . [Quine] envisages will be from any concern with the foundations of science or with the relation between theory and evidence" (223). In fact, Rorty believes that it is only the looseness of such words as 'evidence', 'information', and 'testimony' that allows Quine to link empirical psychology with empiricistic epistemology. "This use permits Quine to say things like 'The nerve endings . . . are the place of input of unprocessed information about the world' and 'It is simply the stimulations of our sensory receptors that are best looked upon as the input of our cognitive mechanism'" (224; notes omitted). Rorty regards such claims as highly unempirical, for he sees no way for empirical psychology to establish experimentally the precise point where, say, mere electrical impulses become information. The problem is, he contends, that "it is hard to see what would count as an experimental criterion of 'information' or 'processing'" (224). Nevertheless, he claims that Quine seems to think that such criteria could be had, for Quine "notes that epistemology has always been torn between two criteria for being 'datal': 'causal proximity to the physical stimulus' and 'the focus of awareness'" (224). However, it appears that Quine does not see himself as attempting to provide such criteria; rather, he apparently wishes to circumvent the problem:

> The dilemma is dissolved, and the strain relieved, when we give up the dream of a first philosophy firmer than science. If we are seeking only the causal mechanism of our knowledge of the external world, and not a justification of that knowledge in terms prior to science, we can settle after all for a theory of vision in Berkeley's style based on color patches in a two-dimensional field. . . . We can look upon man as a black box in the physical world, exposed to externally determinable stimulatory forces as input and spouting externally determinable testimony about the external world as output. Just which of the inner workings of the black box may be tinged with awareness is as may be. (GT, 2–3)

Rorty has two responses to this suggestion of Quine's. First, he declares that if we are to forget about justification and settle for discovering causal mechanisms, then we have dissolved the dilemma only by changing the motive of our inquiry:

> If one were only interested in causal mechanisms, one would never have worried one's head about awareness. But the epistemologists who dreamed the dream Quine describes were not only interested in causal mechanisms. They were interested in making, for example, an invidious distinction be-

tween Galileo and the professors who refused to look through his telescope. (225)

Second, he claims that if there really are no experimental criteria for distinguishing between "the datal" and "the nondatal" (as Rorty himself believes), then Quine's suggestion that we speak causally of nerve endings and epistemologically of observation sentences in no way dissolves the dilemma plaguing epistemology. Rather, Quine's suggestion dissolves epistemology itself. "For if we have psychophysiology to cover causal mechanisms, and the sociology and history of science to note the occasions on which observation sentences are invoked or dodged in constructing and dismantling theories, then epistemology has nothing to do" (Rorty 1979, 225).

Rorty claims that Quine ought to find this conclusion congenial, but that in fact he resists it. Quine's resistance is evidenced, according to Rorty, by his opposition to Michael Polanyi, Thomas Kuhn, and N. R. Hanson's treatment of observation and by his defining 'observation sentence' intersubjectively as "one on which all speakers of the language give the same verdict when given the same concurrent stimulation. To put the point negatively, an observation sentence is one that is not sensitive to differences in past experience within the speech community" (EN, 86–87). Rorty believes that this definition, ironically, only increases empirical psychology's irrelevance to the question of relating evidence to theory:

> What is puzzling is that we have defined "observation sentence" in terms of the *consensus gentium*; we can divide observation from theory without knowing or caring which bits of our body are the sensory receptors, much less how far down the nerves the "processing" begins. We do not need any psychophysiological account of causal mechanisms to isolate what is intersubjectively agreeable—we just do this in ordinary conversation. *So presumably psychology has nothing to tell us about causal proximity which is worth knowing by those who wish to continue "epistemology in a psychological setting."* To put it another way, once we have picked out the observation sentences conversationally rather than neurologically, further inquiry into "how evidence relates to the-

> ory" would seem to be a matter for Polanyi, Kuhn, and Hanson. For what could psychology add to their accounts of how scientists form and discard theories? (226–27; my italics)

Furthermore, Rorty notes, despite Quine's desire to circumvent the issue of locating consciousness by talking only of the input and output of the black box,

> he seems to be bringing it right back again by explicating observationality in terms of intersubjectivity. So he should either let Polanyi, Kuhn, and Hanson say that "observation" is just a matter of what we can agree on these days, or he should show how psychological discoveries can make something more of this notion. If they cannot, then defining "dependence on present sensory stimulation" in terms of intersubjectivity will just be invoking an old epistemological honorific to no psychological purpose. (227–28)

In sum, Rorty makes two major claims against Quine: (1) Quine's naturalized epistemology avoids the traditionalists' dilemma of having to choose between "causal proximity to the physical stimulus" and "awareness" as the "datal" only by changing the motive for inquiry; (2) if there are no experimental criteria for distinguishing the "datal" from the "nondatal," then epistemology loses its point, and Quine's attempt to avoid this conclusion by defining 'observation sentence' intersubjectively only reinforces it, ironically. Let us evaluate each of these points, in turn.

§3.4.1 *Changing the motive*

As we have seen, Rorty interprets Quine as telling would-be epistemologists to "forget justification and look for causal mechanisms" (Rorty 1979, 225). Such an admonition is indeed a change in the motive for inquiry. But is this really Quine's intent? I do not think so. What Quine actually says in the passage Rorty interprets is: "If we are seeking only the causal mechanism of our knowledge of the external world, and not a justification of that knowledge in terms prior to science, we can settle after all for a theory of vision in Berkeley's style" (GT, 2). A better interpretation of Quine's intent would be the following: Forget justification *in terms prior to science* and look for causal mechanisms. In other words, Quine's point about justification is *not* that science needs no justification but that it needs no justification *in terms prior to science*. Science is justified in Quine's eyes by its measuring up to observation and prediction, i.e., the nomological deductive method (see FME, 72). A putative science without such a justification would be no science at all for Quine—regardless of what some society practicing such a putative science might say.

Seen in this light, Quine's position is one that Rorty himself accepts, up to a point, for Rorty construes 'justified' to mean 'in accordance with the norms of certain social practices', *and* he endorses the scientific (social) practices which developed during the Enlightenment as our "best hope" (336). In other words:

> We are the heirs of three hundred years of rhetoric about the importance of distinguishing sharply between science and religion, science and politics, science and art, science and philosophy, and so on. This rhetoric has formed the culture of Europe. It made us what we are today. We are fortunate that no little perplexity within epistemology, or within the historiography of science, is enough to defeat it. (330–31)

So, Rorty can agree with Quine that the social practices of science offer our "best hope" for making predictions. But he cannot go the further step with Quine toward grounding these practices in something firmer, psychology or whatever:

> But to proclaim our loyalty to these distinctions is not to say that there are "objective" and "rational" standards for adopting them. Galileo, so to speak, won the argument [with Cardinal Bellarmine], and we all stand on the common ground of the "grid" of relevance and irrelevance which "modern philosophy" developed as a consequence of that victory. (Rorty 1979, 331)

From Rorty's perspective, the naturalized epistemologist's appeals to mathematics, empirical psychology, cognitive psychology, phys-

76 *Enlightened Empiricism*

ics, neurology, and so on, are simply appeals to just so many sets of social practices—those of mathematicians, psychologists, and so on. Thus what makes a prediction a justified prediction is not that it conforms to some psychological process but, rather, that it conforms to some societal practice(s). There is just no breaking out of the circle of social practices.

Ultimately, for Rorty, to say that a claim or action is justified is just to say that this is the way we do things around here. There is nothing more to be said regarding claims of knowledge, truth, and justification. One has knowledge of p when one is justified in believing p, and one is justified in believing p when society says so. On such a view, truth is simply "'what you can defend against all comers.' Here the line between a belief's being justified and its being true is very thin" (Rorty 1979, 308). Indeed, some would say the distinction is nonexistent. On such a view science is differentiated from nonscience, if at all, only because what is called science is our best line of defense when it comes to justifying our predictions. But, as we shall see below, Rorty thinks it a bad question to inquire *why* science is our "best hope," i.e., to inquire why science works so well.

§3.4.2 *Datal vs. nondatal*

Does Quine's definition of 'observation sentence' render empirical psychology irrelevant to the issue of relating theory to evidence? After all, if observation sentences can be identified conversationally, independently of psychophysiology, why not simply follow Rorty's suggestion and study their relation to theoretical sentences at the level of the sociology and history of science? According to this view, the important relation between evidence and theory is the sociohistorical one, not the psychological one. In short, why not settle for the sociology and history of science and let epistemology, new and old, go?

One response to this challenge is to point out that the sociohistoric approach to the issue of relating evidence to theory fails to explain *why* science works so well. Providing a sociohistoric account of why Galileo won his argument with Cardinal Bellarmine (to use Rorty's example) is one thing, and an important thing, but such an account leaves untouched the question of *why* his science worked so well.

Rorty's reaction to this response to his challenge is to claim that such a question is illegitimate, for we have no idea about how to answer it:

> In the view I am advocating, the question "Why, if science is merely . . . , does it produce powerful new techniques for prediction and control?" is like the question "Why, if the change in moral consciousness in the West since 1750 is merely . . . , has it been able to accomplish so much for human freedom?" In no case does anyone know what might count as a good answer. Retrospectively, "Whiggishly," and "realistically" we will always be able to see the achievement desired (prediction and control of nature, emancipation of the oppressed) as the result of getting a clearer view of what is there (the electrons, the galaxies, the Moral Law, human rights). But these are never the sorts of explanations philosophers want. They are, in Putnam's phrase, "internal" explanations—explanations which satisfy our need to tell a coherent causal story about our interactions with the world, but not our transcendental need to underwrite our mirroring by showing how it approximates to truth. (340–41)

I think it is important to see that while Rorty rejects the *transcendental* question of *why* science works so well, he rejects neither the claim that science works well nor that there can be legitimate scientific inquiry into why science works well. Only he would say that such scientific inquiry into the workings of science is not epistemology (see Rorty 1979, 174). So, if he believes that science is our "best hope" for making justified predictions, and if he countenances the scientific investigation of scientific success, then what is it that he is so intent to deny? He is intent to deny that the objectivity of any alleged account of knowledge goes beyond conformity to current social practices:

> . . . objectivity should be seen as conformity to the norms of justification (for assertions and for actions) we find about us. Such conformity becomes dubious and self-deceptive only

78   *Enlightened Empiricism*

when seen as something more than this—namely, as a way of obtaining access to something which "grounds" current practices of justification in something else. Such a "ground" is thought to need no justification, because it has become so clearly and distinctly perceived as to count as a "philosophical foundation." This is self-deceptive not simply because of the general absurdity of ultimate justification's reposing upon the unjustifiable, but because of the more concrete absurdity of thinking that the vocabulary used by present science, morality, or whatever has some privileged attachment to reality which makes it *more* than just a further set of descriptions. (361)

But what is it that Rorty thinks Quine is after by insisting that empirical psychology can shed light on the relation of evidence to theory? Certainly Quine is not offering psychology as a new first philosophy, a new transcendental perspective. Quine is the first to point out that psychology is a part of the very science he is intent to investigate, and he is the first to admit that science, including psychology, is underdetermined by experience. So it is clear that Quine does not regard the current vocabulary of science to be writ in stone! He sums up his thinking on this matter very nicely in his "Reply to Hilary Putnam":

Finally I should like to clarify what Putnam and others have called my scientism. I admit to naturalism, and even glory in it. This means banishing the dream of a first philosophy and pursuing philosophy rather as part of one's system of the world, continuous with the rest of science. And why, of all natural sciences, do I keep stressing physics? Simply because it is the business of theoretical physics, and of no other branch of science, "to say what . . . minimum catalogue of states would be sufficient to justify us in saying that there is no change without a change in positions or states." ("Facts of the Matter"). If telepathic effects were established beyond peradventure and they were clearly inexplicable on the basis of the present catalogue of microphysical states, it would still not devolve upon the psychologist to supplement physics with an irreducibly psychological annex. It would devolve upon the physicist to go back to the drawing board and have another try at full coverage, which is his business. (RP, 430–31)

In short, Quine seems innocent of the kind of self-deception that Rorty deplores.

§3.4.3 *Common premises, different conclusions*

Perhaps we can get at what is bothering Rorty in another way. Like Quine, Rorty advocates epistemological behaviorism, physicalism, and naturalism. Epistemological behaviorism tells us that no privileged representations justify any of our beliefs; physicalism tells us, according to Rorty, that the world can be completely described in an extensional language; and naturalism tells us that there is no first philosophy, no transcendental perspective regarding knowledge. Now the relevant point is that Rorty only accepts *half* of Quine's naturalism, the negative half: there is no first philosophy, no transcendental vantage point. Rorty does not, however, accept the affirmative half of Quine's naturalism: scientism, the view "that it is within science itself, and not some prior philosophy, that reality is to be identified and described" (TPT, 21).

Another way of stating the same point is to say that Rorty accepts Quine's holism and therewith the rejection of traditional epistemology, but he does not accept Quine's unregenerate realism and therewith Quine's scientism. Reality for Rorty includes not only the *Naturwissenschaften* but also the *Geisteswissenschaften*. As we have seen, the science/nonscience distinction can be drawn by Rorty only along pragmatic lines: science is that set of social practices that offers the "best hope" for justifying predictions. However, he also believes that epistemological behaviorism teaches "that the philosophical attempt to distinguish between 'scientific' and 'unscientific' explanations is needless" (1979, 209). For according to epistemological behaviorism 'true belief' means 'justified belief', and 'justified belief' means 'what society will let us say'. Thus, in particular, justified beliefs about what exists (reality) are not limited to the realm of science. They may inhabit *any* realm where social practices countenance them. Thus, Rorty believes Quine is mistaken in believing that the description of reality is the exclusive province of science.

80   *Enlightened Empiricism*

According to Rorty, it is only because Quine succumbs to "*the* philosophical urge" to talk of "correspondence" that Quine fails to recognize "the Hegelian implications of his own behaviorism and holism" (195). Whereas Rorty, having been completely cured of "*the* philosophical urge," is content to admit that the world can be completely described in an extensional language, "while simultaneously granting that pieces of it can also be described in an intensional one, and simply refraining from invidious comparisons between these modes of description" (204–5). Peaceful coexistence of the *Naturwissenschaften* and the *Geisteswissenschaften*! That's Rorty's battle cry.

How are we to explain the fact that while Rorty and Quine begin with very similar premises (epistemological behaviorism, physicalism, and naturalism) they draw quite different conclusions? I think the key to understanding this is the recognition that they have differing views about holism. Rorty's view of holism is more radical than Quine's. By Rorty's lights, holism applies to *all* of the sentences of a theory *equally*; as we have seen, however, Quine's holism is a mitigated variety that leaves observation sentences virtually unscathed (see RP, 427–28, and RV, 619–21).

This difference in attitude toward holism explains Rorty's rejection of the affirmative aspect of Quine's naturalism, viz., rejection of Quine's claim that it is within science that reality is to be identified and described. So far as Rorty is concerned, knowledge is a matter of "coping," not a matter of truth (read "corresponding to the world"). Reality includes both the *Naturwissenschaften* and the *Geisteswissenschaften* because, while *neither* "corresponds to the world," they *both* help us in "coping" with the world.

This difference in attitude toward holism also explains why Rorty believes that Quine succumbs to "*the* philosophical urge" to talk of "correspondence." Even though Quine quite frankly acknowledges the relativism infecting observation sentences, he writes it off as innocuous:

> 'That's an X-ray machine' will qualify as observational, in the present sense, for an initiate and not for a novice. This relativism, however, is readily transcended. The empirical evidence for a theory is reducible ultimately to what can be conveyed in observation sentences at the novice's level. It just

takes a little stubbornness, a Missourian insistence on being shown. (RA, 293)

The novice's observation sentences are also observation sentences for the initiate. Such sentences are, for Quine, what link theory and world. This is the link that Rorty accuses Quine of infecting with "correspondence." Thus Rorty believes that Quine has merely supplanted the big mirror (viz., theory) with a smaller mirror (viz., observation). However, I believe that Rorty is mistaken in this. Quine does not regard this link as one of "correspondence" (see VITD, 39, and R, 181). For Quine the link is, rather, a matter of conditioning, verbal dispositions conditioned to stimuli. The tug that tows the ship of theory is no more a mirror mirroring the shoreline than is the ship itself a mirror mirroring the shoreline. Rather, the tug is securely tethered to the shoreline via lines of conditioning. Quine does not, therefore, supplant a big mirror with a smaller one. And thus Rorty is mistaken in thinking that Quine succumbs to "*the* philosophical urge" to talk of "correspondence." (I believe that Donald Davidson makes a similar mistake in interpreting Quine. See Davidson 1984b, 189–90; and VITD, 39.) Nor, therefore, is Quine guilty of acquiescing in the traditionalists' myth of the mirroring mind.

Thus Rorty's challenge to Quine that "he should either let Polanyi, Kuhn, and Hanson say that 'observation' is just a matter of what we can agree on these days, or he should show how psychological discoveries make something more of the notion" (227) has been met. Observation sentences are related to the world causally, via conditioning. This relation is not one of mirroring, or corresponding, nor yet even of referring. It is one of responding, of holophrastic observation sentences conditioned to intersubjectively appreciable ranges of physical stimuli. The moral is that the tug towing the ship of theory is *securely moored* to the shoreline. This is the lesson of mitigated holism and empirical psychology.

Even so, we cannot claim to have answered Rorty's chief complaint with Quine's naturalized epistemology. Rorty's chief complaint is that psychology is private (in the sense of providing explanations in terms of private mechanisms and processes) while justification is public (i.e., social), so how can psychology have any relevance to justification, the turf of epistemology?

The answer to this concern is to be found with Quine's externalized empiricism and his genetic method. The externalization of empiricism amounts to focusing on the relation between observation sentences and stimuli *and* the relation between these same observation sentences and theoretical sentences. The genetic approach toward studying these relations amounts to studying language learning. Quine's view is that in learning a language one learns truth conditions of sentences. These truth conditions can be either nonverbal stimuli or verbal stimuli. In the former case sentences are conditioned to the world, in the latter case sentences are conditioned to other sentences. Thus, ranges of nonverbal stimuli become *evidence* for the truth (i.e., justification) of various observation sentences, and these sentences, in turn, become *evidence* for theoretical sentences. Behavioral psychology is the medium for this inquiry, but it is in no way private in Rorty's sense of the term. The quest is not to discover *private* mental processes and mechanisms:

> The uniformity that unites us in communication and belief is a uniformity of resultant patterns overlying a chaotic subjective diversity of connections between words and experience. Uniformity comes where it matters socially; hence rather in point of intersubjectively conspicuous circumstances of utterance than in point of privately conspicuous ones.
>
> . . .
>
> Different persons growing up in the same language are like different bushes trimmed and trained to take the shape of identical elephants. The anatomical details of twigs and branches will fulfill the elephantine form differently from bush to bush, but the overall outward results are alike. (WO, 8)

Determining these overlying patterns of uniformity and the psychological mechanisms that make them possible is the objective of the behavioral investigation of language learning. The patterns are the products of the very social practices of justification that Rorty makes so much of. After all, "[l]anguage is a social art which we all acquire on the evidence solely of other people's overt behavior under publicly recognizable circumstances" (OR, 26).

§3.5 Conclusions

Quine's proposal for naturalizing epistemology is caught in a crossfire between traditionalists who think he has gone too far in his criticisms of traditional epistemology and radicals who believe he has not gone far enough in his criticisms. The traditionalists and the radicals concur that Quine has committed something like the *genetic fallacy*, confusing causes with reasons, explanation with justification. The traditionalists also believe that the radicals (i.e., the sociologists of knowledge) are simply guilty of an *argumentum ad populum*—truth is what the majority say it is! The radicals, in turn, believe that the traditionalists are guilty of succumbing to "*the* philosophical urge" to talk of "correspondence," i.e., to think that truth is separable from justification.

I have attempted to disabuse both the traditionalists and the radicals of their belief that Quine is guilty of the genetic fallacy. In particular, I have tried to show that Stroud's arguments—purporting to show that naturalized epistemology either fails *as* epistemology or fails *to be* epistemology—misfire. His arguments simply overlook two crucial points about Quine's theory of knowledge, viz., that epistemology is contained in ontology and that Quine's genetic approach in answering the central question of epistemology results in the externalization of empiricism. Recognition of the first point blocks Stroud's argument that Quine *does not* and *cannot* answer the skeptic; recognition of the second point blocks Stroud's argument that nerve hits cannot serve as evidence for beliefs. I suspect, however, that Stroud and Quine do a good deal of talking past one another, for Stroud seems to presuppose what Quine denies, viz., that truth is correspondence, that knowledge is incorrigible, and that the existence of the external world needs to be demonstrated.

I have tried to provide Putnam and Siegel with an intelligible account of how naturalized epistemology is, consistently, both descriptive and normative. But it must be remembered that for Quine science requires no stronger justification than what it derives from conforming to observation and the hypothetico-deductive method, for he rejects first philosophy.

Finally, I have suggested that Rorty's failure to see Quine's epistemology as "public" is due to his ignoring Quine's genetic strategy for investigating the relation between evidence and theory. Rorty's charge that Quine also succumbs to "*the* philosophical urge" to talk of "correspondence" is a mistake based on Rorty's misinterpreting Quine's explanation of how observation sentences are related to sensory stimulation. According to Quine, this relation is a matter of *conditioning*, not "correspondence," "mirroring," or "referring." If Rorty could accept this account of the relation between observation sentences and sensory stimulation, then he could accept Quine's *mitigated* holism. And if he could accept the latter, then he could accept the affirmative aspect of Quine's naturalism, viz., scientism. But I do not expect this to come about. Nevertheless, I also do not believe Rorty's radical holism is very plausible. After all, Quine's observation sentences do have their own *unique* stimulus meanings. The claim that there are brick houses on Elm Street is confirmed or refuted by taking a stroll down Elm Street and not, say, by looking under one's bed.

It seems to me that what is most exciting about Quine's naturalized epistemology (enlightened empiricism, externalized empiricism, relative realism) is that it *liberates* the analytically minded philosopher from his self-imposed confinement to the methods of introspection and of scrutinizing the *Oxford English Dictionary*. In short, he no longer has to deliver all of the interesting empirical questions and problems over to the scientist. But there is another, and sterner, side to naturalized epistemology: the philosopher now has the added *responsibility* of learning some science. The *scientific* study of the acquisition of science requires familiarity with relevant areas of science. So, the moral of naturalized epistemology is *freedom with responsibility*.

Analyticity Reconsidered

CHAPTER 4

§4.1 *Introduction*

In chapter 2, we said that Quine's argument in "Two Dogmas of Empiricism" against the analytic-synthetic distinction is two-pronged. One of these prongs, discussed in that chapter, is Quine's argument that any attempt at separating the so-called analytic sentences from the so-called synthetic sentences of a theory is misguided because any such attempt rests on the mistaken assumption that each individual sentence of a theory has its own unique meaning and/or evidence. Quine's holism denies this assumption. Hence the argument from chapter 2:

$$H \longrightarrow (\sim C \cdot \sim D)$$
$$H \:/ \therefore \sim C \cdot \sim D$$

where 'H' stands for holism, 'C' stands for epistemological reductionism, and 'D' stands for the analytic-synthetic distinction. The other prong of Quine's attack on the analytic-synthetic distinction is his argument that the intended distinction has never been clearly drawn and is, therefore, *unfit* to serve the theoretical purposes for which it was intended. Furthermore, Quine argues that any future attempt at drawing the distinction that is similar to those past attempts would suffer the same ignominious fate.

The arguments of the *second prong* are, briefly: (1) Neither Leibniz's truths-of-reason/truths-of-fact distinction, nor Hume's relations-of-ideas/matters-of-fact distinction, nor Kant's analytic-synthetic distinction will bear close analysis. (2) Attempts at reducing putative analytic statements like 'All bachelors are unmarried men' to logical truths like 'All bachelors are bachelors', by relying on definitions like 'unmarried man' *means* 'bachelor', fail. *Lexical definitions* fail because they merely report synonymies, they do not explain them; *explicative definitions* (explications) fail because they presuppose synonymies of contexts of the definiendum and definiens; *stipulative definitions* fail because they define by fiat. (3) Attempts at reducing statements like 'All bachelors are unmarried men' to logical truths like 'All bachelors are bachelors', by substituting synonyms for synonyms *salva veritate*, fail because, in the end, such substitutions presuppose analyticity.[1] In this chapter, we shall examine only a few of the objections that have been raised against Quine's attack on analyticity.

§4.2 *Strawson and Grice*

Among the earliest critics of Quine's "Two Dogmas" are P. F. Strawson and H. P. Grice. In a joint paper entitled "In Defense of a Dogma," Strawson and Grice undertake the defense of the dogma of the analytic-synthetic distinction against Quine's double-pronged attack. Subsequently, Quine counterattacked in the pages of *Word and Object*.

The central intent of Strawson and Grice's paper is "to show that . . . [Quine's] criticisms of the [analytic-synthetic] distinction do not justify his rejection of it" (Grice, 141). In order to show this, Strawson and Grice separate sections 1–4 of "Two Dogmas" from sections 5 and 6. They argue that Quine's intent in sections 1–4 is to demonstrate that the analytic-synthetic distinction is *untenable*; according to Strawson and Grice, all he shows, at best, is that the distinction is *unclear*. Therefore, they conclude, Quine's putative proof in sections 1–4 that the distinction is *untenable* is nothing more than an *ignoratio elenchi*. They argue that Quine's intent in sections 5 and 6 is to demonstrate that the analytic-synthetic dis-

It is regretted that the authorized order of the names of the co-authors has been inadvertently transposed in the text.

tinction is inconsistent with a holism that Quine accepts. Strawson and Grice regard this Quinian argument as another non sequitur, for they believe that the distinction *is* consistent with holism. Let us examine the force of Strawson and Grice's arguments.

§4.2.1 *Unclarity vs. untenability*

Strawson and Grice understand Quine to be claiming that the analytic-synthetic distinction is *unclear*, but, more important, they initially understand him to be making the much stronger claim that the distinction is altogether *illusory*. As support for their interpretation, they quote the following statement of Quine's: "That there is such a distinction to be drawn at all is an unempirical dogma of empiricists, a metaphysical article of faith" (TDE, 37). "It is," say Strawson and Grice, "the existence of the distinction that he here calls in question; so his rejection of it would seem to amount to a denial of its existence" (142). Furthermore, they claim that "such a position of extreme skepticism" (142) regarding the analytic-synthetic distinction is not warranted solely on the proffered grounds that the distinction is unclear, *if* there is a presumption in favor of the distinction. But is there such a presumption? Strawson and Grice believe there is, for not only has the distinction played a significant role in our "not wholly disreputable" (142) philosophical tradition, but it continues to play a role in the contemporary philosophical scene.

> In short, "analytic" and "synthetic" have a more or less established philosophical *use*; and this seems to suggest that it is absurd, even senseless, to say that there is no such distinction. For, in general, if a pair of contrasting expressions are habitually and generally used in application to the same cases, *where these cases do not form a closed list,* this is a sufficient condition for saying that there are *kinds* of cases to which the expressions apply; and nothing more is needed for them to mark a distinction. (Grice, 143)

The source of this semantic/epistemic canon is not revealed. Presumably, its source is intuition, Strawson's and/or Grice's. Whatever its source, the canon does not do what Strawson and Grice claim for it, viz., it does not show that the established philosophical use of 'analytic' and 'synthetic' seems to suggest that it is absurd, even senseless, to say there is no such distinction. We are told that the canon specifies "a sufficient condition for saying that there are *kinds* of cases to which the expressions apply; and nothing more is needed for them to mark a distinction." It should be noted, however, that this assertion is ambiguous. Are we to understand the canon as specifying a sufficient condition for concluding that *the intended distinction exists* or merely that *some distinction or other exists*? Let us see how Strawson and Grice's canon fails of its purpose on either of these proposed interpretations.

If the canon is interpreted as specifying a sufficient condition for establishing that the *intended* distinction exists, then the canon is false. Consider the following counterexample adapted from an example of Gilbert Harman's (see Harman, 125). Even if the pair of contrasting terms 'witch' and 'nonwitch' are "habitually and generally used in application to the same cases," we would not therefore (according to *my* intuitions) regard this as a sufficient condition for saying that the *intended* distinction exists. (I am assuming here that the intended distinction is between women who exercise supernatural powers and women who do not, and that as a matter of fact there are none of the former.) So, while the pair 'witch' and 'nonwitch' may be assumed to fulfill the conditions set forth in the canon in question, we cannot therefore conclude that the *intended* distinction exists. Hence it is neither absurd nor senseless (though it may be false) to deny that an analytic-synthetic distinction exists, despite the presumption (based upon philosophical usage) in favor of the distinction. If, on the other hand, Strawson and Grice's canon is interpreted as specifying a sufficient condition for establishing that some *unintended* distinction exists, then, again, it is neither absurd nor senseless to deny the existence of the *intended* distinction, since, then, philosophical usage would not provide even *prima facie* evidence in favor of the presumption of its existence.

So, on either of the proposed interpretations of their canon, Strawson and Grice's argument fails. Quine's denial of the existence of the analytic-synthetic distinction is neither absurd nor senseless, despite the presumption in its favor based on traditional and current philosophical usage. Strawson and Grice believe otherwise perhaps, because, overlooking the ambiguity concealed in their canon, they mistakenly conflate the truth that established usage is sufficient for showing that *some distinction or other is present* with the falsehood that established usage is sufficient for establishing that the *intended* distinction is present. In short, they conflate established (philosophical) usage and truth. And just as the fact that common usage may distinguish between women who are witches and women who are not does not establish the reality of witches, so the fact that philosophical usage distinguishes between analytic and synthetic statements does not establish the reality of analytic statements.

Unaware that their preceding argument fails, Strawson and Grice believe themselves to have established that if Quine's position is interpreted as denying the existence of the analytic-synthetic distinction, then his position is absurd or senseless. This conclusion suggests to them that perhaps Quine's position is other than as they first suspected. They now suggest that "Quine's thesis might be better represented not as the thesis that there is *no difference at all* marked by the use of these expressions, but as the thesis that the nature of, and reasons for, the difference or differences are totally misunderstood by those who use the expressions, that the stories they tell themselves *about* the difference are full of illusion" (143).

Unlike their first construal of Quine's position, they believe that this construal could be consistent with traditional and current philosophical usage of the terms 'analytic' and 'synthetic'. For example, let us suppose that sentences like 'Bachelors are unmarried men' appear to have a peculiar property that philosophers dub *analytic;* they then proceed to spin out equally peculiar explanations of the truth of such sentences. On the other hand, these same philosophers believe, let us suppose, that sentences like 'There have been black dogs' do not have this peculiar property, nor is their truth explained as before; these are the *synthetic* sentences. Supposing this usage were to become widespread among philosophers, then it is quite intelligible to say that 'analytic' and 'synthetic' have agreed-upon uses. Furthermore, this usage would *not* be inconsistent with the claim that the distinction these philosophers *thought* themselves to be making is nonexistent. In other words, it would not be absurd or senseless to deny the existence of this distinction in the face of the established usage of 'analytic' and 'synthetic' (cf. the 'witch'/ 'nonwitch' example). However, it *would be* inconsistent "with the claim that there simply did not exist a difference of any kind between the classes of statements so characterized" (Grice, 144).

90   *Enlightened Empiricism*

Nevertheless, Strawson and Grice emphasize that even if this second interpretation of Quine's position is the correct interpretation, it still cannot be justified by appealing solely, as Quine does in sections 1–4, to the unclarity of the various philosophical attempts at explaining the distinction in question:

> ... to establish such a claim on the sort of grounds we have indicated evidently requires a great deal more argument than is involved in showing that certain explanations of a term do not measure up to certain requirements of adequacy in philosophical clarification—*and not only more argument, but argument of a very different kind* [my italics]. For it would surely be too harsh to maintain that the *general* presumption is that philosophical distinctions embody the kind of illusion we have described. (Grice, 144)

So far, Strawson and Grice have argued that there is a presumption in favor of the analytic-synthetic distinction, based on traditional and current philosophical usage. However, we have rejected this argument because the semantic/epistemic canon upon which it turns is fallacious. Even if we grant Strawson and Grice their canon, they admit that Quine could counter such a presumption if he could demonstrate that the proponents of the analytic-synthetic distinction have merely misperceived and mischaracterized some innocuous difference between the two classes of statements—like showing that the proponents of witchhood have misperceived and mischaracterized some women's peculiar behavior. Strawson and Grice's further point is that one must go well beyond considering the philosophical clarity of such distinctions in order to establish such things as misperceptions and mischaracterizations. I am willing to admit that in some cases this is true, e.g., in the witch case. But in cases like the analytic-synthetic distinction I am not willing to admit this, for it seems to me that the misperceptions and mischaracterizations that are relevant here are just the kinds of misperceptions and mischaracterizations that considerations of philosophical clarity are designed to reveal.

However, Strawson and Grice believe that a stronger presumption in favor of the analytic-synthetic distinction is to be found in ordinary language. And since this presumption is not based on philosophers' inventions of technical vocabularies and the stories they tell themselves about them, it is not to be countered by moves similar to those by which Quine could counter the presumption based on philosophical usage, viz., on the basis of alleged misperceptions and mischaracterizations by philosophers.

The ordinary language distinction that Strawson and Grice fasten onto is the one marked by the ordinary expressions 'means the same as' and 'does not mean the same as':

> If Quine is to be consistent in his adherence to the extreme thesis, then it appears that he must maintain not only that the distinction we suppose ourselves to be marking by the use of the terms "analytic" and "synthetic" does not exist, but also that the distinction we suppose ourselves to be marking by the use of the expressions "means the same as," "does not mean the same as" does not exist either. At least, he must maintain this insofar as the notion of *meaning the same as,* in its application to predicate-expressions, is supposed to differ from and go beyond the notion of *being true of just the same objects as.* (145)

However, the denial of this ordinary language distinction has paradoxical consequences, according to Strawson and Grice. Among these paradoxical consequences are the following: (1) No distinction could be drawn between meaning and extension; for example, we could not say that 'bachelor' *means the same as* 'unmarried man' but, despite their being coextensive, 'creature with kidneys' *does not mean the same as* 'creature with a heart'. (2) All talk of correct or incorrect translation would be impossible, for all talk of synonymy, including sentence-synonymy, would be senseless. (3) It would no longer be possible even to say that sentences *have* meaning, because "if we are to give up the notion of sentence-synonymy as senseless, we must give up the notion of sentence-significance (of a sentence having meaning) as senseless too" (Grice, 146).

Quine has countered all three of these claims in *Word and Object*. Each is based on a particular misunderstanding or fallacy. The first is based on the misunderstanding that Quine's attack is on our intuitions about the ordinary notions of meaning, synonymy, and analyticity. It is not. Quine does not deny the existence of such intuitions; he merely says "that they do not sustain a synonymy concept suited to identity of propositions, or meanings" (WO, 207).

The second claim is based on a false understanding of the nature of translation. "The notion of proposition [or of meaning, or of statement-synonymy, etc.] seems to facilitate talk of translation precisely because it falsifies the nature of the enterprise" (WO, 208). The third claim is simply a fallacy:

> One of those arguments [in defense of statement-synonymy] involves the fallacy of subtraction: it is argued that if we can speak of a sentence as meaningful, or as having meaning, then there must be a meaning that it has, and this meaning will be identical with or distinct from the meaning that another sentence has. This is urged without any evident attempt to define synonymy in terms of meaningfulness, nor any notice of the fact that we could as well justify the hypostasis of sakes and unicorns on the basis of the idioms 'for the sake of' and 'is hunting unicorns'. (WO, 206–7; notes omitted)

So much for Strawson and Grice's arguments to the effect

> that there is a strong presumption in favor of the existence of the distinction, or distinctions, which Quine challenges—a presumption resting both on philosophical and on ordinary usage—and that this presumption is not in the least shaken by the fact, if it is a fact, that the distinctions in question have not been, in some sense, adequately clarified. It is perhaps time to look at what Quine's notion of adequate clarification is. (Grice, 147)

According to Strawson and Grice, Quine's idea of an adequate clarification of analyticity, synonymy, and related notions is the construction of an explanation of the terms 'analyticity', 'synonymy', etc., which (1) does not include any term from the same family-circle, and (2) must provide necessary and sufficient conditions for the application of the term being explained. Strawson and Grice give arguments for rejecting both of these conditions. "The fact, if it is a fact, that the expressions ['analyticity', 'synonymy', etc.] cannot be explained in precisely the way which Quine seems to require, does not mean that they cannot be explained at all" (149).

However, Quine simply brushes this complaint aside by denying that this notion of clarification is his own. In *Word and Object*, he says, "... we find it argued that the standard of clarity that I demand for synonymy and analyticity is unreasonably high; yet I ask no more, after all, than a rough characterization in terms of dispositions to verbal behavior" (WO, 207; note omitted).

Thus far, Strawson and Grice "have tried to show that sections 1 to 4 of Quine's article—the burden of which is that the notions of the analyticity group have not been satisfactorily explained—do not establish the extreme thesis for which he appears to be arguing" (152). In other words, they have tried to show that even if Quine has proved that such notions are *unclear*, he has not proved that they are *untenable*, and his claiming otherwise is merely an *ignoratio elenchi*. However, for the reasons given, I believe that Strawson and Grice have not succeeded in showing this at all. Be that as it may, let us now turn to their treatment of sections 5 and 6 of "Two Dogmas."

§4.2.2 *Analyticity and holism*

In considering Quine's diagnosis and positive theory, Strawson and Grice focus on the following "two assertions, one of which Quine clearly takes to be incompatible with acceptance of the distinction between analytic and synthetic statements, and the other of which he regards as barring one way to an explanation of that distinction" (154):

> (1) It is an illusion to suppose that there is any class of accepted statements the members of which are in principle "immune from revision" in the light of experience, i.e., any that we accept as true and must continue to accept as true whatever happens.
>
> (2) It is an illusion to suppose that an individual statement, taken in isolation from its fellows, can admit of confirmation or disconfirmation at all. There is no particular statement such that a particular experience or set of experiences decides once for all whether the statement is true or false, independently of our attitudes to all other statements. (154)

Strawson and Grice intend to show that the first of the above assertions "is not incompatible with acceptance of the distinction, but

94 *Enlightened Empiricism*

is, on the contrary, most intelligibly interpreted in a way quite consistent with it, and the second assertion leaves the way open to just the kind of explanation which Quine thinks it precludes" (154).

Taking the second assertion first, Strawson and Grice argue as follows: If we accept assertion (2), then, Quine maintains, we cannot say with the verificationists that two statements are synonymous if and only if they are confirmed and disconfirmed by just the same sets of experiences. Thus we would also be barred from explaining analyticity in terms of statement-synonymy, i.e., we would be barred from saying, for example, that a statement, S, is analytic if it is synonymous with a logical truth, L. However, Quine is wrong about this; we could still say "that two statements are synonymous if and only if any experiences which, *on certain assumptions about the truth-values of other statements,* confirm or disconfirm one of the pair, also, *on the same assumptions,* confirm or disconfirm the other to the same degree" (156). In other words, while it may be true, as assertion (2) above claims, that individual statements are never confirmed or disconfirmed in isolation, still, the *relativistic* sort of statement-synonymy explained above is consistent with its acceptance. Strawson and Grice are not concerned to defend such a notion of statement-synonymy; they are merely "concerned to show that acceptance of Quine's doctrine of empirical confirmation does not, as he says it does, entail giving up the attempt to define statement-synonymy in terms of confirmation" (156).

What about this relativistic notion of statement-synonymy? First, it is difficult to see how one is to determine whether or not two statements are confirmed or disconfirmed *to the same degree.* Strawson and Grice give no hint as to how this might be achieved. So far as this remains unclarified, the same is true of their notion of relativistic statement-synonymy. Second, even if we could solve the aforementioned difficulty, such a relativistic notion of statement-synonymy is hardly going to lead to the notion of analyticity of the desired type. What empiricists have yearned for is an *absolute* distinction between the analytic and the synthetic, not a relativistic one. Nothing is gained, epistemologically speaking, if each theorist is free to circumscribe the class of analytic statements as he sees fit, constrained only by prior subjective commitments to other sentences. Thus, while Strawson and Grice's proposal may not be inconsistent with (2), nevertheless it lacks any epistemological significance.[2]

With respect to assertion (1), Strawson and Grice argue that contrary to Quine's belief, "the doctrine that there is no statement which is in principle immune from revision, no statement which might not be given up in the face of experience . . . is quite consistent with adherence to the distinction between analytic and synthetic statements" (157). This is so *if* one also distinguishes "between that kind of giving up which consists in merely admitting falsity, and that kind of giving up which involves changing or dropping a concept or set of concepts" (157). The former kind of *giving up* "happens as the result of a change of opinion solely as to matters of fact" (157); the latter kind of *giving up* "happens at least partly as a result of a shift in the sense of the words" (157). Thus if "a shift in the sense of the words is a necessary condition of the change in truth-value, then the adherent of the distinction will say that the form of words in question changes from expressing an analytic statement to expressing a synthetic statement" (157). So, if this distinction between kinds of *giving up* can be maintained, then so can the analytic-synthetic distinction, despite the fact that no statement is in principle immune from revision.

However, it does not seem possible to maintain Strawson and Grice's two kinds of *giving up,* unless one assumes senses, or meanings, or propositions, or statement-synonymy, or the like. But, if we are going to do that, then why all this hocus-pocus? Why not just say that a statement, *S,* is analytic if it has the *same sense as*, or has the *same meaning as*, or expresses the *same proposition as*, or is *synonymous with* a logical truth, *L*.

In conclusion, I believe that Strawson and Grice have not established their thesis that Quine's criticisms of the analytic-synthetic distinction do not justify his rejection of it. In sections 1–4 of "Two Dogmas," Quine shows that various ingenious attempts at drawing the distinction fail and that a similar fate awaits any similar attempt. As we have seen, Quine's standard of clarity that any successful attempt must measure up to is avowedly behavioristic: "no more . . . than a rough characterization in terms of dispositions to verbal behavior." However, because of the indeterminacy of translation, no such behavioristic characterization is forthcoming. Furthermore, Strawson and Grice's proposed semantic/epistemic canon notwithstanding, there is no absurdity in denying the existence of the philosophers' analytic-synthetic distinction, anymore than there is an absurdity in denying the witch/nonwitch distinction. Thus, Quine's demonstration that the analytic-synthetic distinction lacks behavioristic clarity is sufficient evidence for its rejection (supposing, with Quine, that behavioristic evidence is the only admissible evidence). So, I believe that Quine is not guilty of an *ignoratio elenchi* in arguing from *unclarity* to *untenability*. Furthermore, I believe that Strawson and Grice are incorrect in their belief that Quine is committed to denying that members of the same speech community have more or less uniform synonymy and analyticity intuitions. But Quine does deny that such intuitions are sufficient for establishing an analytic-synthetic distinction suitable for fulfilling philosophers' epistemological dreams.

Lastly, Strawson and Grice's criticisms of sections 5 and 6 of "Two Dogmas" does nothing to undercut the inference from holism to the rejection of the analytic-synthetic distinction. Strawson and Grice are able to show that holism and the analytic-synthetic distinction are compatible only by either relativizing the notion of statement-synonymy and analyticity or by assuming the separability of facts and meanings. The former move is possible, but it is without epistemological import; the latter move is also possible but only by assuming what is supposedly being proved (viz., meanings, propositions, statement-synonymy, etc.). The move is impossible to make on behavioristic grounds, i.e., we are unable to separate fact from meaning behavioristically. In sum, I am unmoved by Strawson and Grice's criticisms of "Two Dogmas." My own belief is that if one is to have any hope of overturning Quine's position in "Two Dogmas," it must reside with the hope of overturning his behavioristic orientation toward language: in particular, the NB thesis.

§4.3 *Priest*

Graham Priest is another philosopher who argues that holism, "rather than dispensing with the notion of analyticity, requires it." Furthermore, he accepts holism and, thus, argues "that there are analytic truths and that these are true by convention" (Priest, 301). Priest begins his argument by drawing a distinction between entailment and inference: "Premises may imply or entail a conclusion: implication is a relationship between sentences. But an inference, or better, drawing an inference [deductively] is something that one does, an action." Moreover, inferring is an activity that "is rule-governed" (291). These rules are rules of inference.

> But rules of inference, being rules, are not beliefs. Rules are not things that one believes or disbelieves but things one acts in accordance with or violates. Hence the rules cannot be members of the set of beliefs. The beliefs may provide the content of the web of belief but the rules provide the structure. Content and structure must of course be distinguished. . . . And the belief/rule distinction is a special case of the content/structure distinction. (Priest, 291–92)

But why aren't rules of inference beliefs? The argument seems to be that if they were beliefs, then they, in turn, would need justifying, which would require further rule-beliefs, which would require further rule-beliefs, and so on. (Priest likens this argument to that found in Lewis Carroll's famous and humorous paper "What the Tortoise Said to Achilles.")

Even though rules of inference are not beliefs, they have statements corresponding to them which can be believed. "Corresponding to the deductive rule A/B is the logical conditional, best expressed as 'That-A entails that-B'"(Priest, 292). (The inference rule may also be stated as the conditional 'From A, B may be inferred', and its corresponding (belief) statement may be stated as the conditional 'If A then, logically, B' [see Priest, 292].) Given this distinction between inference rules and inferences, Priest characterizes analyticity as follows: ". . . an analytic sentence is any sentence which can be validly inferred from conditionals corresponding to valid rules of inference" (292).

Priest summarizes his argument, to this point, as follows:

> Our beliefs form a [holistic] network. The nodes of the network are individual beliefs. The connections between the nodes cannot be the same kind of entity (on pain of the Carroll infinite regress) but are rules of inference. Although rules are not members of the web of belief the logical conditionals corresponding to them may be. In particular, the analytic truths are the logical consequences of the logical conditionals corresponding to the rules of deductive inference governing the web of belief. The Carroll paradox shows that the notion of analyticity is not vacuous. (294)

98   *Enlightened Empiricism*

According to Priest, this account of analyticity shows that sentences such as the following will be analytic: 'If Socrates is a bachelor, he is unmarried'; 'If this is red (all over), it is not blue (all over)'; 'If it is raining and it is snowing, then it is raining'. "These are paradigm examples of positivist analyticity, and I take this," says Priest, "to show that the class of sentences I have characterized as analytic will coincide extensionally (more or less) with the class of sentences positivists called 'analytic'" (295).

Thus does Priest arrive at a class of philosophically interesting analytic statements: Quinian holism requires a belief/rule distinction, and this distinction provides the means for distinguishing the analytic sentences from the synthetic ones. But there remains a story to be told about how analytically true sentences are true by *convention*.

Recall that analytically true sentences are ones which can be *validly* inferred from conditionals corresponding to *valid* rules of inference. According to Priest, the truth of such sentences is wound up with the conventionality of validity:

> ... validity is to be identified with the norms that are in force. However, these are, in a sense, conventional. A rule of deductive inference "in force" does not force us to act in a certain way. Rather, that a rule of inference is in force is the result of the concurrence of human actions: that people agree in the way to proceed. Thus, which rules are valid is a matter which depends upon human agreement (of action). In this sense it is conventional. (296)

On this account, validity is a notion derived from the social practice (or convention) of inferring; and analytic truth is derived from validity. Thus is analytic truth conventional.

As we have seen, Priest's argument that Quinian holism "requires" that there be analytic sentences turns on his belief/rule distinction. The idea is that beliefs cannot be used to justify entailments among beliefs, on pain of an infinite regress, so there must be some other justificatory device, namely, inference rules. Such rules or, better, their corresponding conditional statements represent the fixed points, the "structure," of the web of belief, while beliefs represent its revisable "content." The suppressed premise of this argument is, of course, a foundationalist theory of justification. Is such a theory consistent with the Quinian holism that Priest professes to accept? (See Priest, 290.) I do not believe that it is. According to Quinian holism, the rules of inference, or the inferential relations among sentences, are themselves justified holistically and pragmatically. Furthermore they, too, are susceptible to revision, right along with the sentences they connect. Priest, also, claims that rules of inference are revisable, in the sense that the social practice of inferring may change (thereby changing which sentences count as analytic, presumably). But Quine's holism is more radical since he insists that rules of inference are revisable without there being a change in behavior. Even the lowly truth-functional connections among a subject's sentences transcend what is evidenced in his behavior, viz., his verdict functions:

> Two-valued logic is a theoretical development that is learned, like other theory, in indirect ways upon which we can only speculate. Some theorists, notably intuitionists, favor another logic, and there is nothing in the observable circumstances of our utterances that need persuade them to assign meaning to our two-valued scheme. (RR, 78)

From all of these considerations, I conclude that despite his good intentions, Priest really does not accept Quinian holism. So, while Priest may have demonstrated that *his* brand of holism may require the belief/rule distinction, he has not demonstrated that Quine's brand does.

If one gives up what I allege to be Priest's commitment to a foundationalist theory of justification, then there doesn't seem to be any good reason for not regarding the rules of inference he speaks of as just further *beliefs,* in Quine's sense, viz., behavioral dispositions. For example, the inference rule 'From A, B may be inferred' represents a generalization over a population's dispositions to act thusly, within a certain time frame.

One last point regarding Priest's position that inference rules are revisable (and, therefore, analytic sentences are true by convention) because the social practice of inferring may change: As Priest explains, this position commits him to the view that we do not call a rule of inference (e.g., 'From A, B may be inferred') valid *on the grounds* that the truth of A guarantees the truth of B; rather, we say that the truth of A guarantees the truth of B *on the grounds* that the rule of inference is valid. ". . . we are able to determine that a particular inference is (materially) truth-preserving (even if we do not know the truth values of the premises and conclusion) since we have a prior ability to recognize valid inferences" (Priest, 297). Thus the price of establishing the conventionality of analytic truths is nothing short of turning standard logical theory on its head. Priest is fully aware of the price, and, unlike myself, he is quite willing to pay it.

§4.4 Conclusions

"Two Dogmas of Empiricism" was published in 1951. Since then, countless rejoinders have been published. These rejoinders fall into two broad camps. One camp argues for an analytic-synthetic distinction that is epistemologically significant (e.g., Priest); the other camp argues for an analytic-synthetic distinction that is epistemologically insignificant (e.g., Putnam 1975a). Indeed, of late, Quine himself has come around to the view that there may very well be a tenable analytic-synthetic distinction that is epistemologically insignificant. In *The Roots of Reference*, Quine suggests that "a sentence is analytic if *everybody* learns that it is true by learning its words" (RR, 79). An example of such a sentence might be 'No bachelor is married'. "At any rate it would seem that we all learned 'bachelor' uniformly, by learning that our elders are disposed to assent to it in just the circumstances where they will assent to 'unmarried man'" (RR, 80).

> Even so, we have here no such radical cleavage between analytic and synthetic sentences as was called for by Carnap and other epistemologists. In learning our language each of us learns to count certain sentences, outright, as true; there are sentences whose truth is learned in that way by many of us, and there are sentences whose truth is learned in that way by few or none of us. The former sentences are more *nearly* analytic than the latter. The *analytic* sentences are the ones whose truth is learned in that way by all of us; and these extreme cases do not differ notably from their neighbors, nor can we always say which ones they are. (RR, 80)

Thus, ironically, is Quine led by his own theory of language learning to the conclusion that some sentences are indeed analytic. The irony is doubled, however, for the same theory of language learning that admits analyticity denies it any substantial epistemological significance. The concluding remark in our discussion of Strawson and Grice bears repeating: If one is to have any hope of overturning Quine's position in "Two Dogmas," it must reside with the hope of overturning his behavioristic orientation toward language.

Indeterminacy, Underdetermination, and Facts of the Matter

CHAPTER 5

§5.1 *Introduction*

Quine's *indeterminacy of translation thesis* asserts that translations of a language can be set up in such ways that, while each is consistent with the speech dispositions of everyone concerned, they nevertheless can have different sentence-to-sentence correlations even to the point where two translations of some sentence can be correlated with sentences having opposite truth values; *and* there is no answer to the (pseudo-) question of which translation is the *uniquely* correct one—they are *all* correct insofar as they measure up to the speech dispositions of all concerned. Quine's *underdetermination thesis* asserts that our system of the world is bound to have empirically equivalent alternatives which, if we were to discover them, we would see no way of reconciling by a reconstrual of predicates; *and* only one such system can be correct.

According to Quine, the chief difference between these two theses is, then, that there is no fact of the matter to the question of which translation is *the* correct one, but there is a fact of the matter to the question of which physical theory is *the* correct one. His critics persistently maintain that this alleged difference is spurious, and even his defenders cannot agree on how to construe Quine's claim.

Thus, both the truth and the meaning of Quine's claim are hotly contested.

In this chapter, I hope to shed some light on these matters. I shall begin by considering first the arguments of two of Quine's critics (Noam Chomsky and Richard Rorty), who maintain that the distinction that Quine draws between translation and physics is spurious, thereafter turning to consider analyses by two other philosophers (Dagfinn Føllesdal and Bruce Aune), who are more sympathetic to Quine's distinction. I shall argue that *none* of these thinkers has securely grasped Quine's point, essentially, because none has understood the central roles that naturalism and physicalism play in connection with Quine's notion of *fact of the matter*.

Next, I shall offer my own analysis of Quine's position. I shall show how Quine's thoughts regarding underdetermination have changed over the years, landing him in a contradiction—a contradiction that he acknowledges. Afterward, I will examine the thought of one of Quine's fellow physicalists (Michael Friedman), who, appreciating the central roles played by naturalism and physicalism in Quine's argument for indeterminacy, nevertheless rejects Quine's indeterminacy thesis. Finally, I will examine the views of two other philosophers (Saul Kripke and Harry Beatty), who claim that Quine's indeterminacy thesis is logically independent of his behaviorism.

In particular, my hope in this chapter is to contribute something toward answering the following two important questions: (1) What moves Quine to say that there is a fact of the matter to physics but none to translation? (2) Is Quine's indeterminacy thesis logically independent of his behaviorism?

§5.2 *Translation vs. physics*

Noam Chomsky is among the earliest critics of the indeterminacy thesis. However, his claim is *not* that the indeterminacy thesis is false. Rather, he claims "it is true and uninteresting" (Chomsky 1980, 15; note omitted). He thinks that Quine believes the thesis is interesting only because Quine draws an illicit distinction between analytical hypotheses and genuine hypotheses. In this regard, Chomsky writes in "Quine's Empirical Assumptions":

> To understand the thesis [of indeterminacy] clearly it is necessary to bear in mind that Quine distinguishes sharply between the construction of analytical hypotheses on the basis of data and the postulation of "stimulus meanings of observation sentences" on the basis of data. The latter, he states, involves only uncertainty of the "normal inductive" kind. . . . The same is true, apparently, about the inductive inference involved in translation (similarly, 'learning' and understanding) of sentences containing truth-functional connectives. In these cases, induction leads us to "genuine hypotheses", which are to be sharply distinguished from the "analytical hypotheses" to which reference is made in the discussion of indeterminacy of translation. Hence Quine has in mind a distinction between 'normal induction', which involves no serious epistemological problem, and 'hypothesis formation' or 'theory construction', which does involve such a problem. Such a distinction can no doubt be made; its point, however, is less than obvious.
>
> . . .
>
> . . . there can surely be no doubt that Quine's statement about analytical hypotheses is true, though the question arises why it is important. It is, to be sure, undeniable that if a system of "analytical hypotheses" goes beyond evidence then it is possible to conceive alternatives compatible with the evidence, just as in the case of Quine's "genuine hypotheses" about stimulus meaning and truth-functional connectives. Thus the situation in the case of language, or "common sense knowledge", is, in this respect, no different from the case of physics. (Chomsky 1969, 61)

Putting Chomsky's point briefly, we can say that since translation and physics are on a par epistemologically, then there is no reason to think they are not on a par ontologically. In short, there is no "special indeterminacy," epistemological or ontological, infecting translation. I shall argue later on that Chomsky is half-right in this claim: translation and physics are on a par epistemologically, that is, they both go beyond their evidence.[1] But, as we shall see, he is mistaken in thinking that they are on a par ontologically.

A point similar to Chomsky's is made by Richard Rorty in his paper "Indeterminacy of Translation and of Truth." Rorty is, perhaps, more sympathetic than is Chomsky to Quine's general philosophical orientation, but, like Chomsky, he believes that translation and physics are on an epistemological *and* ontological par.

In that paper, Rorty focuses upon the third of the following three theses, which he believes are connected with Quine's views about indeterminacy:

(1) A person's dispositions to accept sentences do not determine a unique interpretation of those sentences.
(2) The notions of meaning, propositional attitudes, etc., do not possess the explanatory power often attributed to them by philosophers.
(3) Though linguistics is of course a part of the theory of nature, the indeterminacy of translation is not just inherited as a special case of underdetermination of our theory of the world; it is parallel but additional.

In effect, (3) suggests that *there is a fact of the matter* to the question of which of two physical theories (both being consistent with all possible observations) is *the* correct one; but that *there is no fact of the matter* to the question of which of two translation manuals (both being consistent with the speech dispositions of all parties concerned) is *the* correct one.

While Rorty accepts (1) and (2), he rejects (3). He sees no way for Quine to maintain that there is a fact of the matter to physics but no fact of the matter to linguistics (i.e., translation). Thus, he is puzzled by what he takes to be Quine's suggestion that "accepting (2) should lead to accepting (3), or *vice versa,* or both" (Rorty 1972, 443). And, in order to show that one can consistently accept (2) while rejecting (3), Rorty argues that the *best* interpretation of (3)—namely, "Non-inferential knowledge is always the result of the 'internalization' of some theory or other, and so we cannot appeal to the existence of such knowledge for an exemption from the usual 'underdetermination of our theory of nature'" (450)—is *not* inconsistent with (2). However, Rorty acknowledges that Quine would *not* accept this interpretation of (3). Nevertheless, he believes that Quine's reluctance in this matter is traceable to Quine's untenable distinction between canons and laws. Rorty wonders how

Quine can "grant that the linguists' analytical hypotheses are 'not capricious' and also say that 'where indeterminacy of translation applies... there is no fact of the matter'? What more does it take for there to be a 'fact of the matter' than a rational procedure for reaching agreement about what to assert?" (453). In other words, how can the Quine who rejected the analytic-synthetic distinction turn around and support a canon-law (heuristic-substantive) distinction?

Rorty concludes by posing what he perceives as a dilemma for Quine: "he should either give up the notion of 'objective matter of fact' all along the line, or reinstate it in linguistics" (459). In other words, in order to be consistent, Quine should either deny that there is a fact of the matter to both physics and linguistics or he should affirm that there is a fact of the matter to both.

> On the first alternative, he can say that the notion of 'being about the world', which the positivists used to explicate both 'analytic' and 'meaningless', was as empty as these latter notions themselves, and cannot survive in their absence. On the second alternative, he can say that the linguists discover 'substantive laws' just as the chemists do, remarking merely that these discoveries are likely to hold few surprises.... So far in this paper I have been suggesting the second, but either alternative would make sense. (459–60)

Thus, while both Chomsky and Rorty would have a *consistent* Quine maintaining that physics and linguistics are on an ontological par, they seem to be pointing that Quine in different directions: Chomsky wants Quine to conclude that neither physics nor linguistics has a fact of the matter, while Rorty wants Quine to conclude that both do. In short, Chomsky seems to think that there is no fact of the matter to physics, while Rorty seems to think that there is a fact of the matter to linguistics! Both thinkers are, I maintain, confused. Chomsky is confused in saying that there is no fact of the matter to physics simply on the ground that physics is underdetermined by evidence, and Rorty is confused in saying there is a fact of the matter to linguistics simply on the ground that there exists a rational procedure for reaching agreement about what to assert. Neither thinker has understood Quine's notion of *fact of the matter*. I shall return to this theme below, but now let us turn to two writers who are sympathetic to Quine's thesis of indeterminacy of translation.

One such writer is Dagfinn Føllesdal. In his paper "Indeterminacy of Translation and Under-Determination of the Theory of Nature," Føllesdal isolates what he takes to be Quine's two arguments for indeterminacy of translation: "One that proceeds via holism and a verificationist theory of meaning, and one that is based on certain differences between a theory of nature and the analytic [*sic*] hypotheses used in translation" (Føllesdal, 290). The former argument claims that *evidence* cannot be allocated uniquely to individual sentences of theories (holism), and since evidence for the truth of a sentence is identical with the meaning of a sentence (verificationism), it follows that *meaning* cannot be allocated uniquely to individual sentences of theories (indeterminacy). In short, Duhem plus Peirce equals indeterminacy. However, Føllesdal regards this argument as being "to little avail" (291) since he believes that the verificationist theory of meaning, upon which it turns, is "inadequate" (291). However, Quine's latter argument is independent of the verificationist theory of meaning, and therefore Føllesdal sees it as the more fundamental of the two. He also regards it as the "crucial" (291) argument for indeterminacy, since he rejects the verificationist argument.[2]

This second argument for indeterminacy turns upon the possibility of making plausible the claim that while there is a fact of the matter to physics, there is no fact of the matter to translation. Føllesdal attempts to do just that. He claims

> that the only entities we are justified in assuming are those that are appealed to in the simplest theory that accounts for all the evidence. These entities and their properties and interrelations are all there is to the world, and all there is to be right or wrong about. All truths about these are included in our theory of nature. In translation we are not describing a further realm of reality, we are just correlating two comprehensive language/theories concerning all there is. (295)

But why are we not describing a further realm of reality in translation? Føllesdal's answer to this question seems to be connected with the different roles that he sees simplicity playing in physics and translation. Simplicity does not determine truth in either physics or translation. However, simplicity is a "guide to truth" (Føllesdal, 295) in physics, but not in semantics. In other words, "[w]hile simplicity overrides almost every other consideration in our choice between scientific theories, this is not so for translation" (296). At times, "the simplest translation is not always regarded as the best, simplicity is sometimes considered less crucial than, for example, agreement" (296). Further, if

> in translation, simplicity were a guide to truth, then translation would be on a par with empirical theory. Translation would be underdetermined: several alternative translations would yield the required correlations of observation sentences etc. But translation would not be indeterminate, since one of the translations would be the true one. (295)

So, on Føllesdal's reading of Quine, the difference between underdetermination and indeterminacy can be traced back to the different roles played by simplicity considerations in the two domains, physics and translation. This analysis of the difference leads Føllesdal to conclude that "indeterminacy of translation seems to follow from empiricism alone without the need for any extra dogma [of physicalism]" (296), and that "the indeterminacy of translation seems to be with us to stay" (300; note omitted).

Føllesdal's paper is something of a direct response to Chomsky and Rorty. In particular, Føllesdal may be read as responding to Rorty's claim that Quine cannot consistently ascribe to a canon-law (heuristic-substantive) dichotomy. Føllesdal's answer is that a consistent Quine can do so, *if* he is willing to assign simplicity a role in physics different from the role assigned to it in translation, a notion Føllesdal seems to countenance even while admitting that "[t]he argument is not stated in this way in any of Quine's writings, but it seems to fit in well with what Quine says on this topic" (296). As we have seen, according to Føllesdal, simplicity's role in physics is that of "a guide to truth," overriding almost every other consideration in our choice between specific scientific theories; while simplicity's role in translation pales by contrast, being itself overridden by such things as mere agreement. Hence, in Rorty's terms, physics discovers laws while translation constructs canons—such is the work wrought by simplicity, according to Føllesdal.[3]

Føllesdal's account of the difference between physics and translation with respect to facts of the matter, given in terms of simplicity considerations, is certainly clever, but it is just as certainly not Quine's view (see RG, 155). Føllesdal shares with Rorty (and Chomsky) the mistaken notion that Quine is using the expression 'fact of the matter' in some methodological (i.e., epistemological) sense. But this is erroneous; Quine's understanding of this term is decidedly *naturalistic* and *physicalistic.* When Quine says that there is a fact of the matter to physics and no fact of the matter to translation, he is talking about physical facts, and he is talking from within an already accepted naturalistic-physicalistic theory. Thus, the error that Føllesdal, Rorty, and Chomsky share in their debate regarding facts of the matter is the assumption that the question before them is methodological (i.e., epistemological) when in fact "it is ontological, a question of reality, and to be taken naturalistically within our scientific theory of the world" (TPT, 23). As I shall further explain below, physics and translation are on a par methodologically (i.e., epistemologically), but they are not on a par ontologically. And, since they are on a methodological par, one cannot therefore distinguish between them in terms of simplicity considerations, as Føllesdal is wont to do.

Another writer who is somewhat sympathetic to Quine's indeterminacy thesis and has tried his hand at explaining Quine's position is Bruce Aune. In his paper "Quine on Translation and Reference," Aune's aim "is to clarify and elaborate Quine's key arguments for translational and referential indeterminacy" (Aune, 221). He begins by giving an exposition of the behavioristic procedure used by Quine in chapter 2 of *Word and Object* to explain and support his indeterminacy thesis. However, Aune centers on the question of what Quine means by his claim that there is a fact of the matter to physics but none to translation. Presumably, to say that there is a fact of the matter to physics is to claim that if we could not choose between two physical theories on such grounds as observation, simplicity, familiarity of principle, conservatism, and so on, one of them might *still* be correct. According to Aune's Quine,

> [t]he fact that we might not *know* that it is correct would not show that it is in some sense incomplete. The theory would (or could) be objectively right, because there would be an ob-

jective matter to be right about—namely, the objects whose existence the theory postulates. If those objects exist and have the appropriate features, then the theory would be objectively right, whether we could ever know it or not. (Aune, 223)

But why should rival translations be treated any differently? In other words, "[w]hy does Quine think that there is no objective 'fact of the matter' about whether an expression *E* has a particular translation in some other language" (Aune, 223)? According to Aune, the answer to this question begins with recognizing that "Quine's thesis of translational indeterminacy seems to rest squarely on his view that language is to be viewed 'naturalistically'" (224). Quine's naturalistic orientation, we are rightly told, "supports his view that a 'fact of the matter' concerning the synonymy of expressions must be found *in* observable behavior, not in a supposed reference to something nonbehavioral, such as an idea or Idea" (225). And, unfortunately, observable behavior will never be able to arbitrate a conclusive settlement among competing manuals of translation:

> Since, in Quine's opinion, the most we can expect of a translation manual is that it provide . . . a systematization of native utterances and a correlation of them (or segments of them) with words of our language, there is no alternative, he thinks, to concluding that countless incompatible translation manuals are, in principle, equally good. Consequently, there can be, for him, no such thing as *the* right or correct manual and no such thing (absolutely speaking) as *the* right or correct translation of a given utterance. Considered absolutely, translation must be regarded as indeterminate: the totality of relevant behavioral facts does not 'determine', or single out, any *particular* form of translation. (Aune, 225–26)

Aune's account of why Quine believes there is no fact of the matter to translation is correct. However, Aune's account of Quine's doctrine of underdetermination (which claims that two theories may be empirically equivalent but logically incompatible and yet one might be *the* correct one) is suspect, for it could be construed as presupposing that there is a thing-in-itself (*Ding an sich*), a view that Quine explicitly rejects (see TPT, 22). Recall that Aune says that one of the theories "would (or could) be objectively right, because there would be an objective matter to be right about—namely, the objects whose existence the theory postulates. *If those objects exist and have the appropriate features, then the theory would be objectively right, whether we could ever know it or not*" (223; my italics). This way of putting the matter certainly is not Quine's way, for it at least seems to construe 'fact of the matter' transcendentally. It also suggests that a true theory is one that "fits the facts," which is another view that Quine explicitly rejects (see VITD, 39). As we shall see later, the explanation of why there is a fact of the matter to physics lies elsewhere; it has to do with the circumstance that facts of the matter and truth are both immanent notions.

As we have seen, Chomsky's account goes wrong because he construes 'fact of the matter' methodologically, concluding that neither physics nor translation has a fact of the matter. Rorty's account goes wrong because he construes 'fact of the matter' methodologically, concluding instead that both physics and translation have a fact of the matter because methodology is the final arbiter of ontology (i.e., no canon-law dichotomy is possible). Føllesdal's account goes wrong because he construes 'fact of the matter' methodologically, assigning to simplicity dubiously different roles in physics and linguistics. Aune's account goes wrong because he construes 'fact of the matter' transcendentally, making the truth of physics dependent upon a thing-in-itself. None of these accounts of Quine's position accords naturalism and physicalism the central roles they deserve, for the proper construal of 'fact of the matter' is neither methodological (i.e., epistemological) nor transcendental; it is naturalistic and physicalistic. We have yet to eke out, however, the sense in which Quine believes there is a fact of the matter to physics but none to translation.

§5.2.1 *No fact of the matter to translation*

We noted in chapter 2 that ontology and epistemology are concerned with different issues. Ontology focuses on the issue of what there is; and what there is is a question of *truth*. Epistemology focuses on the issues of how we know what there is; and how we know what there is is a question of *method* and *evidence*. So, from the point of view of *epistemology*, underdetermination of physical theory and indeterminacy of translation *are* on a par: just as alternative *ontologies* can be erected on the same observational basis, so alternative *translations* of a native expression can be erected on the same observational basis. All are equally warranted by the evidence, let us suppose. How is it supposed to follow, then, that there is a fact of the matter to physics but no fact of the matter to translation?

In order to understand Quine's argument, we must recognize that for Quine facts of the matter are neither epistemological nor transcendental; they are ontological (i.e., naturalistic and physicalistic). Another way of making this same point is to say that facts of the matter are immanent: "Factuality, like gravitation and electric charge, is internal to our theory of nature" (TPT, 23).

The just-noted immanent nature of facts of the matter must be kept clearly in mind if we are to understand Quine's claim that there is no fact of the matter to translation:

> I have argued that two conflicting manuals of translation can both do justice to all dispositions to behavior, and that, in such a case, there is no fact of the matter of which manual is right. The intended notion of matter of fact is not transcendental or yet epistemological, not even a question of evidence; it is ontological, a question of reality, and to be taken *naturalistically within our scientific theory of the world*. Thus suppose, to make things vivid, that we are settling still for a physics of elementary particles and recognizing a dozen or so basic states and relations in which they may stand. Then when I say there is no fact of the matter, as regards, say, the two rival manuals of translation, what I mean is that both manuals are compatible with all the same distributions of states and relations over elementary particles. In a word, they are physically equivalent. (TPT, 23; my italics)

The current theory of the world is physicalistic—and with good reason, Quine thinks. And this physicalistic world-view settles, for the present, the physical facts of the matter and thereby what can be said to be true or false given these facts. Any putative meanings, therefore, that fall between the cracks of the physical facts just aren't meanings at all. And, further, since there just aren't any facts for such putative semantical statements to be about, it follows that such statements are indeterminate, that is, they are neither true nor false.

> My thesis of the indeterminacy of translation is [says Quine] that mutually incompatible manuals of translation can conform to all the same distributions of speech dispositions. *But the only facts of nature that bear on the correctness of translation are speech dispositions.* Thus mutually incompatible manuals of translation can conform to all the same overall states of nature, hence all the same distributions of microphysical states. Yet, being incompatible, both manuals can scarcely be right. Which one is, if either? I say there is no fact of the matter. This illustrates my identification of facts of the matter with distribution of microphysical states. (RP, 429; my italics)

In this straightforward, naturalistic-physicalistic sense, then, there is no fact of the matter to the question of which of the two manuals is *the* right one. But how, then, can there be a fact of the matter to the parallel question about physical theories?

§5.2.2 *A fact of the matter to physics*

In order to fully understand the answer that Quine gives to the above question, we must embark on a fascinating odyssey, a trip traversing some twenty or so years of Quine's ratiocinations regarding underdetermination of physical theory. As we shall see, Quine's thinking on this matter has vacillated: he begins by saying that of two empirically equivalent but logically incompatible world theories only *one* can be true; next, he adopts the opposite point of view, namely, that they are *both* true; and, finally, he reverts to his first position, that only *one* is true.

Quine calls the position that only one such theory is true the *sectarian position;* he calls the position that both such theories are true the *ecumenical position.* Thus, Quine's odyssey comprises three argumentative phases but only two positions. The first argumentative phase I shall call his *semantical argument,* the second his *trivial expedient* argument, and the third his *economy and mean-*

114   *Enlightened Empiricism*

ingfulness argument. Let us now examine each of these three argumentative phases, in turn.

§5.2.2.1 *Quine's semantical argument*

The semantical argument begins with the distinction drawn above between ontology and epistemology: ontology is the theory of what there is, and the question of what there is is a matter of *truth;* epistemology is the theory of method and evidence, and questions of method and evidence are matters of *warranted belief*. Ontology is that theoretical structure that links past and present sensory stimulations to future ones—it is a theory of objects. Underdetermination of theory is, therefore, underdetermination of ontology; it is the thesis that *different* systems of objects (or systems of sentences about objects) may link past and present sensory stimulations to future ones. "But it is a confusion to suppose that we can stand aloof and recognize all the alternative ontologies as true in their several ways, all the envisaged worlds as real. It is a confusion of truth with evidential support. Truth is immanent, and there is no higher. We must speak from within a theory, albeit any of various" (TPT, 21–22).

In other words, despite the fact that it is meaningful to say of alternative theories that they are *equally warranted* by the same sensory evidence, it makes no sense to say that they are *equally true*. It makes sense to say they are equally warranted, because we are speaking *from within* the same (physicalistic) theory of evidence: given all the (possible) evidence, *this* ontology is warranted, *that* ontology is warranted, and so on. However, it makes no sense to say they are equally true, because we are *not* speaking from within the same theory of objects (i.e., ontology).

The trouble here isn't with 'equally', it is with 'true'. Such an extratheoretical, or transcendental, usage is without meaning, for, like facts of the matter, truth is an immanent notion. In order for such a transcendental usage to be meaningful, there would have to be, presumably, a successful first philosophy, but there isn't, according to Quine. And since there is no such cosmic vantage point from which we could survey all competing, equally warranted ontologies, we are destined to occupy the position of some historical theory of what there is, which settles for us, at that time, the facts of the matter, what there is. In just this sense, and in just the words of our historically occupied theory, then, there is a fact of the matter to physics; it is just here that we feel the force of the figure of Neurath's boat, the full weight of Quine's naturalism.

The key to this semantical argument, as I have called it, is the claim quoted above that one confuses truth with evidential support if one supposes it possible to recognize all the ontologies as true in their several ways. Such a use of 'true' is meaningless because transcendental. But how are we to square this claim with the following claim, which Quine makes a mere eight pages later (but in a different essay):

> Still, let us suppose that the two [theory] formulations are in fact empirically equivalent even though not known to be; and let us suppose further that all of the implied observation categoricals are in fact true, although, again, not known to be. Nothing more, surely, can be required for the truth of either theory formulation. Are they both true? I say yes. (EC, 29)

To repeat: If it is "a confusion to suppose that we can stand aloof and recognize all the alternative ontologies as true" (TPT, 21–22), then how can we legitimately say of two such ontologies that "they [are] both true" (EC, 29)?

In short, we are confronted with contradictory claims. A choice must be made; Quine cannot have it both ways. However, this poses something of a dilemma for Quine. If he chooses to acquiesce in the former, sectarian position, then he must recant the latter, ecumenical position.[4] But this will not be easy to do for an empiricist like Quine. For what further requirement for the truth of a theory could such an empiricist want besides its ability to make all possible true (and no false) predictions? On the other hand, if he chooses to give up the former, sectarian position, then he must also give up the *semantical argument* for the factuality of physics. Thus he would be required to explain anew how there can be a fact of the matter to physics. I shall return to this point, but now let us examine Quine's argument in favor of his ecumenical position. Doing so involves our surveying a number of Quine's writings on underdetermination.

§5.2.2.2 Quine's trivial expedient argument

One of Quine's early statements of the thesis of underdetermination is found in his reply to Chomsky in *Words and Objections:* "The totality of possible observations of nature, made and unmade, is compatible with physical theories that are incompatible with one another" (RC, 302). The first thing to notice here is that when Quine is talking of underdetermination, he is doing so only in connection with global world theories and not in connection with any lesser theories. Further, even if one's global world theory is underdetermined, it does not follow from this that any component theory is underdetermined. The second thing to notice is that underdetermination is not identical with holism (i.e., the Duhem-Quine thesis):

> This doctrine of empirical under-determination is not to be confused with holism. It is holism that has rightly been called the Duhem thesis and also, rather generously, the Duhem-Quine thesis. It says that scientific statements are not separately vulnerable to adverse observations, because it is only jointly as a theory that they imply their observable consequences. Any one of the statements can be adhered to in the face of adverse observations, by revising others of the statements. This holism thesis lends credence to the underdetermination theses. If in the face of adverse observations we are free always to choose among various adequate modifications of our theory, then presumably all possible observations are insufficient to determine theory uniquely. (OEES, 313)

Perhaps Quine's clearest early exegesis of the thesis of underdetermination is in "On the Reasons for Indeterminacy of Translation":

> Naturally, it [physical theory, or our theory about the world] is underdetermined by past evidence; a future observation can conflict with it. Naturally it is underdetermined by past and future evidence combined, since some observable event that conflicts with it can happen to go unobserved. Moreover, many people will agree, far beyond all this, that physical theory is underdetermined even by all *possible* observations. Not to make a mystery of this mode of possibility, what I mean is

the following. Consider all the observation sentences of the language: all the occasion sentences that are suited for use in reporting observable events in the external world. Apply dates and positions to them in all combinations, without regard to whether observers were at the place and time. Some of these place-time sentences will be true and the others false, by virtue simply of the observable though unobserved past and future events in the world. Now my point about physical theory is that physical theory is underdetermined even by all these truths. Theory can still vary though all possible observations be fixed. Physical theories can be at odds with each other and yet compatible with all possible data even in the broadest sense. In a word, they can be logically incompatible and empirically equivalent. This is a point on which I expect wide agreement, if only because the observational criteria of theoretical terms are commonly so flexible and fragmentary. (RIT, 178–79; note omitted)

Here Quine is claiming that a theory is underdetermined by past observations because a future observation may conflict with the theory; that a theory is underdetermined by past *and* future observations because some conflicting observation may go unnoticed; and that a theory can still be underdetermined by all possible observations because the observational criteria of theoretical terms are commonly flexible and fragmentary. It is noteworthy that this last form of underdetermination is quite different from the first two forms. In the first two cases Quine is claiming that physical theory is *in fact* underdetermined; in the third case he is claiming that physical theory is *in principle* underdetermined. It is this third form of underdeterminism that is philosophically important for Quine.

In "On Empirically Equivalent Systems of the World" Quine undertakes a closer examination of underdetermination, for "[t]he doctrine is plausible insofar as it is intelligible, but it is less readily intelligible than it may seem" (OEES, 313). Here Quine investigates underdetermination more precisely in terms of *theory formulations* entailing *observation conditionals*. Theory formulations are, roughly, sets of axioms; observation conditionals are standing sentences of the form ⌜If ϕ then ψ⌝. The antecedents of such conditionals refer to boundary conditions, while their consequents refer to predicted observations. The class of observation conditionals entailed by a theory formulation composes the *empirical content* of the theory formulation. Thus, the general thesis of underdetermination alleges that for *any* theory formulation, say, TF_1, there is (in principle) another theory formulation, say, TF_2, which has the same empirical content (that is, which entails just the same true observation conditionals) as TF_1, *and* that TF_1 and TF_2 are irremediably logically incompatible. To say that two theory formulations are *irremediably* logically incompatible is to say that there is no reconstrual of predicates that would render the two logically *equivalent*. And by 'a reconstrual of predicates' Quine means "any mapping of our lexicon of predicates into our open sentences (n-place predicates to n-variable sentences)" (OEES, 320).

Quine's investigations in OEES led him to conclude therein that this *general version* of underdetermination is untenable. It is simply false that for *any* theory formulation there is, even in principle, another that is empirically equivalent to it but irremediably logically incompatible with it. Take, for instance, a theory formulation whose implied observation conditionals are finite in number. The conjunction of this finite set of sentences would be its own theory formulation. It would be implied by every empirically equivalent theory formulation but inconsistent with none. Another difficulty with the general thesis is that in particular instances there may be no way to determine that a reconstrual of predicates (which would render the two logically equivalent) is impossible. However, these difficulties do not persuade Quine to abandon the doctrine of underdetermination altogether. Rather, he reformulates the doctrine as the claim that *some* theory formulations are bound to have empirically equivalent but logically incompatible alternatives, and if we should happen upon such, we would see no way to render them equivalent by a reconstrual of predicates. Quine explains further:

> The only hope for a thesis of under-determination, evidently, is in application to theories that imply observation conditionals infinite in number and too ill-assorted to be exactly encompassed by any finite formulation; tightly encompassed, that is, without theoretical foreign matter. The thesis needs to be read as a thesis about the world. It needs to be read as saying, for one thing, that the observation conditionals that are in fact true in the world are thus ill-assorted. And it needs to be read as saying, further, that we can encom-

pass more of these true observation conditionals in a loose formulation than in any tight one. And it needs to be read as saying, finally, that for any such loose formulation there will be others, empirically equivalent but logically incompatible with it and incapable of being rendered logically equivalent to it by any reconstrual of predicates.

Here, evidently, is the nature of under-determination. There is some infinite lot of observation conditionals that we want to capture in a finite formulation. Because of the complexity of the assortment, we cannot produce a finite formulation that would be equivalent merely to their infinite conjunction. Any finite formulation that will imply them is going to have to imply also some trumped-up matter, or stuffing, whose only service is to round out the formulation. There is some freedom of choice of stuffing, and such is the under-determination. (OEES, 324)

Stated in these terms, the underdetermination thesis seems to be the result of the nature of finite theory formulations. Thus why not jettison the theory formulations and retain the infinite number of observation conditionals? Quine's answer is that there is no practical way to specify the class of such conditionals without using some theory formulation (see OEES, 324ff.). Thus, the net effect of Quine's refinements in OEES amounts to reducing the doctrine of underdetermination from the status of a *theoretical* claim (which it seemed to enjoy in RIT) to that of a *practical* claim about what is humanly possible.

In "Empirical Content" Quine again takes up the challenge of making intelligible the doctrine of underdetermination. The observation conditionals of OEES were rather sophisticated sentences: they were understood as assuming an ontology of place-times, and they came along quite late in one's history of language learning. These observation conditionals give way in EC to what Quine now calls "*observation categoricals*—sentences like 'Where there is smoke there is fire' or 'When it rains it pours' or 'When night falls the lamps are lit'" (EC, 27). These observation categoricals are eternal sentences which are composed of observation sentences. "These enjoy generality over places and times, but [unlike the observation conditionals of OEES] they do not need to be read as assuming a prior ontology of places and times or any implicit universal quantification over them" (EC, 27). Pursuant to this change, the *empirical content* of a theory formulation can now be construed as the class of observation categoricals entailed by the theory formulation. "Here, then, is further progress in relating scientific theory to its sensory evidence. The relation consists in the implying of true observation categoricals by the theory formulation" (EC, 28).

There is one further refinement of the OEES analysis of underdetermination given in EC. Suppose there are two theory formulations having the same empirical content; suppose, further, that they are logically incompatible and we see no way to render them equivalent by a reconstrual of predicates. Must we regard both as true? "Nothing more, surely, can be required for the truth of either theory formulation. Are they both true? I say yes" (EC, 29). But doesn't this admission entail the acceptance of cultural relativism: "each [theory] is evidently true only from its own point of view" (EC, 29)? This Quine denies:

> Being incompatible, the two theory formulations that we are imagining must evaluate some sentence oppositely. Since they are nevertheless empirically equivalent, that sentence must contain terms that are short on observational criteria. But then we can just as well pick out one of those terms and treat it as if it were two independent words, one in the one theory formulation and another in the other. We can mark this by changing the spelling of the word in one of the two theory formulations.
>
> Pressing this trivial expedient, we can resolve all conflict between the two theory formulations. Both can be admitted thenceforward as true descriptions of one and the same world in different terms. The threat of relativism of truth is averted. (EC, 29–30)

But isn't this *trivial expedient* argument merely a backhanded rejection of underdetermination itself? *No*, for the thesis of underdetermination asserts that two theory formulations can be empirically equivalent and yet logically incompatible and cannot be rendered logically *equivalent* by a reconstrual of predicates. Note that Quine's trivial expedient does not render the incompatible theory formulations logically *equivalent* but merely logically *compat-*

ible. Hence, speaking legalistically, this measure does not belie underdetermination; its core intuition remains intact:

> Might another culture, another species, take a radically different line of scientific development, guided by norms that differ sharply from ours but that are justified by their scientific findings as ours are by ours? And might these people predict as successfully and thrive as well as we? Yes, I think that we must admit this as a possibility in principle; that we must admit it even from the point of view of our own science, which is the only point of view I can offer. I should be surprised to see this possibility realized, but I cannot picture a disproof. (R, 181)

However, more significantly, Quine not only advocates rendering incompatible theory formulations compatible via the trivial expedient, *he also pronounces them all true*. What then of physics' factuality? Initially, to say there is a fact of the matter to physics was to say of two rival global physical theories that only one of them is *the* correct one (the sectarian position). But, now, having traced out Quine's ratiocinations over the last twenty or so years on underdetermination, we are told that they are *both* true (the ecumenical position). So, again, what are we to make of physics' claim to factuality now? Here are Quine's latest thoughts on the matter:

> Gibson points out a startling contradiction between consecutive essays in *Theories and Things* [see Gibson 1986b, n. 2]. There was an appreciable lapse of time in my writing of the two essays, and the more so in that the first one developed from still earlier lectures. I was aware of my change in attitude, but not of so abrupt a conflict. In the first passage I had held that one of two systems of the world must be deemed false even if we know them to be empirically equivalent. I shall call this the *sectarian* position. My reason for it was naturalism: my disavowal of any higher tribunal than science itself. In the later and conflicting passage, as Gibson relates, I opted for truth of both systems of the world, finding it offensive to my empiricist sensibilities to declare otherwise. This I shall call the *ecumenical* position. It raises two questions that can be satisfactorily dealt with, we shall see, and a third that seemingly cannot.

One apparent difficulty with it is that two empirically equivalent systems of the world may be *logically incompatible,* and hence incapable of being simultaneously viewed as true. This difficulty was met in *Theories and Things* (pp. 29f) by the following expedient, due to Davidson. When a sentence is affirmed in one of two empirically equivalent theories and denied in the other, the incompatibility is resoluble simply by reconstruing some theoretical term in that sentence as a pair of distinct homonyms. If the two theories have unlike ontologies, we can reconcile them by distinguishing two styles of variables.

A second apparent difficulty with the ecumenical position is the naturalistic restraint cited just now in support of the sectarian view. But this again can be accommodated. Once the two empirically equivalent systems of the world have been rendered logically compatible, they can be treated as a single big tandem theory consisting perhaps of two largely independent lobes and a shared logic. Its lobes describe the world in two equally correct ways, and we can simultaneously reckon as factual whatever is asserted in either. What can be known of the world is the common denominator of all the world systems, logically reconciled, that conform to all possible observation. (RG, 156)

So, at this point, objections based on the semantical argument are overcome. The semantical argument maintains that while it is possible to say of two empirically equivalent systems of the world that they are both equally *warranted* by the evidence, one cannot legitimately (i.e., from a naturalistic perspective) say that both are *true*. Such a usage of 'true' was considered to be transcendental, i.e, meaningless. But now, with the trivial expedient in full force, we can simply regard the two world theories as a single tandem theory. 'True' reverts to its legitimate, naturalistic-immanent usage.

§5.2.2.3 *Quine's economy and meaningfulness argument*

Have we thereby successfully moved from the sectarian to the ecumenical position? After all, we have been able to avoid the relativity of truth without giving up our naturalism.

But there is a third difficulty, raised by Føllesdal in a recent conversation. To exhibit it I must distinguish cases. In the tandem theory just now contemplated, a sentence in the added lobe may or may not be couched wholly in the vocabulary of our original lobe. Those that are so couched are either already affirmed also in the original lobe or can be freely added, for they treat of the same matters without contradiction. They might even be welcome additions, as settling the truth values of some old but hitherto unadjudicated sentences.

The picture changes when we come to sentences of the added lobe that do contain alien terms, perhaps created by Davidson's expedient of forging homonyms or perhaps present in the rival theory to begin with. Can we systematically so reinterpret this deviant lexicon as to render it in our own language without distorting empirical content? If so, we are back in the benign first case and can cheerfully annex the whole lobe to our original theory. All is ecumenical still.

But the remaining case, and the sticky one, is where the alien terms of the annexed lobe are irreducible. The sentences containing them constitute a gratuitous annex to the original theory, since the whole combination is still empirically equivalent to the original. It is as if some scientifically undigested terms of metaphysics or religion, say, 'essence' or 'grace' or 'Nirvana', were admitted into science along with all their pertinent doctrine, and tolerated on the ground merely that they contravened no observation. It would be an abandonment of the scientist's quest for economy and of the empiricist's standard of meaningfulness.

The sectarian position, then, is my newly recovered stance on these precarious slopes. It is called for in that last case, where no way is evident of annexing the rival system of the world without adding new terms. Our own system is true by our lights, and the other does not even make sense in our terms.

And what if, even so, we have somehow managed to persuade ourselves that the two are empirically equivalent? Then surely we must recognize the two as equally *warranted*. Having got the swing of the alien jargon without benefit of translation, we might even oscillate between the two for the sake of an enriched perspective on nature. But whichever system we are working in is the one for us to count at the time as true, there being no wider frame of reference. (RG, 156–57)

Thus, to this point, Quine has come full circle in his thinking on underdetermination of physical theory. There is a fact of the matter to physics because it is within physics—*our* physics, the physics we all know and love—that ascriptions of reality, truth, and factuality make sense. We are back to something like the semantical argument, after all. The offending paragraph of "Empirical Content" in the first printing of *Theories and Things*, which asserts the ecumenical position, has been replaced in a later printing by the following paragraph, which is consistent with Quine's *economy and meaningfulness argument:*

> Suppose, however, two empirically equivalent theory formulations that we see no way of reconciling by such a reinterpretation of terms. We probably would not know that they are empirically equivalent, for the usual way of finding them so would be by hitting upon such a reinterpretation. Still, we might succeed somehow in persuading ourselves of the empirical equivalence of the two formulations despite finding no way of intertranslation. Then we should indeed recognize the two as equally well *warranted*. We might even oscillate between them, for the sake of a richer perspective on nature. But we should still limit the ascription of truth to whichever theory formulation we are entertaining at the time, for there is no wider frame of reference. (EC, 29; note omitted)

At last, Quine is now speaking with one voice, a sectarian one. This history of vacillation between the sectarian and ecumenical views is a symptom of a tension deep within Quine's philosophy, between naturalism-cum-realism, on the one hand, and empiricism-cum-instrumentalism, on the other. As we have seen, maintaining both positions simultaneously, as Quine is wont to do, requires a subtle, delicate balancing act.

§5.3 *Physicalism and translational determinacy*

We noted earlier that in their respective accounts of Quine's views on indeterminacy, neither Chomsky, nor Rorty, nor Føllesdal, nor

Aune gives Quine's naturalism and physicalism the central roles they deserve. Thus each of these thinkers interprets 'fact of the matter' either methodologically (i.e., epistemologically) or transcendentally—that is, erroneously. I have attempted to correct these misinterpretations by emphasizing that 'fact of the matter' is properly interpreted naturalistically and physicalistically. Quine's naturalism rules out Aune's transcendental interpretation, and Quine's physicalism rules out Chomsky's, Rorty's, and Føllesdal's methodological (epistemological) interpretations. However, even if my account of things is correct, not all of the critics of Quine's indeterminacy thesis have thereby been silenced. For example, in his "Physicalism and the Indeterminacy of Translation," Michael Friedman intends to show that one can accept Quine's naturalism and physicalism and yet still reject the thesis of indeterminacy of translation. Friedman prefers a *causal* theory of meaning and reference, according to which questions regarding the meanings and reference of expressions do have *determinate*, naturalistic-physicalistic answers.

Friedman begins by pointing out that there are two nonequivalent versions of Quine's indeterminacy thesis: an epistemological version and an ontological version. According to the epistemological version of the thesis, the data and methods of translating are insufficient for determining a unique choice of translation. In other words, the *totality of evidence* does not epistemologically determine translation. Friedman goes on to specify what is meant by 'totality of evidence', and he offers two interpretations of 'epistemologically determines', a weak version and a strong version.

However, this epistemological version of indeterminacy does not fully capture Quine's main point concerning translation, namely, that there is no fact of the matter about a uniquely correct translation. (In other words, this version of the indeterminacy is indistinguishable from the doctrine of underdetermination of theory.) To capture this point, we must move on to the ontological version of the indeterminacy thesis. According to this version, the *totality of the world's truths* (i.e., the totality of physical facts) is insufficient for ontologically determining a unique choice of translation. Friedman goes on to specify what is meant by 'totality of physical facts', and he again offers two interpretations of 'ontologically determines', a strong version and a weak version.

Concentrating for the rest of his paper on the ontological version of the indeterminacy thesis, Friedman argues that Quine may have shown that translation is ontologically underdetermined by the totality of *behavioral facts,* but he has not shown that translation is ontologically underdetermined by the totality of *physical facts.* Using words that echo Chomsky and Rorty, Friedman claims that "Quine has not provided us with a reason for thinking that linguistic theory is different from any other higher-level theory—like chemistry or biology—in this respect" (Friedman, 356).

According to Friedman, if Quine is to make a convincing case for indeterminacy, he must give us some reason for thinking that nonbehavioral, physical facts are not relevant and/or sufficient for determining translation. Friedman points out two attempts by Quine to do just this; both are based on Quine's behavioristic theory of language learning. However, Friedman argues that both of these attempts fall short of their objective: Quine has not shown that the science of linguistics (and, specifically, translation) is limited to the realm of behavioral evidence.

Friedman believes that if this analysis is correct, it also demonstrates that, while there is a historical connection between Quine's rejection of the antiphysicalistic Frege-Church-Carnap tradition in semantics on the one hand, and his advocacy of indeterminacy on the other, the issue of indeterminacy is actually *independent* of that dispute. In other words, as a naturalist and physicalist, one can reject the mentalist tradition in semantics without being thereby committed to indeterminacy. The reason Quine is so committed, according to Friedman, is his behaviorism-cum-verificationism, which Friedman rejects.

I have no real complaint with Friedman's analysis of Quine's position on indeterminacy; in fact, I think it is one of the best analyses of the matter in print. So long as one believes that a *causal* theory of meaning and reference is possible, I see no reason why one cannot accept Quine's naturalism and physicalism and reject his indeterminacy (cf. Newton-Smith and Putnam 1975b). The question is, of course, whether such a *causal* theory is intelligible and plausible. Unlike Friedman, I am not convinced that it is. Nor is Quine:

> The suggestion seems to be that the meaning of a term is the thing or mechanism that causes the stimulatory data that leads us to apply the term. I have three problems here: how much causal background should we include? how does the

suggestion work for terms for whose application there are no separable data? and when there are such separable data, why not just take them as the meaning instead of the causes? Evidently, I have not grasped the idea. (RN, 365)

§5.4 *Indeterminacy and behaviorism*

In essence Friedman's position is that Quine's indeterminacy thesis is *logically wedded* to his behaviorism-cum-verificationism, but since Quine has not demonstrated that the *behavioral* facts are *all* the facts relevant to translation, he has not demonstrated that indeterminacy occurs. However, others of Quine's readers, who are more sympathetic to Quine's indeterminacy thesis than is Friedman, have denied that Quine's behaviorism-cum-verificationism is essential to his indeterminacy thesis. For example, in his *Wittgenstein on Rules and Private Language* Saul Kripke suggests that there might indeed be a sound nonbehavioristic basis for Quine's indeterminacy thesis:

> For those of us who are not as behavioristically inclined as Quine, Wittgenstein's problem may lead to a new look at Quine's theses [of indeterminacy of translation and inscrutability of reference]. Given Quine's own formulation of his theses, it appears open to a non-behaviorist to regard his arguments, *if* he accepts them, as demonstrations that any behavioristic account of meaning must be inadequate—it cannot even distinguish between a word meaning rabbit and one meaning rabbit-stage. But if Wittgenstein is right, and no amount of access to my mind can reveal whether I mean plus or quus, may the same not hold for rabbit and rabbit-stage? So perhaps Quine's problem arises even for non-behaviorists. This is not the place to explore the matter. (Kripke, 57)

Unfortunately, being a man of his word, Kripke does not explore the matter further.

However, Harry Beatty published a paper some ten years before the appearance of Kripke's book on Wittgenstein in which he develops an argument very much along the lines suggested by Kripke. In that paper, "Behaviourism, Mentalism, and Quine's Indeterminacy Thesis," Beatty raises and answers the following four questions:

(a) What is the role of *behaviorism* in Quine's defense of the indeterminacy thesis?
(b) Who are Quine's *real* opponents?
(c) Why does Quine *himself* distinguish the indeterminacy thesis from the underdetermination of theory by data?
(d) Can Quine legitimately extend the indeterminacy thesis to "translation" between speakers' versions of the *same* language?

With respect to question (a) Beatty argues that Quine's behaviorism is at best inessential to and at worst an obfuscation of the point of the indeterminacy thesis, namely, that no one possesses privileged semantic knowledge, i.e., no one knows even his own meanings or references (cf. Kripke's 'plus' and 'quus'). Beatty believes that Quine's gratuitous behavioristic methodology further detracts from Quine's argument by opening Quine to three lines of criticism. These three are: (1) Quine does not give a *real* behavioristic account of radical translation; (2) Quine's concept of stimulus meaning is inconsistent with strict behaviorism; and (3) Quine's indeterminacy thesis is a form of skepticism.

Beatty attempts to defuse all three lines of criticism. In the midst of doing so he answers question (b) by claiming that Quine's *real* opponents are those persons who believe that they possess private evidence on such semantic matters as reference, e.g., persons who claim to know what their words are referring to, even if no one else does. Furthermore:

> it should be noted that this answer to (b), if acceptable, has clear implications about (a), the question about the role of behaviourism in the indeterminacy thesis. If Quine really intends to direct the indeterminacy thesis only against those who accept that there is privileged knowledge on semantic matters, then it follows that *any* view which rejects such privileged knowledge is compatible with Quine's position, even if this view is in some sense 'mentalistic'. One could accept as rich an ontology of mental states as he liked and still accept indeterminacy, just as long as he did not hold that his

ontology of mental states committed him to the view that we have privileged private access to semantic information. So, on my interpretation, Quine does not *need* behaviourism to defend the indeterminacy thesis. (Beatty, 104)

Beatty also answers question (c) by claiming that even if there were a uniquely correct and comprehensive theory of nature, indeterminacy would persist, for there still would be no semantic knowledge to use to decide which translation manual is *the* correct one. Lastly, with respect to question (d), Beatty explains how Quine can indeed extend the indeterminacy thesis from the interlinguistic context to cover intralinguistic translation. Beatty concludes his essay by suggesting that Quine has "picked up on Wittgenstein's 'no private language' theme" (109) and by lamenting, again, Quine's "bringing behaviourism into his defense of indeterminacy" (109).

I believe that Beatty's analysis of the matter is both correct and misleading. He is correct in his identification of Quine's *real* opponents: Quine is directing his argument against those who believe in privileged semantical knowledge, that is, against those who "regard a man's semantics as somehow determinate in his mind beyond what might be implicit in his dispositions to overt behavior" (OR, 27). But Beatty's discussion of Quine's behaviorism is misleading, for he seems to saddle Quine with a form of behaviorism that is alien to Quine.

Beatty, and for that matter Kripke, seem to take Quine's behaviorism to be more profound than it actually is. The crucial point that needs making is succinctly put by Quine as follows: "When I have stressed that language is learned through observation of overt behavior without telepathic aids, I have encapsulated the point by saying that linguistics has to be behavioristic; but if the term does not fit my account, the term is what should be dropped."[5] I claim that it is in this sense of behaviorism that Quine's indeterminacy thesis is *logically wedded* to his behaviorism. And, while there may indeed be other avenues of argument leading to indeterminacy, as Beatty conjectures, still Quine would not accept them if they contradicted the behavioristic parameters of language learning. (This same point militates against Kripke's *reductio* interpretation of Quine's behaviorism, as given in the quotation from Kripke. See Quine's remarks concerning the verification theory of meaning and language learning in EN, 81.)

§5.5 Conclusions

At the beginning of this chapter, we raised two questions: (1) What moves Quine to say there is a fact of the matter to physics but none to translation? and (2) Is Quine's indeterminacy thesis logically independent of his behaviorism? What are we now prepared to say in response to these two questions?

Re: (1). As we have seen in this chapter, Quine's use of the expression 'fact of the matter' is neither epistemological nor transcendental; it is ontological (i.e., naturalistic and physicalistic). We noted in chapter 2 that Quine's philosophy is nothing if not naturalistic, and the same can be said, now, regarding facts of the matter. The physical facts relevant to semantics manifest themselves as verbal dispositions, hence Quine's preoccupation with behavioristic semantics. This is not to say that verbal dispositions do not have their underlying physiological and microphysical states. Certainly, they do. But the point is that such underlying states, except as manifested in (possible) behavior, are irrelevant to semantics. Thus the facts relevant to translation are behavioral facts, mainly verbal dispositions. Any ascription of meaning or reference that goes beyond the behavioral facts is, therefore, indeterminate: there simply is no fact of the matter to the (pseudo-) question of which of two fully behaviorally adequate translations of some expression is *the* correct one. Quine believes that all of this follows from adopting a naturalistic view of language and a behavioral view of meaning (see OR, 26ff., and PPE, 35–36).

So far as physics is concerned, we have traversed the tortuous path of Quine's intellectual odyssey over the difficult terrain of underdetermination only to find him ending up just where he began. He moved from his sectarian position to his ecumenical position and back to his sectarian position by means of the *semantical*, the *trivial expedient*, and the *economy and meaningfulness* arguments. According to his "newly recovered stance on these precarious slopes" (RG, 157), Quine's naturalism-cum-realism, again, looms large: it is only within *our* single, overall world theory that ascriptions of truth and falsity make sense.

Most philosophers who have pondered question (1) have, I believe, regarded translation's lack of factuality as the obscure part of Quine's claim. On the contrary, I believe *that* part of Quine's claim is crystal clear; it is, ironically, physics' factuality (not translation's) that has been difficult to pin down!

Re: (2). It seems to me that Quine would be willing to accept *any* argument for indeterminacy just as long as that argument did not violate the behavioristic principle that "[l]anguage is a social art which we all acquire on the evidence solely of other people's overt behavior under publicly recognizable circumstances" (OR, 26). In this sense the indeterminacy thesis is *not* logically independent of Quine's behaviorism. It is the *behavioral* facts, after all, that serve as *the* facts for semantics (see RP, 429, and RN, 365). Nevertheless, this is a pretty weak form of behaviorism, and Quine's indeterminacy thesis certainly *is* logically independent of stronger forms.

These days, to call someone a behaviorist is to heap scorn and derision upon them! However, there are behaviorists and there are behaviorists. And, ironically, post-Chomsky psycholinguistics, with its deemphasizing of innatism and emphasizing of social interaction between child and caretaker, sounds congenial to Quine's weak behaviorism. Even so, if it helps to make Quine's views more palatable, read 'externalized empiricist' for 'behaviorist'. My view is that Quine would countenance no argument for indeterminacy that is inconsistent with externalized empiricism.

Ontological Relativity

CHAPTER 6

§6.1 *Introduction*

Quine's doctrine of ontological relativity is most assiduously proclaimed and elaborated in his 1969 essay "Ontological Relativity." In that essay he claims that there are three aspects or levels to the ontological (or referential) relativity of theories. The first of these is expressed by the claim that it makes no sense to say what the objects of a theory are, beyond saying how to interpret or reinterpret that theory in another. There is no sense to specifying the objects of a theory *absolutely*. Consider the answer to a question like 'What is an F?': 'An F is a G'. 'What is a gavagai?': 'A gavagai is a rabbit'. "The answer makes only *relative* sense: sense relative to the uncritical acceptance of 'G' [and of 'rabbit']" (OR, 53; my italics).

The second aspect or level of ontological relativity has to do with the choices among competing manuals for translating talk of Fs into talk of Gs—translating the talk of the object theory into talk of the background theory. In Quine's radical translation context, for example, the field linguist has a choice among rival sets of analytical hypotheses, which would translate 'gavagai' as either, say, 'rabbit' or as 'undetached rabbit part'. It is only relative to some such set of analytical hypotheses that object-theory talk can be translated into background-theory talk. "Commonly of course the background theory will simply be a containing theory, and in this case no question of a manual of translation arises. But this is after all just a degenerate case of translation still—the case where the rule of translation is the homophonic one" (OR, 55).

The third aspect of the doctrine of ontological relativity emerges when we attempt to distinguish between substitutional and referential (or objectual) quantification in the object theory relative to a background theory and some manual for translating. Sometimes it is possible to show within a theory having an infinite number of names, and having the means for treating of the theory's notations and proofs within the terms of the theory, that the quantifications of the theory are referential (or objectual) rather than substitutional. If it can be shown, for example, that every time a name is substituted for the variable in a certain open sentence the resulting sentence is true, but at the same time we prove that the universal quantification of the open sentence is false, then we have thereby shown that the universe of the theory contains some nameless objects. "This is a case where an absolute decision can be reached in favor of referential quantification and against substitutional quantification, without ever retreating to a background theory" (OR, 64).

On the other hand, however, it is possible that in such a theory as outlined above there is no such open sentence: whenever an open sentence is such that each result of substituting a name in it can be proved, its universal quantification can be proved in the theory as well. Under these circumstances one would be likely to construe the universe of the theory as devoid of nameless objects, but one need not do so. One could still maintain that the theory's universe contains nameless objects. "It could just happen that the nameless ones are *inseparable* from the named ones, in this sense: it could happen that all properties of nameless objects that we can express in the notation of the theory are shared by named objects" (OR, 65).

Quine cites as an example of this kind of thing a theory containing all real numbers. Since the real numbers are indenumerable, and yet their names are denumerable, some of the reals are nameless. But it still might be the case that within this theory the nameless reals are inseparable from the named reals. If so, then it would be impossible, within the theory, to prove a distinction between referential and substitutional quantification. Every quantification expressible in the theory that is true when referentially construed remains true when substitutionally construed, and vice versa.

> We might still make the distinction from the vantage point of a background theory. In it we might specify some real number that was nameless in the object theory; for there are always ways of strengthening a theory so as to name more real numbers, though never all. Further, in the background theory, we might construe the universe of the object theory as exhausting the real numbers. In the background theory we could, in this way, clinch the quantifications in the object theory as referential. But this clinching is doubly relative: it is relative to the background theory and to the interpretation or translation imposed on the object theory from within the background theory. (OR, 65)

Even though, as noted, Quine most assiduously proclaimed and elaborated the doctrine of ontological relativity in his 1969 Dewey Lectures, he has lately acknowledged that his argument therein is obscure:

> The thesis of "Ontological relativity" is a natural sequel to my "Ontological reduction and the world of numbers" of 1964. Proxy functions, as I called them, map one ontology onto another. They served in 1964 to disqualify certain shifts of ontology, but they serve equally to change the ontology of a theory at will, without disturbing any sentences or any supporting evidence. Such was ontological relativity, but it was still foggy in my Dewey Lectures. (TL, 345)

In "Things and Their Place in Theories," Quine puts forth the proxy-function argument for ontological relativity as follows:

> All that is needed . . . is a rule whereby a unique object of the supposedly new sort is assigned to each of the old objects. I call such a rule a proxy function. Then, instead of predicating a general term 'P' of an old object x, saying that x is a P, we reinterpret x as a new object and say that it is the f of a P, where 'f' expresses the proxy function. Instead of saying that

x is a dog, we say that x is the lifelong filament of space-time taken up by a dog. Or, really, we just adhere to the old term 'P', 'dog', and reinterpret it as 'f of a P', 'place-time of a dog'. . . .

The apparent change is twofold and sweeping. The original objects have been supplanted and the general terms reinterpreted. There has been a revision of ontology on the one hand and of ideology, so to say, on the other; they go together. Yet verbal behavior proceeds undisturbed, warranted by the same observations as before and elicited by the same observations. Nothing really has changed.

The conclusion I draw is the inscrutability of reference. To say what objects someone is talking about is to say no more than how we propose to translate his terms into ours; we are free to vary the decision with a proxy function. The translation adopted arrests the free-floating reference of the alien terms only relatively to the free-floating reference of our own terms, by linking the two. (TPT, 19–20)

The proxy-function argument is a welcome one, for, "propounded independently of the indeterminacy of translation" (RPR, 460), it is clearer than the protracted argument given in "Ontological Relativity" (Dewey Lectures).

Quine's doctrine of ontological relativity has, of course, not been without its critics. In the next four sections, we shall examine some criticisms that have gained wide currency in the Quinian literature.

§6.2 Field

In his essay "Quine and the Correspondence Theory," Hartry Field maintains that Quine's doctrine of ontological relativity is succinctly stated as follows:

> (I) What makes sense is to say not what the terms of a theory denote or signify, absolutely speaking, but how one theory is interpretable or reinterpretable in another. (Field, 200)

Field regards (I) to be a "very radical contention, for it seems to preclude the possibility of a correspondence theory of truth" (200).

By a correspondence theory of truth Field has in mind "a theory that says that the notion of truth can be explained by appealing to the relation between words on the one hand and the objects that they are about on the other" (200). It is just this word-world relationship that (I) denies, for, according to Field, (I) "says that the only interesting correspondence you can get is a correspondence between the words of one theory and the words of another" (200). In short, Field's preferred (correspondence) theory of truth requires a word-world theory of reference, whereas Quine's doctrine of ontological relativity is, according to Field, a word-word theory of reference.

Furthermore, "Quine's only argument for (I) is based on his thesis that semantics is radically indeterminate" (200), and Field has doubts about the truth of Quine's claim of semantic indeterminacy. However, waiving those doubts, Field argues "that *even if semantics is as indeterminate as Quine says it is,* we ought to believe in a correspondence theory of truth and reject (I)" (200). Field is confident that if he is right about this and about several other points he makes about indeterminacy, then "it will follow that Quine's radical indeterminacy thesis is of considerably less philosophical interest than is usually supposed" (201).

In what follows, I shall argue that Field is wrong on at least three counts. First, (I) does not preclude the possibility of a correspondence theory of truth. Second, Quine's argument for (I) is not based solely on his thesis that semantics is radically indeterminate. Third, Field is wrong to assume that the truth or falsity of the doctrine of ontological relativity is the measure of the philosophical import of Quine's indeterminacy thesis. However, before giving these arguments against Field's claims, we need to examine the arguments he gives in support of his claims.

Let us recall the difficulty that the doctrine of ontological relativity is intended to resolve: inscrutability of reference. Inscrutability of reference is the doctrine that a term's reference can be construed in a variety of ways, and that so long as these ways are consistent with all possible behavioral evidence, there is no fact of the matter to the question of which construal is *the* correct one. For example, if the term 'gavagai' can be construed according to one set of analytical hypotheses (consistent with all possible behavioral evidence) as referring to rabbits, and according to another set of analytical hypotheses (consistent with all possible behavioral evidence) as referring to undetached rabbit parts, then *both* construals are correct. Quine finds this doctrine "plausible because of the broadly structural and contextual character of any considerations that could guide us to native translations of the English cluster of interrelated devices of individuation" (OR, 34).

According to Quine, we cannot say *absolutely* that 'gavagai' refers to rabbits, nor that 'gavagai' refers to undetached rabbit parts. But we can say that *relative to* one manual of translation 'gavagai' refers to rabbits, and *relative to* a different manual of translation 'gavagai' refers to undetached rabbit parts. So, while talk of *absolute* reference is nonsense, talk of *relative reference* is not. Such, in brief, is Quine's doctrine of ontological relativity, or (I).

As noted previously, Field does not accept Quine's indeterminacy and inscrutability claims. Not that Field is a mentalist; rather, he is a physicalist who believes that there is a physical fact of the matter to questions of translation and reference. Nevertheless, his immediate quarry here is ontological relativity and not indeterminacy or inscrutability. Thus, he is willing to pretend that he accepts indeterminacy and inscrutability so as to consider the consequences that such indeterminacy and inscrutability would have for the correspondence theory of truth. So, what is Field's complaint with ontological relativity?

His complaint is that Quine's notion of relativized reference is nonsense:

> The difficulty is obvious: the whole point of relativizing the notions of denotation and signification to a translation manual was that due to the indeterminacy of reference (or "inscrutability of reference," to use Quine's phrase) the unrelativized notions of denotation and signification are not physicalistically acceptable. But the foregoing remarks show that once the indeterminacy is taken seriously and applied to our own current language, as well as other languages, the manual-relative notions of denotation and signification are not acceptable, either. By employing them, Quine himself has become a victim of "the myth of the museum." (207)

In short, Field argues that the very same considerations of indeterminacy that give rise to the doctrine of inscrutability of reference undercut Quine's attempted solution to this difficulty, viz., onto-

138   *Enlightened Empiricism*

logical relativity. If 'gavagai' is inscrutable, then so is 'rabbit', 'undetached rabbit part', and so on. Thus, at best (I) yields only word-word correspondences and not the word-world correspondences that a correspondence theory of truth requires. Within the framework of (I) no link has or can be established between 'rabbit' and the world, 'undetached rabbit parts' and the world, and so on. To think otherwise is, ironically, merely to succumb to the myth of the museum.

What are we to make of Field's argument? It seems to me that the argument is a non sequitur, for it overlooks that all-important distinction that we drew in chapter 2—the distinction between ontology and epistemology.

It is from his epistemological reflections, viz., reflections on method and evidence, that Quine arrives at the doctrines of indeterminacy of translation, inscrutability of reference, and ontological relativity. Moreover, the important point that must not be lost sight of is that his epistemological reflections occur *within* an ontological setting. The ontological setting is that of contemporary science, and "it is within science itself, and not in some prior philosophy, that reality is to be identified and described" (TPT, 21). Furthermore, to recognize that indeterminacy, inscrutability, and ontological relativity occur "is not to repudiate the ontology in terms of which the recognition took place" (TPT, 21).

> We *can* repudiate it. We are free to switch [ontologies], without doing violence to any evidence. If we switch, then this epistemological remark itself undergoes appropriate reinterpretation too; nerve endings and other things give way to appropriate proxies, again without straining any evidence. But it is a confusion to suppose that we can stand aloof and recognize all the alternative ontologies as true in their several ways, all the envisaged worlds as real. It is a confusion of truth with evidential support. Truth is immanent, and there is no higher. We must speak from within a theory, albeit any of various. (TPT, 21–22)

Now how do these remarks about epistemology and ontology relate to Field's argument? Just so: Field argues that it makes no sense to say that relative to a translation manual the foreigner's term 'gavagai' refers to rabbits, for example; for the home term 'rabbit' is just as inscrutable as the foreigner's 'gavagai'. But, as we have just explained, to recognize that the foreigner's 'gavagai' is inscrutable is not to repudiate the ontology in terms of which the recognition took place. We *can* repudiate it. That is, we can call into question the reference of 'rabbit', but we need not. As Quine insists, the inscrutability of a term of the home language "differs none from radical translation ordinarily so called except in the willfulness of this suspension of homophonic translation" (OR, 47). Thus, by one's acquiescing to homophonic translation in the home language, the reference of 'rabbit' remains fixed: 'rabbit' refers to rabbits, and reference remains a word-world relation.

In responding to a remark by J. N. Mohanty, Quine makes clear that his notion of reference is of the word-world variety, and not of the word-word variety:

> 'Refer' has various uses, and Mohanty rightly cautions against confusing mine with others. I use the word to relate linguistic expressions to objects. *Real* objects, I am tempted to say, despite the redundancy. When language is regimented in the familiar way, reference in my sense has three species: *denotation* by general terms, *designation* by singular terms, and *taking as value* by bound variables. (REE, 229)

But how can Quine say that he is using the word 'refer' to relate linguistic expressions and objects, *real* objects, when he also says:

> By the inscrutability doctrine, what the terms of a given language denote is not a question of fact; so, when we interpret those terms as denoting such and such objects, all we are really doing is to propound translations of those terms into terms of our language. All we are really doing, in effect, is combining Ramsey sentences with Ramsey sentences under shared quantifiers. We have arrested the free-floating reference of the alien terms only relatively to the free-floating reference of our own terms, by linking the two. (REE, 243)

It would appear from the last two quotations that Quine has succumbed to an inconsistency: reference is a word-world relation (first quotation), *and* reference is a word-word relation (second quotation).

140 *Enlightened Empiricism*

The key to reconciling these apparently conflicting claims can be found, I believe, in the following passage, where Quine, having just completed a discussion of his notion of *fact of the matter* in connection with indeterminacy of translation, turns to a discussion of the same notion in connection with inscrutability of reference:

> It is in the same [nonepistemological, ontological, i.e., naturalistic-physicalistic] sense that I say there is no fact of the matter of our interpreting any man's ontology in one way or, via proxy functions, in another. Any man's, that is to say, except ourselves. We can switch our own ontology too without doing violence to any evidence, but in so doing we switch from our elementary particles to some manner of proxies and thus reinterpret our standard of what counts as a fact of the matter. Factuality, like gravitation and electric charge, is internal to our theory of nature. (TPT, 23)

The above quotation can be used as follows to dispel the apparent conflict in Quine's views regarding reference. Suppose linguist A translates 'gavagai' into his mother tongue, English, as 'rabbit'. Suppose linguist B translates 'gavagai' into his mother tongue, English, as 'undetached rabbit part'. Supposing that both translations are consistent with all possible behavioral evidence, Quine's point is that there is no naturalistic-physicalistic fact of the matter to the question of which word-word relation is *the* correct one. Both are correct in the only reasonable (by Quine's behavioristic lights) sense of 'correct'. However, so long as linguists A and B continue to conform unquestionably in their usages of 'rabbit' and 'undetached rabbit part', just so long do 'rabbit' and 'undetached rabbit part' refer, respectively, to rabbits and undetached rabbit parts. And this latter pair of relations, unlike the pair of relations 'gavagai'/'rabbit' and 'gavagai'/'undetached rabbit part', is *not* of the word-word type but of the word-world type: 'rabbit'/rabbits, 'undetached rabbit part'/undetached rabbit parts. Quine's point is that these latter word-world relations, too, can be disturbed, but they need not be. And so long as they remain undisturbed, it makes perfectly good sense to say that 'rabbit' refers to (i.e., denotes) rabbits and 'undetached rabbit part' refers to (i.e., denotes) undetached rabbit parts. (See RP, 429.)

If the view just explained is indeed Quine's, then there is no justification for Field's charge that he has succumbed to the fallacy of the museum myth. The claim that 'rabbit' refers to rabbits, even while accepting indeterminacy and inscrutability, does not commit one to the dubious position that reference is fixed somehow extra-theoretically. But the view just explained does call for paying careful attention to Quine's distinction between epistemology and ontology. From an epistemological perspective, indeterminacy and inscrutability render the word-word–word-world distinction dubious indeed, for from this perspective *any* word-world relation can be reduced to a word-word relation. However, from an ontological perspective the distinction continues to makes sense, if only immanent sense. And the important point to keep in mind is that Quine's naturalism precludes the possibility of embracing an exclusively epistemological perspective, a perspective outside of all ontological frameworks: epistemology presupposes ontology (cf. chapter 2). Quine very aptly draws all this together when he says:

> To call a posit a posit is not to patronize it. A posit can be unavoidable except at the cost of other no less artificial expedients. Everything to which we concede existence is a posit from the standpoint of a description of the theory-building process, and simultaneously real from the standpoint of the theory that is being built. Nor let us look down on the standpoint of the theory as make-believe; for we can never do better than occupy the standpoint of some theory or other, the best we can muster at the time.
>
> What reality is like is the business of scientists, in the broadest sense, painstakingly to surmise; and what there is, what is real [i.e., ontology], is part of that question. The question how we know what there is [i.e., epistemology] is simply part of the question . . . of the evidence for truth about the world. The last arbiter is so-called scientific method, however amorphous. (WO, 22–23)

In concluding this section on Field's argument against ontological relativity, I will respond briefly to the three claims that I attributed to Field toward the beginning of this section. First, it should be obvious from what has been said that (I) does not preclude the possibility of a correspondence theory of truth, at least in some general (e.g., Davidsonian) sense of 'correspondence'. "What is it that makes one complete physical theory true and another false? I can only answer," says Quine, "with unhelpful realism, that it is the nature of the world" (R, 179–80). Second, Field's claim that the only argument that Quine has for ontological relativity is based on indeterminacy is incorrect, for there is also the proxy functions argument. Third, it is a mistake to think, as Field does, that ontological relativity is *the* measure of the philosophical import of indeterminacy. This is a mistake because indeterminacy has philosophical consequences quite apart from considerations of ontological relativity. For example, the doctrine has implications for the theory of meaning, the theory of translation, the philosophy of logic, and the philosophy of the natural and social sciences. These implications of indeterminacy suffice by themselves to endow the thesis of indeterminacy with ample philosophical import.

§6.3 *Davidson*

As we have noted, Field, like Quine, is a physicalist. However, he rejects Quine's doctrines of indeterminacy and inscrutability, along with ontological relativity. Similarly, Donald Davidson is a physicalist. And, while Davidson too rejects Quine's doctrine of ontological relativity, unlike Field he accepts Quine's doctrines of indeterminacy and inscrutability. He believes that Quine has pretty well established the truth of inscrutability by means of example (e.g., the Japanese classifiers, for which see OR, 35–38), and he believes that the general thesis of indeterminacy follows from inscrutability. All this is summed up very succinctly by Davidson in his essay "The Inscrutability of Reference":

> To make my general position clear from the start, I accept Quine's thesis of unscrutability [*sic*] of reference and therefore of indeterminacy of translation. And I think that I accept both these mainly on the basis of arguments that I have learned from Quine. But I do not see how these arguments show reference to be relative in the way that Quine believes it is; indeed, I think Quine's own views undermine the idea that ontology can be relativized. (Davidson 1984a, 227–28)

It is important to understand that Davidson is not denying that reference can be relativized at all. Indeed, he himself proposes a way in which it can be. Rather, he is objecting to "the idea that reference can be relativized in such a way as to fix ontology" (232). He construes Quine's doctrine of ontological relativity to be advocating just such a "fixing" of ontology.

There are two sources of Davidson's objection: one is a misreading of Quine, the other is a faulty analogy used by Quine. Davidson's misreading of Quine concerns the following passage: "What makes sense is to say not what the objects of a theory are, absolutely speaking, but how one theory of objects is interpretable or reinterpretable in another" (OR, 50). Davidson is bothered by this passage, "since the 'absolutely speaking' suggests that there is a way of relatively speaking that will decide, perhaps arbitrarily, what the *objects* are, and this I have strongly denied" (238).

Here, Davidson's charge against Quine is the same as Field's, previously noted: Quine's doctrine of ontological relativity re-institutes the myth of the museum. However, Davidson's reading of Quine on this point is a misreading. Quine did not intend his term 'relativity' to be construed in the manner of Davidson:

> Davidson expresses agreement with this thesis [viz., inscrutability of reference], but boggles at the relativity of reference. The trouble lies in faulty communication, traceable to an unfortunate word; for *relativity* as I meant it is a corollary of the inscrutability. By the inscrutability doctrine, what the terms of a given language denote is not a question of fact; so, when we interpret those terms as denoting such and such objects, all we are really doing is to propound translations of those terms into terms of our language. (REE, 243; my italics)

Thus, despite the "unfortunate word," Quine did not intend to be understood as claiming that relativizing reference confers factuality on reference, even relatively. But caution must be exercised here, if we are to understand Quine's position. When Quine is writing about reference in an *epistemological* vein, he can claim that "what the terms of a given language denote is not a question of fact . . ." (REE, 243). For example, given all the behavioral evidence, the linguist of radical translation fame can translate 'gavagai' as 'rabbit', or as 'undetached rabbit parts', or as 'rabbithood', and so on. However, when Quine is talking in an *ontological* vein, he can also claim that what the terms of one's uncritically accepted language denote *is* a question of fact. For example, it is a behavioral fact, let us assume, that the uncritical speaker of English would reply affirmatively to the query "Does 'rabbit' refer to rabbits?". Notice that there is no corresponding disposition to be had in the radical translation case: the native has no disposition to reply affirmatively (or negatively) to the query "Does 'gavagai' refer to rabbits?". Hence, his 'gavagai' can be translated multifariously. Of course, the inscrutability of reference *can* be brought to bear upon 'rabbit' directly: the uncritical English speaker can "go critical," refusing to take 'rabbit' any longer at face value. But he need not do this. The difference at home and abroad is just that abroad the linguist of radical translation has no choice but to "go critical" with respect to the native.

The second source of Davidson's objection to ontological relativity has to do with the analogy that Quine draws between his doctrine and the relational theory of space:

> Very well; in the case of position and velocity, in practice, pointing breaks the regress. But what of position and velocity apart from practice? what of the regress then? The answer, of course, is the relational doctrine of space; there is no absolute position or velocity; there are just the relations of coordinate systems to one another, and ultimately of things to one another. And I think that the parallel question regarding denotation calls for a parallel answer, a relational theory of what the objects of theories are. What makes sense is to say not what the objects of a theory are, absolutely speaking, but how one theory of objects is interpretable or reinterpretable in another. (OR, 49–50)

Davidson points out that this analogy with space is faulty, because within a coordinate system, position is absolute, but reference is not absolute within a background language. Quine takes this one on the chin:

> As Davidson observes, my analogy with position in space was poor. Position is relative, but relative position is absolute; that is, there is a fact of the matter of an object's position relative to other objects or relative to a coordinate system. Not so in translating terms into terms; there is free choice within the indeterminacy of translation. (REE, 243)

Again, the central *epistemological* point to be acknowledged is that ontological relativity does not confer factuality upon reference, absolutely or relatively. All the physical facts may remain just what they are and yet 'gavagai' may be construed as referring to rabbits, undetached rabbit parts, rabbithood, and so on. Even so, *ontologically,*

> The point is not that we ourselves are casting about in vain for a mooring. Staying aboard our own language and not rocking the boat, we are borne smoothly along on it and all is well; 'rabbit' denotes rabbits, and there is no sense in asking 'Rabbits in what sense of "rabbit"?' Reference goes inscrutable *if,* rocking the boat, we contemplate a permutational mapping of our language on itself, or *if* we undertake translation. (TPT, 20; my italics)

Reference goes inscrutable *if* we either rock the boat or undertake translation; otherwise there is a fact of the matter to rather otiose questions in the home language like "Does 'rabbit' refer to rabbits?".

Thus far we have focused on three major criticisms of Quine's doctrine of ontological relativity. There is a fourth major criticism of Quine's doctrine advanced separately by Michael Levin and Stephen Leeds. We shall examine both writers' views in the next two sections.

§6.4 *Levin*

In his paper "Length Relativity," Michael Levin argues "that the 'alternative ontologies' that Quine tells us are indeterminate vis-à-vis other speakers, are in reality alternative sets of conventions for the description of 'stimulations,' or, more simply, things" (Levin 1971, 171). Levin supports his contention by constructing a clever parody of Quine's doctrine.

He asks us to imagine a situation where two linguists, working independently of each other, undertake to translate a native's term, 'agee'. The native is measuring a rabbit with a stick. He gives both linguists to understand that the stick's length is one agee, and the rabbit's length is three agees. However, this is where the agreement

146   *Enlightened Empiricism*

between the two linguists terminates. In particular, they disagree over how to translate 'agee'. Linguist *A*, after having measured the native's stick, formulates the following analytical hypotheses:

'1 agee' translates as '3.42 inches'
'A gavagai is 3 agees long' translates as 'A rabbit is 10.26 inches long'

On the other hand, linguist *B*, after having measured the native's stick, formulates the following analytical hypotheses:

'1 agee' translates as '8.18 centimeters'
'A gavagai is 3 agees long' translates as 'A rabbit is 24.54 centimeters long'

The first set of analytical hypotheses construes 'agee' in terms of inches; the second set construes 'agee' in terms of centimeters; and nothing in the native's repertoire of (present) speech dispositions can be used by the linguist to decide which of these two construals is *the* correct one. Clearly, there is no fact of the matter to the question of which of the two is *the* correct construal; they are both correct.

Levin believes that the situation just described is completely analogous in its relevant respects to the inscrutability that Quine alleges for 'gavagai': 'gavagai' translates as 'rabbit'; 'gavagai' translates as 'undetached rabbit part'; and so on. Levin then argues by analogy that, just as his measuring example represents the philosophically trivial truth that one may adopt different conventions of measurement for the purpose of describing the native's agee, so Quine's 'gavagai' example represents the philosophically trivial truth that one may adopt different conventions of entification for describing the native's gavagai. Furthermore, in *neither* case do different *ontologies* come into play. Rather, it is the self-same agee that can be conventionally construed in terms of inches or conventionally construed in terms of centimeters. Similarly, it is the self-same gavagai that can be conventionally construed in terms of rabbits or conventionally construed in terms of undetached rabbit parts.

Levin summarizes his argument as follows:

So far as I have been able to determine, Quine rests his case on the thesis that having alternative hypotheses constitutes a difference because the "units" of the two ontologies differ. What the native thinks rabbits are "made of," or what they "really are," differs as he holds two ontologies. But this does not show that having two ontologies means more than having two conventions; for the inch-measurer thinks that agees are "made of" inches, the centimeter measurer thinks that agees are "made of" centimeters. The stage-ontologist thinks that rabbit-stages are "what there is," that stages are what we should quantify over; but the inch-measurer thinks that extension comes in inches, that inches are what we should multiply by. It is Quine himself who is dividing the unit of meaning too fine by concentrating on the "unit" in different ontologies.

Superficially, this guess seems not to be correct; for surely people who think in terms of undetached parts disagree with people who think in terms of bounded portions of space-time, in ways in which inch-users do not disagree with centimeter users. Even waiving the question of whether Quine, as a behaviorist, would admit this formulation of a defense—is this so? In what way does this difference make itself felt? Different descriptions of stimulation proffered by pairs from the first two populations are paralleled by the different descriptions of lengths given by our metrically divergent populations. Moreover, the trivial translation procedure for reconciling "differences" in the second case is replicated in the first. (172)

So, is Levin correct? Are Quine's "'alternative ontologies' . . . in reality alternative sets of conventions for the description of 'stimulations,' or, more simply, things—just as our 'alternative metrics' are alternative conventions for describing 'interval stimulations,' or, more simply, intervals" (171)? I, for one, remain unconvinced of the truth of Levin's claim. I will try to explain why.

For Quine a term is an expression marking out a category of objects in its own right; a nonterm does not. Terms have categorematic use, nonterms have syncategorematic use (see WO, 103). Now, are we to understand Levin's 'agee' as a term or as a nonterm? There are difficulties for Levin's argument, no matter which answer is given to this question.

Suppose that 'agee' is construed as a term. Then it marks out a category of objects, inches or centimeters. But if this is so, then why should we understand these as "alternative metrics" rather than "alternative ontologies"? To merely assume that we should do so is to beg the question at issue. Thus, if Levin's 'agee' is taken as a term analogous to 'gavagai', then there is absolutely no justification for his assumption that translations of 'agee' are merely "alternative conventions for describing . . . intervals" (171).

Suppose, on the other hand, that 'agee' is construed as a nonterm, as not marking out a category of objects. Then, again, Levin's analogical argument breaks down, for it becomes impossible for him to extrapolate from the "conventionality" of the *usage* governing (the syncategorematic) 'agee' to the "conventionality" of the *reference* of (the categorematic) 'gavagai'. For example, if 'agee' is a defective noun (see WO, 244) in the native's language, then its *usage* is "conventional," but surely it is fallacious to conclude from this circumstance that the *reference* of 'gavagai' is "conventional" (in the same sense of the word). In short, if 'agee' is a nonterm and 'gavagai' is a term, then Levin's analogical argument is a matter of comparing apples with oranges.

The vague use of the term 'convention' in the discussion above points to another difficulty with Levin's argument. He unfortunately never explains what he has in mind by his use of this term. In what sense, for example, are "alternative metrics" "conventional"? Does his understanding of this term presuppose resurrecting the analytic-synthetic distinction? the internal-external distinction? the formal-mode–material-mode distinction? If so, then he may have won the battle only at the cost of losing the war!

The motivating force behind Levin's attack on ontological relativity comes out in his subsequent paper entitled "Relativity, Spatial and Ontological": "If I read Quine right, the moving intuition behind OR [ontological relativity] is the neo-idealist view that *reality is accessible only through a conceptual framework*" (1975, 260). This reading of Quine offends Levin's (metaphysical?) realist scruples! Levin was not the first person, nor will he be the last, alas, to read Quine as though he were some kind of idealist. I believe this idealistic interpretation of Quine to be a mistaken one. Furthermore, I believe that philosophers like Levin are prone to give this misinterpretation because they have failed to grasp how thoroughly naturalistic Quine's approach to philosophy is. Like Stroud, for example, Levin does not give due consideration to the fact that for Quine epistemology (i.e., the theory of method and evidence) is contained in ontology (i.e., the theory of what there is). Quine illustrates this mode of containment nicely in the following remarks regarding underdetermination of physical theory:

> The truth of physical theory and the reality of microphysical particles, gross bodies, numbers, sets, are not impugned by what I have said of proxy functions and of wildly deviant but empirically equivalent theory formulations. Those remarks had to do not with what there is and what is true about the world, but only with the evidence for what there is and what is true about the world. I was showing that scientific discourse radically unlike our own, structurally and ontologically, could claim equal evidence and that we are free to switch. Still we can treat of the world and its objects only within some scientific idiom, this or another; there are others, but none higher. Such, then, is my absolutism. Or does it ring relativistic after all? (RA, 295; note omitted)

Although these remarks are ostensibly intended to shed light on underdetermination, they are equally applicable to ontological relativity and reference. The relevant point is that one can question the reference of certain terms only if the reference of other terms remains fixed. (Compare this point with a similar one made in chapter 3, that Stroud's "act of appreciation" is not Quine's.) The conclusion to be drawn, in the present context, is that Levin's claim that Quine is a neoidealist is somewhat anachronistic. For the previous quotation not only suggests that Quine's philosophy transcends the absolutist-relativist dichotomy, it also suggests that his philosophy transcends Levin's realist-idealist dichotomy. In short, Quine's naturalism renders the old-time realist-idealist controversy obsolete; he is neither a neorealist nor a neoidealist.

§6.5 *Leeds*

In his essay "How To Think About Reference," Stephen Leeds claims that on the most plausible reading of Quine's "Ontological Relativity," the doctrine of ontological relativity is trivial:

The most natural—and frequent—reading of Quine runs as follows: Talk of reference makes sense only relative to a background language, in precisely the same way that all talk, whatever its subject matter, makes sense only relative to a background language: a string of signs standing alone, and not taken as uttered in some language, says nothing. This simple fact gives rise to a regress: if one tries to say what a word in a language L refers to, one's answer must be couched in some language L'; however the language L' can itself be translated in several ways into other languages—one's answer therefore does not make absolute sense, but only sense relative to yet another background language, etc.

I think that if this reading is the best that can be given, then ontological relativity is scarcely worth our attention. I must confess, however, that this really does seem to be what Quine is after. (488)

Interpreted thusly, the doctrine of ontological relativity amounts to the philosophically uninteresting triviality that "questions must be asked and answered in some language" (Leeds, 489), i.e., "that *all* speech makes sense only relative to a background language" (489). In other words, "it shows nothing about reference that it does not show about any other relation" (489).

In order for Quine's doctrine of ontological relativity to be rendered philosophically interesting, it must be interpreted as making a claim about the relativity of ontology that is stronger than the interpretation just given; it must somehow distinguish referential talk from talk in general. Leeds suggests the following as a plausible way of doing just this:

> . . . talk of reference makes sense, not merely against the background of a language, but against the background of certain assumptions we make about the background language. To speak of reference, we must pretend that certain questions about our language have been answered—these questions are questions about the reference of the terms in our language; the answer is given by the Tarski schema for reference in the background language. (490)

Leeds provides no further details of what this involves, but the idea seems to be that when ascertaining the reference of terms of a language other than our own, we must *pretend* that the references of the terms of our own language are fixed à la Tarski: "'Snow' refers to snow" is true *if* 'Snow' refers to snow. And, "although it is not in general necessary, when one speaks a language, to beg the truth of the Tarski schema for that language, it is necessary when one is talking about reference" (Leeds, 491). Such, then, is the rationale for distinguishing referential talk from talk in general. Thus, according to Leeds, is the doctrine of ontological relativity saved from trivialization.

Leeds compares the pretense of the referential relativist to that of the spatial relativist: just as the latter believes that all positions and velocities are relative but pretends, for the sake of convenience, that local position and velocity are absolute, so the former believes that all reference is relative but pretends, for the sake of convenience, that local reference is absolute. And, just as talk of absolute position and velocity can be eliminated in a more accurate, relational account of space, so talk of absolute reference can be eliminated in a more accurate, relational account of reference. Leeds explains:

> Let us take inscrutability of reference as having shown that there is no such relation as reference; the subject matter of ontology is not the relations between language and the world but rather certain important relations—intertranslatability is one such—which hold between languages. Now, although it is in principle possible to discuss these relations without ever speaking of reference, in practice, we use the notion of reference as a harmless convenience. Here is what we do: Suppose we are interested in comparing the language we are currently speaking (or the theory we currently believe) with some other language or theory. We assume that there is a relation, reference, which obeys two laws: for our language, the Tarski schema is true, and reference is preserved by correct translation. We then find that we are in a position to say a great deal about the possible reference of terms in the other language. What we say, although couched in the misleading terminology of reference, will be useful and informative, for it will reflect—and perhaps be paraphrasable by—certain important

facts about relations between our language and the other. (491–92)

Leeds believes that "this view has much to recommend it, both as a reading of Quine and as an account of reference" (492). Even so, he rejects it as an account of reference:

> Let us agree with Quine that inscrutability of reference has shown the necessity of giving a new account of reference; let us agree also that we can justify most of what we are inclined to say about reference by supposing that talk of reference is really talk about the relations between theories; where are the arguments to show that this is the only justification open to us? Where are the arguments to show that we must give up thinking of reference as a relation between words and objects? (493)

Where are they, indeed? Leeds believes Quine attempts such arguments, but that they "prove little or nothing" (493). But this is mistaken, for as we noted in discussing Field's arguments, Quine uses the word 'refer' "to relate linguistic expressions to objects" (REE, 229). In short, Quine construes reference as a word-world relation, not as a word-word relation. It is puzzling why Leeds thinks otherwise, for his analysis of Quine's account of reference is otherwise highly accurate, and it does not appear to support the word-word interpretation at which Leeds arrives. After all, the Tarski reference schema that Leeds invokes is not a word-word relation.

Perhaps the best explanation lies with Leeds's use of the analogy of reference and space. But as we noted in discussing Davidson's arguments, Quine now admits the *disanalogy* between the relativity of reference and the relativity of space. Relative position can be absolute in the sense that "there is a [physical] fact of the matter of an object's position relative to other objects or relative to a coordinate system" (REE, 243). However, relative reference cannot be absolute in this sense, for there is no physical fact of the matter of a term's reference relative to other terms or relative to a set of analytical hypotheses. *Nevertheless,* the *undisturbed* terms of the home language do refer to objects: ". . . 'rabbit' denotes rabbits, and there is no sense in asking 'Rabbits in what sense of "rabbits"?'

Reference goes inscrutable if, rocking the boat, we contemplate a permutational mapping of our language on itself, or if we undertake translation" (TPT, 20). This was the moral, I thought, of Leeds's Tarski schema. It was also the point at which Field and Davidson charged that Quine was surreptitiously invoking the museum myth. But we have seen that this charge overlooks, and is deflected by, Quine's naturalism together with his distinguishing epistemology from ontology: "It is . . . [epistemology] that reveals that displacements of our ontology through proxy functions would have measured up to that neural input no less faithfully. To recognize this is not to repudiate the ontology in terms of which the recognition took place" (TPT, 21).

§6.6 Conclusions

In this chapter, we have examined a number of criticisms of Quine's doctrine of ontological relativity. The first of these, coming from Field, was that Quine's doctrine is inconsistent since, in the end, it assumes what it allegedly rejects, viz., the myth of the museum. The second, coming from Davidson, was that Quine's doctrine is inconsistent since it asserts both that there is and is not a fact of the matter to the question of a term's reference. In responding to both of these criticisms I have urged that Quine's doctrine is not inconsistent, in either of the above ways. Quine does not commit himself to the museum myth when he claims that reference is a word-world relation. Reference remains a theoretical relation, for all that: 'rabbit' refers to rabbits only by virtue of its multifarious but undisturbed connections to other parts of language. Nor is there an inconsistency in the claim that reference is and is not inscrutable, or that there is and is not a fact of the matter to the question of a term's reference. From an epistemological perspective, reference is inscrutable—there is no fact of the matter. From an ontological perspective, reference is scrutable—there is a fact of the matter. The epistemological perspective is that of the linguist of radical translation and of anyone who rocks the boat at home; the ontological perspective is that of most speakers, most of the time. The overriding moral of Quine's naturalism is that no one can occupy *only* the epistemological perspective. The epistemological perspective, like the skepticism that gives rise to it, presupposes the ontological perspective. Neither epistemology nor skepticism is intelligible outside of all ontologies. The ontological planks of the ship of theory may be replaced piecemeal, but only by shipboard theorists.

The third criticism, from Davidson, concerns Quine's spatial analogy. The point is that the analogy is a poor one since relative position is absolute, but relative reference is not. This is a point that Quine frankly concedes.

Finally, the criticism from Levin and Leeds—that ontological relativity is trivial for one reason or another—also misfires. Levin's charge makes essential use of an undefined notion of convention, which may very well presuppose something like the analytic-synthetic distinction. Leeds conflates the epistemological and ontological perspectives, leading to the erroneous conclusion that Quine is committed to a word-word theory of reference.

In chapter 2, I remarked that Quine's philosophy is nothing if not naturalistic. The import of this remark in the present context is that Quine's doctrine of ontological relativity presupposes an uncritically accepted background language. In the uncritically accepted language, reference is a word-world relation. For the linguist translating a foreign language, this is his home language. For the speaker of the home language, this is that part of his home language that he accepts uncritically. Without an uncritically accepted background language, inscrutability of reference, ontological relativity, epistemology—indeed, language itself—would be impossible.

Quine on Ethics

CHAPTER 7

§7.1 *Introduction*

Until fairly late in his philosophical career, Quine published nothing on the topic of morality. To date, he has published but one essay devoted entirely to the subject of moral values, namely, "On the Nature of Moral Values." What other scanty remarks he has made on the topic are to be found in *The Roots of Reference, The Web of Belief,* "What I Believe," "Reply to Morton G. White," and a few lines scattered here and there in various essays. In this chapter, I shall focus primarily on his essay "On the Nature of Moral Values," in which he discusses the epistemological status of ethics.

It has now been over two decades since Quine drove a contentious wedge between physics and translation by claiming that there is a fact of the matter to the former but not to the latter. With the publication of "On the Nature of Moral Values," however, he has driven a similar wedge between physics and ethics by claiming therein that the former has some title to a correspondence theory of truth, while a coherence theory of truth is the lot of the latter. Another way of putting his point is to say that ethics is methodologically infirm as compared to science.

As we saw in chapter 5, ever since Quine published his views about underdetermination of physical theory and indeterminacy of translation, a controversy has raged concerning the meaning and justification of his claim that there is a fact of the matter to physics but none to translation. As noted in chapter 5, many philosophers have erroneously construed Quine's claim as having to do with methodology: the methodology of physics confers factuality, the methodology of translation does not. Moreover, finding no relevant methodological difference between the two, these philosophers have concluded that Quine's contention is mistaken; either there is a fact of the matter to both physics and translation, or there is a fact of the matter to neither. This erroneous conclusion results from taking Quine's claim to be a methodological claim; it isn't. The claim is an ontological one, "to be taken naturalistically within our scientific theory of the world" (TPT, 23). It asserts that factuality is immanent and that within some accepted physical theory, when all the physical facts are in, there is still no physical fact of the matter to the question of which of two fully (behaviorally) adequate but incompatible translation manuals is *the* correct one; they are both correct. Thus, the difference Quine alleges between physics and translation is an ontological one, not a methodological (i.e., epistemological) one.

I pause to recount this point because, as we shall see, Quine's more recent distinction between physics and ethics *is* a methodological one. In sum, Quine believes that translation and physics are on a methodological par but not on an ontological par; and he believes that ethics and physics are on an ontological par but not on a methodological par. Thus it would be a mistake to infer that Quine is lumping translation and ethics together in opposition to physics; the opposition among the three is more complex. To repeat: The opposition between translation and physics is ontological; the opposition between ethics and physics is methodological.

Just as Quine's allegation of the ontological opposition between translation and physics has generated controversy, so too (but to a much lesser extent) has his allegation of the methodological opposition between ethics and physics. In this chapter, after giving an account of Quine's views on the nature of morality, we shall examine the controversy that his views have spawned.

§7.2 Quine on moral values

It will come as no surprise to the readers of these pages to be told that Quine views the institution of morality and the values it presupposes as natural phenomena and that they (like knowledge, mind, and meaning) "are to be studied in the same empirical spirit that animates natural science" (OR, 26). Thus does Quine offer a *naturalistic* account of his topic in "On the Nature of Moral Values." In particular, he offers naturalistic accounts of (1) the institution of morality, (2) the nature and origins of moral values, (3) the nature of moral conflicts, and (4) the epistemological status of ethics. So, his essay is best classified as belonging to meta-ethics rather than to normative ethics, but to meta-ethics of a distinctively scientific (as opposed to philosophical-cum-conceptual) kind. For example, he does not offer naturalistic definitions of ethical terms. After all, that preoccupation of old style meta-ethics presupposed the analytic-synthetic distinction!

§7.2.1 The institution of morality

If Quine were asked to explain why humankind has developed the institution of morality, his answer would focus on the theory of evolution—the idea being that ethical behavior has generally proven to be conducive to the survival of the race (see NMV, 65–66), and therefore the propensity to behave morally has been selected for.

Caution must be exercised, however, when interpreting Quine's position. First, he does not claim that whatever is conducive to survival is therefore morally good; nor does he claim that whatever is morally good is therefore conducive to survival. Second, he defines neither 'moral' nor 'good' in terms of survival value, e.g., 'conducive to survival of the race'. In fact, he offers no definitions of 'moral' or of 'good', at all. Third, while Quine acknowledges that there are *ultimate* moral goods, some of which are "higher" than others, he offers neither survival value nor anything else as the *summum bonum* of morality.

§7.2.2 The nature and origins of moral values

Values, both moral and nonmoral, play a role, of course, in motivating human behavior. Quine's theory about such motivation is intimately intertwined with his general theory of learning. Both theories share the same two aspects, an epistemological and a valuational aspect:

> Imagine a dog idling in the foreground, a tree in the middle distance, and a turnip lying on the ground behind the tree. Either of two hypotheses, or a combination of them, may be advanced to explain the dog's inaction with respect to the turnip: perhaps he is not aware that it is there, and perhaps he does not want a turnip. Such is the bipartite nature of motivation: belief and valuation intertwined. It is the deep old duality of thought and feeling, of the head and the heart, the cortex and the thalamus, the words and the music. (NMV, 55)

The epistemological aspect involves standards of perceptual similarity. Some of these standards are innate, others are acquired. Man's ability to recognize that a sensory episode a is more similar to an episode b than is an episode c, with respect to, say, gaudy color, is probably innate. On the other hand, his ability to recognize that a is more similar to b than is c, with respect to, say, chemical composition, is acquired.

The valuational aspect involves pleasure (or the absence of pain) and pain (or the absence of pleasure). Certain episodes innately elicit pleasure, while others innately elicit pain. Mother's milk may belong to the former category, intense heat to the latter. Beyond these innate likes and dislikes are acquired likes and dislikes: an acquired taste for beer, an acquired distaste for milk. All these examples are of sensual values, but Quine believes that this account holds true for *all* values, moral as well as nonmoral.

The pleasures and pains come encoded in episodes right along with the perceptual similarities, of course. Physiologically normal subjects naturally strive to replicate pleasurable episodes and to avoid replicating painful ones. "The drive to increase or decrease the similarity will . . . vary with the degree of pleasantness or unpleasantness of the earlier episode" (RR, 28). Further, "[t]he drive will vary also with the degree of perceptual similarity that already obtains" (RR, 28).

> Learning, thus viewed, is a matter of learning to warp the trend of episodes, by intervention of one's own muscles, in such a way as to simulate a pleasant earlier episode. To learn is to learn to have fun. Behaviorally, the shoe is on the other foot: an episode counts as pleasant if, through whatever unidentified mechanism of nerves and hormones, it implants a drive to reproduce it. The pleasure is measured by the strength of this drive. And all this applies also in reverse, to the avoiding of the unpleasant. (RR, 28–29)

We have been speaking glibly of *moral* values and of *nonmoral* values, but how does Quine distinguish between these? "The distinction between moral values and others is not an easy one. There are easy extremes: the value that one places on his neighbor's welfare is moral, and the value of peanut brittle is not" (NMV, 57–58). There are other cases, however, whose classifications are more problematic:

> It is hard to pick out a single distinguishing feature of moral values, beyond the vague matter of being somehow irreducibly social. We do better to recognize two largely overlapping classes of moral values. *Altruistic* values are values that one attaches to satisfactions of other persons, or to means to such satisfactions, without regard to ulterior satisfactions accruing to oneself. *Ceremonial* values, as we might say, are values that one attaches to practices of one's society or social group, again without regard to ulterior satisfactions accruing to oneself. (NMV, 58)

In short, moral values are those which a person attaches to other persons' satisfactions and/or to society's practices.

Quine goes on to point out that these two classes of moral values are overlapping in two ways. First, "[a]ltruistic values are in part institutionalized and so may take on an added ceremonial appeal. Conversely, there is altruistic value in so behaving as not to offend against a neighbor's ceremonial values" (NMV, 60). Second, the origins of both altruistic and ceremonial values are the same:

> Some values, in the altruistic category, perhaps issue freely from an innate faculty of sympathy, unless this class is empty and sympathy is an acquired taste. Some, in the ceremonial category, are embraced out of sentiments of solidarity; thus the dietary observances in some cases, and the old school tie. The basis here is perhaps sympathy still, in an attenuated way. Further, in any event, there are both altruistic and ceremonial values that are inculcated by precept, unsupported still by palpable reward or punishment. This is already a case of training in its mild way, a case of transmutation of means [to pleasure] into ends [i.e., pleasure]; the good behavior is indulged in at first as a means to the ethereal end of parental or social approval, and only afterward comes to be valued as an end in itself. Finally, there is moral training by recourse to palpable reward or punishment over and above parental or social attitudes. Few of us are of such saintly docility as to need no training of this earthier kind. But in due course, here again, means get transmuted into ends, and conscience is further fortified. (NMV, 60)

Thus, altruistic values and ceremonial values have shared origins: heredity, learning from precept, and training. Evolution has (possibly) selected for "an innate faculty of sympathy," and because moral values matter to society, much effort is expended to ensure that new generations acquire the moral values of their elders.

Quine has claimed that moral values are "irreducibly social" in the sense that they are values attached to the satisfactions of *others*, or to the means to such satisfactions, or to the practices of one's *society*, without regard to ulterior satisfactions accruing to oneself. However, as we have seen, in the very learning of values, including moral values, it is the *learner's* pleasure that is causally efficacious. Does this represent a conflict in Quine's account? Not really. According to his account, a child, say, who performs a morally right act because he fears his parents' wrath if he does not do it, or because he anticipates their approval if he does, has not yet attached a *moral* value to the act in question. However, if and when the child transmutes the means to the parents' pleasurable approval (viz., the act in question) into a pleasure-giving end in itself, say, by transfer of conditioning or whatever, *then* the value he attaches to the act becomes a moral one. Quine explains this harmonizing of the child's private satisfactions with society's thusly:

> I remarked that this account places the moral values in among the sensual and aesthetic [i.e., nonmoral] ones. By the same token it represents each of us as pursuing exclusively his own private satisfactions. Thanks to the moral values that have been trained into us, however, plus any innate moral beginnings that there may have been, there is no clash of interests as we pursue our separate ways. Our scales of values blend in social harmony. (NMV, 60)

Quite apart from relying on this Quinian *invisible hand* argument, however, the apparent conflict noted above can be dispelled simply by keeping in mind that the pleasure that the child accrues from performing the act in no wise makes his act a moral one, nor the value he attaches to the act a moral value. Indeed, once the transmutation of means into ends takes place, the child may subsequently perform such acts habitually, without experiencing the slightest pleasure; but the value attached to such acts would be moral value nonetheless. Again, the pleasure that the child gets from performing the act may be causally efficacious in his acquiring a particular moral value, and it may serve as his motivation for performing such acts in the future, but it is concern for the satisfactions of *others,* without regard to *ulterior* satisfactions accruing to oneself, that constitutes the moral value attached to the act.

Let us summarize Quine's views on the nature and origins of moral values. Moral values, as opposed to nonmoral values, are "irreducibly social," i.e., they are oriented toward the satisfactions of others. Quine recognizes two overlapping classes of moral values, the altruistic and the ceremonial. They overlap in two ways. Altruistic values may become institutionalized, thereby accruing ceremonial value, and observance of ceremonial values may be altruistic. Also, the origins of both kinds of moral values are the same: some are innate (perhaps); some are acquired by precept; some are acquired by moral training. We are now prepared to consider Quine's account of moral conflicts.

162 *Enlightened Empiricism*

§7.2.3 *The nature of moral conflicts*

According to Quine, we can expect various cultures to share a common core of moral values, "since the most basic problems of societies are bound to run to type" (NMV, 62). Nevertheless, "[m]oral contrasts are not, of course, so far to seek. Disagreements on moral matters can arise at home, and even within oneself" (NMV, 63). Besides classifying moral conflicts as intersubjective and intrasubjective, Quine classifies them as they relate to ultimate values or derivative values. By merging these two classifications we arrive at the following four classes of moral conflicts: (1) the intersubjective derivative, (2) the intersubjective ultimate; (3) the intrasubjective derivative; (4) the intrasubjective ultimate.

§7.2.3.1 *Intersubjective moral conflicts*

Suppose that two individuals, A and B, have a disagreement regarding action *a*: A claims that *a* is moral, B claims the opposite. Sometimes such conflicts are resoluble by means of causal reduction. For example, A may attempt to convince B that action *a* is moral because doing *a* will cause *b*, where *b* represents a moral value that both A and B accept. B may or may not be persuaded by A's causal reduction. In either case, the moral conflict has been transformed into an empirical, scientific question about what causes what.

> This way of resolving moral issues is successful to the extent that we can reduce moral values causally to other moral values that command agreement. There must remain some ultimate ends, unreduced and so unjustified. Happily these, once identified, would tend to be widely accepted. For we may expect a tendency to uniformity in the hereditary component of morality, whatever it may be, and also, since the basic problems of societies are much alike, we may expect considerable agreement in the socially imposed component when it is reduced to fundamentals. (NMV, 64)

But what is one to do in those cases where the moral conflict does not concern derivative moral values but, rather, ultimate ones?

> Even in the extreme case where disagreement extends irreducibly to ultimate moral ends, the proper counsel is not one of pluralistic tolerance. One's disapproval of gratuitous torture, for example, easily withstands one's failure to make a causal reduction, and so be it. We can still call the good good and the bad bad, and hope with [Charles L.] Stevenson that these epithets may work their emotive weal. In an extremity we can fight, if the threat to the ultimate value in question outweighs the disvalue of the fighting. (NMV, 64–65)

Quine's point that "the proper counsel is not one of pluralistic tolerance" when it comes to conflicts involving "ultimate moral ends" is clear enough. However, his particular example is infelicitous, for elsewhere he has denied that this very example represents a moral conflict at all: "One may oppose torture categorically; another may condone it for punishment or for extorting information beneficial to society. *One who favours torture for its own sake, however, represents no moral position,* and indeed conflict usually reflects rather an aloofness from moral values than disagreement over them" (WIB, 74; my italics). Thus, the conflict between one who condones gratuitous torture and one who does not is *not* a conflict about "ultimate moral ends," for condoning gratuitous torture "represents no moral position."

Quine's position regarding intersubjective conflicts about "ultimate moral ends" raises the question of whether he is a normative ethical relativist. Is he saying, for example, that whatever an individual or a society *thinks* is right/wrong *really* is right/wrong for him or it, and whatever a different individual or society *thinks* is right/wrong *really* is right/wrong for him or it, such that one individual or society could hold that ultimate moral value *a* is right while another individual or society could hold that *a* is wrong, and both individuals or societies would be justified in their moral beliefs? In short, does Quine equate what-an-individual-or-a-society-believes-to-be-right/wrong with what-really-is-right/wrong-for-that-individual-or-society?

First, with respect to individuals, since Quine regards moral values as "irreducibly social" to the extent that they are oriented toward the "satisfactions of other persons, without regard to ulterior satisfactions accruing to oneself," and as socially shared and inculcated, it would seem to follow that no individual can be the source of his own *moral* values. Nor, therefore, can a conflict of the idiosyncratic values of two individuals be termed a conflict of *moral* values. This is not to say, however, that an individual cannot be the source of some of his own values, which can *become* moral values by virtue of becoming moral values of his society. For example, Socrates' claim, recorded in Plato's *Republic,* that one ought not injure his enemies may be viewed in this light. Socrates, let us suppose, is the source of this value, but it does not become a *moral* value, on Quine's analysis, unless and until it becomes "irreducibly social." In this way does Quine's analysis of moral values, despite their being "irreducibly social," leave room for moral reformers like Socrates. In sum, so far as individuals are concerned, we must answer the question of the preceding paragraph with "No, Quine does not equate whatever-the-individual-thinks-is-morally-right/wrong with what-really-is-morally-right/wrong-for-that-individual."

Second, with respect to societies as opposed to individuals, Quine makes the following interesting observations:

> Directed as it is to the welfare of a society, morality hinges on demarcation of the pertinent society. An isolated tribe could rest with a crystalline moral law, seemingly absolute and eternal, recognized by all and obeyed by most. Conflict between societies is outside of society and is thus morally neutral, until we widen our horizons and fuse many societies as one. For most of us the demarcation of society is manifold, marking tighter societies that variously overlap within looser ones; thus family, clan, nation, culture, species, phylum, posterity. Besides the moral issues over the weighting of benefits, therefore, there arise moral issues over the weighting of beneficiaries. Moral dilemma is rife. (WIB, 74–75)

Quine's claim that "conflict between societies is outside of society and is thus morally neutral" suggests that we answer the question of the penultimate paragraph with "Yes, Quine does equate whatever-a-society-thinks-is-right/wrong with what-really-is-right/wrong-for-that-society." Thus, if one society believes that *a* is an ultimate moral value and another society does not, then they are both justified in their beliefs. This point is reminiscent of Quine's thesis of indeterminacy of translation, according to which two equally justified but incompatible translation manuals of some language are both deemed correct. The analogous point in morality is that two equally justified but incompatible systems of morality are, from the point of view of Quine's naturalism, both deemed correct, i.e., the point in morality is normative ethical relativism.

To sum up: Intersubjective moral conflicts may be about derivative or ultimate moral values. If the parties involved in a conflict about derivative moral values share ultimate moral values, then sometimes the conflict may be resolved by causal reduction. On the other hand, if the conflict is about ultimate moral values (e.g., the value of personal freedom versus the value of life, as in the abortion debate), then the method of causal reduction is unavailable. In an extreme case, resolution of such conflicts may call for fighting. Insofar as personal values are not moral values, i.e., are not "irreducibly social," conflicts among individuals regarding such values are not moral conflicts. Also, conflicts between societies are outside of society and are thus morally neutral, until such societies are viewed as one. Thus does Quine's account of intersubjective moral conflicts eventuate into normative ethical relativism.

§7.2.3.2 *Intrasubjective moral conflicts*

Quine only briefly addresses the question of resolving intrasubjective moral conflicts regarding *derivative* moral values. Presumably, he believes that such conflicts can be resolved in a manner similar to the manner in which intersubjective moral conflicts regarding derivative moral values are resolved, viz., by causal reduction. However, the question of resolving intrasubjective moral conflicts regarding *ultimate* moral values remains:

> The basic difficulty is that the altruistic values that we acquire by social conditioning and perhaps by heredity are vague and open-ended. Primitively the premium is on kin, and primitively therefore the very boundary of the tribe itself in its isolation constitutes a bold boundary between the beneficiaries of one's altruism and the alien world. Nowadays the boundary has given way to gradations. Moreover, we are prone to extrapolate; extrapolation was always intrinsic to induction, that primitive propensity that is at the root of all science. Extrapolation in science, however, is under the welcome restraint of stubborn fact: failures of prediction. Ex-

trapolation in morals has only our unsettled moral values themselves to answer to, and it is these that the extrapolation was meant to settle. (NMV, 65)

Quine goes on to point out that most of us, today, "unhesitatingly extrapolate our altruism beyond our close community . . . to all mankind" (NMV, 65). Still, there remains a question regarding the degree of altruism so extended: Must we love our neighbors as we love ourselves? Also, there are questions about extending altruistic concern to unborn generations of humans and to members of other species. Are abortion, vivisection, and eating meat to be ruled out?

Now the chief point that Quine wants to make regarding such conflicts is that their resolutions are exacerbated by the methodological infirmity of ethics: "Thus we do what we can with our ultimate values, but we have to deplore the irreparable lack of the empirical checkpoints that are the solace of the scientist. Loose ends are untidy at best, and disturbingly so when the ultimate good is at stake" (NMV, 66).

§7.2.4 *The epistemological status of ethics*

We noted in the introduction to this chapter that Quine has driven an epistemological wedge between ethics and science: ethics as compared with science is methodologically infirm. And, in the previous section, we witnessed Quine deploring ethics' "irreparable lack of the empirical checkpoints that are the solace of the scientist." It is time to lay Quine's cards on the table:

> The empirical foothold of scientific theory is in the predicted observable event; that of a moral code is in the observable moral act. But whereas we can test a prediction against the independent course of observable nature, we can judge the morality of an act only by our moral standards themselves. Science, thanks to its links with observation, retains some title to a correspondence theory of truth; but a coherence theory is evidently the lot of ethics. (NMV, 63)

To illustrate Quine's point, suppose that two scientists disagree about whether a certain beaker contains acid. In order to settle their dispute they immerse blue litmus paper into the liquid in the beaker; subsequently, the paper turns red. They agree that the beaker contains acid. In short, the test for the claim that the beaker contains acid is whether, or not, it *corresponds* to the world.

Now suppose that two persons disagree about whether some particular action is moral or immoral. This disagreement may take either of two forms. On the one hand, the two persons might agree that all actions of kind ABC are moral and that all actions of kind ABD are immoral yet disagree about whether the particular action in question is of kind ABC or kind ABD; and there very well may be no "independent course of observable nature" against which to decide the matter. On the other hand, the two persons might agree that the action in question is of kind ABC yet disagree about the morality of acts of that kind; and there very well may be no "independent course of observable nature" against which to decide the matter. In short, the test for the claim that the action in question is moral/immoral is whether, or not, it *coheres* with one's moral standards.

Quine's views on ethics, and in particular his position on the epistemological status of ethics, have not received a great deal of attention. However, in sections 7.3 and 7.4 we shall examine the arguments of two thinkers who have given the matter some thought: Owen J. Flanagan, Jr., and Morton G. White. Both Flanagan and White share Quine's general naturalistic orientation, yet both argue that Quine's contention that ethics is epistemologically infirm is mistaken.

§7.3 *Flanagan*

In his essay "Quinean Ethics," Owen J. Flanagan, Jr., argues that Quine's ethical theory is actually inconsistent with Quine's systematic philosophical naturalism, i.e., with the rest of Quine's philosophical system. The "crux of my argument is that Quine's concern with the 'methodological infirmity of ethics as compared to science' is unwarranted" (56; note omitted). It is unwarranted, Flanagan contends, because "the two characteristics of ethics which lead

168   *Enlightened Empiricism*

Quine to contrast scientific and moral discourse, namely, (1) that 'we can judge the morality of an act only by our own moral standards themselves', and (2) that 'there must remain some ultimate ends unreduced and so unjustified' are attributes which . . . [Quine] himself has shown are characteristic of all significant discourse and thus do not serve to distinguish ethics from science at all" (Flanagan, 56; note omitted).

Flanagan develops his essay in three sections. In the first section he makes "some remarks about Quine's general philosophical position, highlighting the theses of holism and naturalism since these will be used later on to undermine the thesis that 1 and 2 [above] uniquely afflict ethics" (56). In the second section he discusses and fills out "the unproblematic part of Quine's ethical theory" (56). In the final section he provides "a critique and a naturalistic reformulation of the problematic part of Quine's ethical theory" (56).

In the next two sections I shall argue that Flanagan's critique of Quine's claim that ethics is methodologically infirm is misdirected. It is misdirected, first, because it erroneously presupposes that Quine is committed to a radical form of holism (7.3.1). Second, it is misdirected because Flanagan's attempted "naturalistic reformulation" of Quine's ethical theory is unsuccessful (7.3.2).

§7.3.1 *Holism and coherence*

One should be clear about what it is, precisely, that Flanagan is claiming. He is not claiming, he warns his reader, that it is "impossible to be a consistent philosophical naturalist and hold that ethics is methodologically infirm compared to science" (64). Indeed, philosophers there have been who were consistent naturalists and who maintained that ethics is methodologically infirm on the grounds that ethical utterances are noncognitive. Rather, Flanagan's claim is specific to Quine: "Quine's naturalism precludes counting ethics as one of the underprivileged modes [of discourse] since the grounds he cites for contrasting science and ethics rest on an archaic philosophical view of scientific discourse, a view which he himself rejects" (64). In spelling out Flanagan's argument for this claim we shall come to see that it amounts to the denial and replacement of Quine's claim that "science, thanks to its links with observation, retains some title to a correspondence theory of truth; but a coherence theory is evidently the lot of ethics" with the claim that a coherence theory is evidently the lot of *both* science and ethics. Thus, ethics is no more and no less "methodologically infirm" than is science.

Flanagan's argument against Quine proceeds, in general, as follows:

> P1: Quine's rejection of the two dogmas of empiricism (viz., the analytic-synthetic distinction and radical epistemological reductionism) supports and is implied by holism.
>
> P2: Holism precludes *any* talk of correspondence obtaining between the sentences of a theory and the world.
>
> P3: Holism eliminates first philosophy, thereby opening the way for naturalism.
>
> P4: Naturalism applies equally to science and to ethics.
>
> P5: Just like naturalized epistemology, naturalized ethics has both a descriptive side and a normative side.
>
> P6: Quine denies P5.
>
> ∴ C: Quine's denial of P5 is inconsistent with P2.

I believe that the argument sketched above has a certain cogency, but it is nevertheless unsound. The problem occurs at P2. Flanagan there misconstrues the nature and scope of Quine's holism. Flanagan writes that holism is "the thesis that sentences are brought to experience as a system which is ultimately constrained *only by* consistency considerations, our tendency toward epistemic conservationism, and the needs of practice" (57; my italics). Again, Flanagan writes, "Quine has shown that the thesis of determinate meaning is untenable and that the thesis of exhaustive reduction to observation [i.e., radical epistemological reductionism] is mythical *even for those [observation] sentences on the periphery of our systematic scientific theories*" (65; my italics). And, finally, Flanagan writes, "Quine has spent his philosophical career convincing us that *all* checks are ultimately intersystematic" (70; my italics). Now, this conception of holism is a form of *radical* holism, and it may very well preclude any talk of correspondence obtaining between the sentences of a theory and the world (P2). However, as we saw in chapter 2, Quine rejects this form of holism, opting instead for a form of *mitigated* holism which allows, nay, insists that observation sentences have their own individual empirical (stimulus) meanings: "I must caution against over-stating my holism. Observation sentences do have their empirical content individually, and other sentences are biased individually to particular empirical content in varying degrees" (RP, 427). Indeed, it is only by virtue of the fact that observation sentences do have their own individual empirical meanings that Quine can say that observation "is the tug that tows the ship of theory" (WB, 29) and that "[s]cience . . . retains some title to the correspondence theory of truth" (NMV, 63). Thus, because he overstates Quine's holism, Flanagan's argument fails: he does not show that Quine's claim (that ethics as compared to science is methodologically infirm) is inconsistent with *Quine's* holism-cum-naturalism, and therefore he fails to show that the coherence theory of truth is the lot of both ethics and science.

§7.3.2 *"Practice" and correspondence*

Flanagan is not insensitive to the possibility that the foregoing argument may fail because therein he may have overstated Quine's holism. In this regard, he writes:

> But perhaps I am drawing too simple a picture. Quine is not an idealist. We are not entirely intersystematically constrained in our scientific theorizing, although it is in principle impossible to tell exactly when we are not so constrained. Holism is dialectical. Our theories have what Quine likes to refer to as an oddly reciprocal relationship with experience. Theories break through the linguistic barrier now and again, and thanks to some feedback from nature we adjust our accounts. The feedback is never, of course, totally free of theoretical static. Nonetheless it is this feedback which constitutes the "empirical foothold," the "empirical controls," "the predicted observable event" which, according to Quine, science courts from time to time. But is ethics really so empirically uninvolved as to be worthy of disparagement by these standards? (71)

Clearly, Flanagan wants his reader to answer this question with a resounding "No." If we can justify this answer, then we can deny Quine's claim that ethics is methodologically infirm as compared to science—not, however, as before, on the grounds that the *coherence* theory of truth is the lot of both ethics and science, but now on the grounds that both science and ethics have some title to the *correspondence* theory of truth. But if science *corresponds* (in this weak sense) to observation, to what does Flanagan believe ethics *corresponds?* The answer is, in a word, practice:

> The corresponding role to observation [in science], of course, is played [in ethics] by practice. The theory of the *summum bonum* . . . [the normative side of naturalized ethics, according to Flanagan] is the theory of the form(s) of life which most comprehensively maximizes our aims, our interests. The best way to find out whether some particular hunk of the theory of the good life is correct is to try it, to practice it. The value of truth telling, for example, is ultimately not merely maintained because of intersystematic consistency considerations. It is maintained because of these and because it works; truth telling tends to help maximize our aims, our interests. So Quine is wrong that the empirical foothold of a moral code is "in the observable moral act." It is in the consequences of the observable moral act. These consequences break the hold of the system, and they undercut the thesis that we can judge our values "only by our moral standards themselves." (71)

Does the appeal to the *consequences* of observable moral acts, rather than to the moral acts themselves, put ethics *fully* on a methodological par with science, as Flanagan here maintains? So far as nonultimate, or instrumental, moral values are concerned, Flanagan's claim may be true. Indeed, Quine has written that "[t]here is a legitimate mixture of ethics with science that somewhat mitigates the methodological predicament of ethics" (NMV, 64). And what is this mixture of ethics with science? Causal reductionism. "Ethical axioms can be minimized by reducing some values causally to others; that is, by showing that some of the valued acts would already count as valuable anyway as means to ulterior ends. Utilitarianism is a notable example of such systematization" (NMV, 64). "This way of resolving moral issues is successful to the extent that we can reduce moral values causally to other moral values that command agreement" (NMV, 64). However, Quine warns, "[t]here must remain some ultimate ends, unreduced and so unjustified" (NMV, 64). Quine does not believe that appeals to science can resolve conflicts over ultimate ends.

The further point that must be noted now is that Flanagan's appeal to "our aims, our interests" does nothing toward resolving conflicts regarding ultimate ends, for such conflicts are over just what "our aims, our interests" are or ought to be. Thus, again, I cannot agree with him that he has undermined Quine's thesis of the methodological infirmity of ethics.

§7.4 White

Like Flanagan, Morton G. White is another philosophical naturalist who is generally sympathetic to Quine's philosophical orientation, but who cannot accept Quine's claim that ethics is methodologically infirm as compared to science. In his interesting paper "Normative Ethics, Normative Epistemology, and Quine's Holism," White hopes to "persuade Quine to abandon a dualism between the methods of testing normative and descriptive statements which is as untenable as that between analytic and synthetic statements" (650). He attempts to get Quine to admit that, just as sensory hits serve as evidence for descriptive claims, so feelings (or emotions) serve as evidence for normative claims and, in particular, for ethical claims. Once this is understood and accepted, then it is an easy matter to demonstrate that heterogeneous collections of (descriptive and normative) statements can be tested holistically, just as homogeneous collections of (descriptive) statements can be tested holistically. Thus, White concludes, ethics is not methodologically infirm as compared to science.

It might be helpful in understanding White's position to recount one of his examples. Consider the following heterogeneous collection of (descriptive and normative) statements:

> (1) Whoever takes the life of a human being does something that ought not to be done.
> (2) The mother took the life of the fetus in her womb.
> (3) Every living fetus in the womb of a human being is a human being.

Therefore,

(4) The mother took the life of a human being.

Therefore,

(5) The mother did something that ought not to be done.
(652–53)

Now, suppose that the woman in question "does not have the feeling of being obligated *not* to have done what she did" (653). In other words, she denies (5).

> As soon as we grant that after denying (5) the mother may deny the conjunction that implies it, we may say that the mother, or anyone else engaged in such thinking, may amend or surrender a law of logic such as that which gets us from (2) and (3) to (4); an ethical principle such as (1); or a descriptive statement such as (2), (3), or (4). Any one of these moves will bring about what may be called a Duhemian alteration of the original body of beliefs in response to a recalcitrant feeling. (653)

White's point is that there is "an analogy between Quine's permitting a recalcitrant experience to lead to the abandonment of a logical statement and my permitting the abandonment of a descriptive statement because of a recalcitrant feeling" (654). And, if Quine were to agree that feelings can play an evidential role in ethics *analogous* to the role that sensory hits play in science, then "he would have to withdraw his remark that a coherence theory is the lot of ethics. For if science—that is to say, descriptive science—retains some title to the correspondence theory of truth 'thanks to its links with observation', then ethics should retain some title to a correspondence theory of truth thanks to its links with *observation and feeling*" (654–55). Putting the matter the other way around, White writes: "Once we let feeling play the part that I assign to it, a coherence theory is *not* the lot of ethics, and it does not suffer from the 'methodological infirmity' of which Quine speaks" (655).

Is White correct? I do not think that he is. In order for White's argument to work, certain moral statements must count as observation sentences. However, as Quine explains, the notion of moral observation sentences is problematic:

An observation sentence is an occasion sentence that commands the same verdict from all witnesses who know the language. Consider, then, the moral occasion sentence 'That's outrageous'. In the hope of getting it to qualify as an observation sentence, let us adopt an unrealistic "best-case" assumption about our linguistic community, to the effect that all speakers are disposed to assent to 'That's outrageous' on seeing a man beat a cripple or furtively snatch a wreath off a door or commit any other evil that can be condemned on sight without collateral information. (The malefactor would be foreign, since our fellow speakers are assumed to deplore all such acts.) Would 'That's outrageous' then qualify as an observation sentence? It would still not, simply because it applies also and indeed mostly to other acts whose outrageousness hinges on collateral information not in general shared by all witnesses of the acts.

The sentence 'It's raining', in contrast, almost never hinges on information not shared by present witnesses, and the sentence 'That's a rabbit' does so only seldom. These two consequently qualify well enough as observational, a status that is somewhat a matter of degree. 'He's a bachelor', at the other extreme, depends on collateral information that is seldom widely shared. 'That's outrageous' is intermediate between 'That's a rabbit' and 'He's a bachelor'. *Even our best-case assumption is insufficient, we see, to qualify it as an observation sentence.* Moral judgments differ thus from cognitive ones in their relation to observation.

The difference is due to a difference between sensation and emotion. . . . Sensation is nicely coordinated with concurrent, publicly accessible stimulation. Impacts on a certain range of surface receptors produce the sensation, and conversely, apart from occasional illusion, the sensation occurs only when thus produced. It is not so with emotions. The emotion of revulsion matches up only half way even under the best-case assumption, for the converse condition still fails: revulsion is commonly aroused also by acts that are visibly evil only in the light of collateral information not generally shared. Hence the lack of moral observation sentences. Natural science owes its objectivity to its intersubjective checkpoints in observation sentences, but there is no such rock bottom for moral judgments. (RW, 664; my italics)

Another way of putting Quine's point against White's proposal is to say that the causal mechanisms involved in sense perception and those involved in emotional reactions differ substantially and relevantly. The latter allow for a certain plasticity that the former do not. Further, even if a fair number of types of emotional reactions that are relevant to ethics are innate, still they are—as J. B. Watson showed long ago in connection with "innate fears" of spiders and snakes—susceptible to modification through conditioning. Thus, White's conclusion that ethics "does not suffer from the 'methodological infirmity' of which Quine speaks" (655) is not justified.

§7.5 Conclusions

In our discussion of Quine's naturalistic accounts of the institution of morality, the nature and origins of moral values, the nature of moral conflicts, and the epistemological status of ethics, we have seen that his approach to these topics is clearly meta-ethical and—much to Flanagan's disappointment—not normative. Furthermore, his meta-ethical approach differs radically from the kinds of meta-ethics practiced either by those philosophers engaged in first philosophy or by philosophical naturalists writing during the heyday of positivism. Quine disagrees with the former by denying their claim that ethical values have some sort of nonnaturalistic foundation; he disagrees with the latter by denying their notion of conceptual analysis—a notion that presupposes the analytic-synthetic distinction. Quine's meta-ethics is decidedly scientific and is, therefore, of a piece with his entire systematic philosophy.

Is Quine a normative ethical relativist? If that doctrine is defined as the view that what is *really* morally right/wrong for one society at some time and place may *really* be the opposite for a different society (or the same society at a different time/place), then it certainly appears that Quine is committed to this view. It does not follow from this doctrine, however, that different societies do not share many or even most of their ethical values. Indeed, common genetic factors and common environmental factors would seem to nurture a common core of ethical values for all human societies. Even so, as Quine says, moral conflict is rife.

Granting Quine his mitigated holism-cum-naturalism for the sake of argument, is he correct in saying that ethics as compared to science is methodologically infirm, that science retains some title to the correspondence theory of truth while the coherence theory of truth is apparently the lot of ethics? If we further grant him that science is linked to the world via sense experience and that the mechanisms of sense experience are pretty much as we have characterized them, and that ethics is linked to the world via feelings (or emotions) and the mechanisms of feeling are pretty much as we have characterized them, then it is clear that there is likely to be a great deal more intersubjective agreement about what is seen, say, than about what is felt. It is a matter accounted for by reference to the long-known distinction between an unconditioned response to a stimulus versus a conditioned response to a stimulus. Thus, it seems quite right to point out that putting the moral sense on a par with the five senses would be an extravagant departure from the causal realities. Consequently, it appears that ethics is indeed methodologically infirm.

AFTERWORD

From the 1930s to the 1970s, Anglo-American philosophy was dominated first by logical positivism and then by various forms of linguistic philosophy. Both of these movements took the analytic-synthetic distinction seriously, using the distinction to erect a barrier between science and philosophy. Positivists argued that epistemology, that is, the logic of science, ought to restrict itself to the context of justification, eschewing the context of discovery. Thus did they gleefully hand over all synthetic statements to the sciences, thereby relegating philosophy to the realm of analytic statements. Linguistic philosophy followed suit, claiming that the job of science is to carry out empirical investigations, while the job of philosophy is to carry out conceptual analyses. Whole generations of philosophers accepted, for various reasons, this thesis of the radical separation of science and philosophy.

Quine's rejection of the analytic-synthetic distinction has, I believe, a liberating effect on the theory of knowledge, for it removes a chief impetus for drawing a barrier between science and philosophy. If Quine is right, there simply is no domain of analytic statements to which to confine philosophy; philosophy—the theory of knowledge, anyway—is concerned with synthetic statements and is therefore continuous with science:

> The philosopher's task differs from the . . . [scientist's] in detail; but in no such drastic way as those suppose who imagine for the philosopher a vantage point outside the conceptual scheme that he takes in charge. There is no such cosmic exile. He cannot study and revise the fundamental conceptual scheme of science and common sense without having some conceptual scheme, whether the same or another no less in need of philosophical scrutiny, in which to work. He can scrutinize and improve the system from within, appealing to coherence and simplicity; but this is the theoretician's method generally. He has recourse to semantic ascent [i.e., talking of words rather than of what they purportedly refer to], but so has the scientist. And if the theoretical scientist in his remote way is bound to save the eventual connections with non-verbal stimulation, the philosopher in his remoter way is bound to save them too. True, no experiment may be expected to settle an ontological issue; but this is only because such issues are connected with surface irritations in such multifarious ways, through such a maze of intervening theory. (WO, 275–76).

Such is naturalized epistemology.

I have already remarked that the rejection of the analytic-synthetic distinction has a liberating effect on the theory of knowledge. I now want to claim that it is salutary as well. No longer are epistemologists confined by the walls of their studies or bound by the covers of the *Oxford English Dictionary*. No longer must they content themselves with working out necessary and sufficient conditions for 'S knows that p' or with cataloging uses of the verb 'to know'. There is an empirical world, and it is theirs for the taking; it is no longer the exclusive domain of scientists. Scientific theories regarding perception, reliable belief formation, neural processing, and so on, are now available to the epistemologist. At long last, there is real promise of progress for epistemology.

In the midst of this celebration we ought not, however, lose sight of a remark made at the close of chapter 3. There is another, and sterner, side to naturalized epistemology: the philosopher now has the added *responsibility* of learning some science. The *scientific* study of the acquisition of science requires familiarity with relevant areas of science. So, the moral of naturalized epistemology, or enlightened empiricism, is *freedom with responsibility*.

NOTES

Chapter 1. Quine's Philosophy: A Systematic Overview

1. In calling the thesis an axiom, I do not mean that it is without empirical support. When I say the thesis is central, I mean it is one of those theses Quine would hold *come what may*.
2. For a detailed account of Quine's "scientific semantics," see UPM.
3. This is the first of two "cardinal tenets of empiricism" that Quine accepts and defends.
4. This is the second "cardinal tenet of empiricism."
5. What prompts the "usually" in this formulation of the holism thesis are observation sentences. Observation sentences may be said to possess their individual ranges of confirming and infirming experiences. See OEES, 314.

Chapter 2. Holism, Realism, and Naturalized Epistemology

1. I have argued in Gibson 1982 that this *reductio*—called therein Quine's *pragmatic reductio*—is wanting. The chief difficulty with it is that P3 and P4 are not, conjunctively, logically inconsistent with P1. Thus the argument, while a *reductio ad absurdum*, does not culminate in an "absurdity" of the strictest sort, viz., logical inconsistency. Nevertheless, the argument is not without force. (See Gibson 1982, 103–6, for further discussion of this point.)
2. I count this argument weakest among the three that Quine rolls out in defense of the holism thesis. Of the remaining two arguments I believe the scientific practices argument is somewhat more plausible—if only because clearer—than the language learning argument. The advantage of the language learning argument is that it provides something of an *explanation* of

180 Notes

why holism occurs. Whatever the relative merits of Quine's three arguments, it is important to realize that the holism thesis is an *empirical* claim (about how physical theories are related to their evidence) insofar as it is supported by considerations drawn from the history of philosophy, the history of science, and the science of linguistics. Thus is Quine's commitment to the holism thesis fully consistent with his naturalistic scruples.

Chapter 4. Analyticity Reconsidered

1. For a detailed exposition of Quine's arguments, see Gibson 1982, 96–100.
2. Moves like this one by Strawson and Grice are seen to be no more than clutching at straws when one remembers that philosophers have wanted an analytic-synthetic distinction not as an end in itself, but as a major plank in their epistemological platforms. Empiricists and rationalists alike esteemed the distinction not for itself but as a means for separating the conceptual from the factual, the necessary from the contingent, and so on. (See RH, 207.)

Chapter 5. Indeterminacy, Underdetermination, and Facts of the Matter

1. Actually, Chomsky is probably not even half-right, for he fails to appreciate the "in principle" character of Quine's thesis of underdetermination: the point is *not* that our empirical generalizations go beyond their evidence *as a matter of fact* but that they go beyond *all possible evidence.*
2. I shall here ignore the verificationist argument for indeterminacy only because Føllesdal does. Quine's suspicion that I agree with Føllesdal's repudiation of verificationism is, however, erroneous. (See RG, 155.)
3. Føllesdal takes issue with my interpretation of his position. In a January 1988 letter he writes: "Gibson misinterprets my position and thinks that I want to define truth in terms of simplicity. On the contrary, in the sentence immediately following the passage he quotes from my article, I emphasize: 'considerations of simplicity and methodology cannot give a definition of truth' (p. 295). And two pages earlier I say 'scientific methodology cannot be used to define truth' (p. 293). My point in the passage quoted by Gibson is indicated by the contrafactual: if truth *were* definable in terms of simplicity, then translation would be on a par with empirical theory. However, truth is not thus definable, and while empirical theory aims at full coverage of all facts of the matter, translation is a different kind of enterprise. It is not part of our theory of the world, but aims at correlating various such theories."
4. As we shall see at the end of section 5.2.2.3, Quine *does* recant this position by supplanting the offending paragraph of EC, 29, with a new paragraph in a later edition of that book.
5. Quine to Gibson, December 14, 1984.

REFERENCES

Aune, B. "Quine on Translation and Reference." *Philosophical Studies* 27 (1975): 221–36.
Ayer, A. *Language, Truth and Logic.* 2d ed., paperback. London: Victor Gollancz, 1946.
Beatty, H. "Behaviourism, Mentalism, and Quine's Indeterminacy Thesis." *Philosophical Studies* 26 (1974): 97–110.
Beri, P., R. Horstmann, and L. Kruger, eds. *Transcendental Arguments and Science.* Dordrecht, Holland: D. Reidel Publishing Company, 1979.
Booth, M., ed. *What I Believe.* London: Waterstone, 1984.
Carroll, Lewis. "What the Tortoise Said to Achilles." *Mind* 14 (1895): 278–80.
Chomsky, N. "Quine's Empirical Assumptions." In *Words and Objections: Essays on the Work of W. V. Quine,* edited by D. Davidson and J. Hintikka, 53–68. Dordrecht, Holland: D. Reidel Publishing Company, 1969.
———. *Reflections on Language.* New York: Pantheon Books, Random House, 1975.
———. *Rules and Representations.* New York: Columbia University Press, 1980.
Davidson, D. "The Inscrutability of Reference." In *Truth and Interpretation,* 227–41. Oxford: Oxford University Press, 1984a.
———. "On the Very Idea of a Conceptual Scheme." In *Truth and Interpretation,* 183–98. Oxford: Oxford University Press, 1984b.
———, and J. Hintikka, eds. *Words and Objections: Essays on the Work of W. V. Quine.* Dordrecht, Holland: D. Reidel Publishing Company, 1969.
Descartes, R. *The Philosophical Works of Descartes.* Translated by Elizabeth S.

Haldane and G. R. T. Ross. 2 vols. Cambridge: Cambridge University Press, 1911. Reprints. 1973 (vol. 1), 1970 (vol. 2).
Field, H. "Quine and the Correspondence Theory." *The Philosophical Review* 83 (1974): 200–228.
Flanagan, O. "Quinean Ethics." *Ethics* 93 (1982): 56–74.
Friedman, M. "Physicalism and the Indeterminacy of Translation." *Nous* 9 (1975): 353–74.
Føllesdal, D. "Indeterminacy of Translation and Under-Determination of the Theory of Nature." *Dialectica* 27 (1973): 289–301.
Foster, L., and J. Swanson, eds. *Experience and Theory*. Amherst: University of Massachusetts Press, 1970.
Gibson, R. "Are There Really Two Quines?" *Erkenntnis* 15 (1980): 349–70.
———. "Flanagan on Quinean Ethics." *Ethics* (forthcoming a).
———. "A New Perspective on Quine." *Journal of Thought* 18 (1983): 73–84.
———. *The Philosophy of W. V. Quine: An Expository Essay*. Tampa: University of South Florida Press, 1982. Paperback reprint, 1986.
———. "Quine on Naturalism and Epistemology." *Erkenntnis* 27 (1987): 57–78.
———. "Quine's Dilemma." *Synthese* 69 (1986a): 27–39.
———. "Stroud on Naturalized Epistemology." *Meta-philosophy* (forthcoming b).
———. "Translation, Physics, and Facts of the Matter." In *The Philosophy of W. V. Quine*, edited by L. Hahn and P. Schilpp, 139–54. La Salle, Ill.: Open Court, 1986b.
Grice, H., and P. Strawson. "In Defense of a Dogma." *Philosophical Review* 65, no. 2 (1956): 141–58.
Grunbaum, A. "The Falsifiability of Theories: Total or Partial? A Contemporary Evaluation of the Duhem-Quine Thesis." *Synthese* 14 (1962): 17–23.
Guttenplan, S., ed. *Mind and Language*. Oxford: Clarendon Press, 1975.
Hahn, L., and P. Schilpp, eds. *The Philosophy of W. V. Quine*. La Salle, Ill.: Open Court, 1986.
Harding, S., ed. *Can Theories Be Refuted? Essays on the Duhem-Quine Thesis*. Dordrecht, Holland: Reidel Publishing Company, 1976.
Harman, G. "Quine on Meaning and Existence, I." *Review of Metaphysics* 21 (1967): 124–51.
Kripke, S. *Wittgenstein on Rules and Private Language*. Cambridge: Harvard University Press, 1982.
Leeds, S. "How To Think About Reference." *Journal of Philosophy* 15 (1973): 485–503.
Levin, M. "Length Relativity." *Journal of Philosophy* 68 (1971): 164–74.
———. "Relativity, Spatial and Ontological." *Nous* 9 (1975): 243–67.
Mill, J. *A System of Logic*. New York, 1867.
Mulvaney, R., and P. Zeltner, eds. *Pragmatism: Its Sources and Prospects*. Columbia: University of South Carolina Press, 1981.

References

Newton-Smith, W. *The Rationality of Science.* Paperback. Boston: Routledge & Kegan Paul, 1981.
Priest, G. "Two Dogmas of Quineanism." *Philosophical Quarterly* 29 (1979): 289–301.
Putnam, H. "The Analytic and the Synthetic." In *Mind, Language and Reality*, 33–69. Cambridge: Cambridge University Press, 1975a.
———. "The Refutation of Conventionalism." In *Mind, Language and Reality*, 151–91. Cambridge: Cambridge University Press, 1975b.
———. "Why Reason Can't Be Naturalized." *Synthese* 52 (1982): 3–23.
Quine, W. "Empirical Content." In *Theories and Things*, 24–30. Cambridge: Harvard University Press, 1981.
———. "Epistemology Naturalized." In *Ontological Relativity and Other Essays*, 69–90. New York: Columbia University Press, 1969.
———. "Facts of the Matter." In *American Philosophy from Edwards to Quine*, edited by R. Shahan, 176–96. Norman: University of Oklahoma Press, 1977.
———. "Five Milestones of Empiricism." In *Theories and Things*, 67–72. Cambridge: Harvard University Press, 1981.
———. *From a Logical Point of View.* 2d ed. rev., paperback. Cambridge: Harvard University Press, 1980.
———. "Grades of Theoreticity." In *Experience and Theory*, edited by L. Foster and J. Swanson, 1–17. Amherst: University of Massachusetts Press, 1970.
———. "Intensions Revisited." In *Theories and Things*, 113–23. Cambridge: Harvard University Press, 1981.
———. "Letter to Professor Grunbaum." In *Can Theories Be Refuted? Essays on the Duhem-Quine Thesis*, edited by S. Harding, 132. Dordrecht, Holland: Reidel Publishing Company, 1976.
———. "Natural Kinds." In *Ontological Relativity and Other Essays*, 114–38. New York: Columbia University Press, 1969.
———. "The Nature of Natural Knowledge." In *Mind and Language*, edited by S. Guttenplan, 67–81. Oxford: Clarendon Press, 1975.
———. "On Empirically Equivalent Systems of the World." *Erkenntnis* 9 (1975): 313–28.
———. "On the Nature of Moral Values." In *Theories and Things*, 55–66. Cambridge: Harvard University Press, 1981.
———. "Ontological Reduction and the World of Numbers." *Journal of Philosophy* 61 (1964): 209–16.
———. "On the Reasons for Indeterminacy of Translation." *Journal of Philosophy* 67 (1970): 179–83.
———. "On the Very Idea of a Third Dogma." In *Theories and Things*, 38–42. Cambridge: Harvard University Press, 1981.
———. "Ontological Relativity." In *Ontological Relativity and Other Essays*, 26–68. New York: Columbia University Press, 1969.
———. *Ontological Relativity and Other Essays.* New York: Columbia University Press, 1969.

References

———. "Ontology and Ideology Revisited." *Journal of Philosophy* 80 (1983): 499–502.
———. "On What There Is." In *From a Logical Point of View*, 1–19. 2d ed. rev., paperback. Cambridge: Harvard University Press, 1980.
———. "Philosophical Progress in Language Theory." *Metaphilosophy* 1 (1970): 2–19.
———. "The Pragmatists' Place in Empiricism." In *Pragmatism: Its Sources and Prospects*, edited by R. Mulvaney and P. Zeltner, 21–39. Columbia: University of South Carolina Press, 1981.
———. "Reference and Modality." In *From a Logical Point of View*, 139–59. 2d ed. rev., paperback. Cambridge: Harvard University Press, 1980.
———. "Relativism and Absolutism." *The Monist* 67 (1984): 293–96.
———. "Replies to Eleven Essays." *Philosophical Topics* 12 (1981): 227–43.
———. "Reply to Charles D. Parsons." In *The Philosophy of W. V. Quine*, edited by L. Hahn and P. Schilpp, 396–403. La Salle, Ill.: Open Court, 1986.
———. "Reply to Chomsky." In *Words and Objections: Essays on the Work of W. V. Quine*, edited by D. Davidson and J. Hintikka, 302–11. Dordrecht, Holland: D. Reidel Publishing Company, 1969.
———. "Reply to Geoffrey Hellman." In *The Philosophy of W. V. Quine*, edited by L. Hahn and P. Schilpp, 206–8. La Salle, Ill.: Open Court, 1986.
———. "Reply to Harold N. Lee." In *The Philosophy of W. V. Quine*, edited by L. Hahn and P. Schilpp, 315–18. La Salle, Ill.: Open Court, 1986.
———. "Reply to Hilary Putnam." In *The Philosophy of W. V. Quine*, edited by L. Hahn and P. Schilpp, 427–31. La Salle, Ill.: Open Court, 1986.
———. "Reply to Jules Vuillemin." In *The Philosophy of W. V. Quine*, edited by L. Hahn and P. Schilpp, 619–22. La Salle, Ill.: Open Court, 1986.
———. "Reply to Morton White." In *The Philosophy of W. V. Quine*, edited by L. Hahn and P. Schilpp, 663–65. La Salle, Ill.: Open Court, 1986.
———. "Reply to Paul A. Roth." In *The Philosophy of W. V. Quine*, edited by L. Hahn and P. Schilpp, 459–61. La Salle, Ill.: Open Court, 1986.
———. "Reply to Robert Nozick." In *The Philosophy of W. V. Quine*, edited by L. Hahn and P. Schilpp, 364–67. La Salle, Ill.: Open Court, 1986.
———. "Reply to Roger F. Gibson, Jr." In *The Philosophy of W. V. Quine*, edited by L. Hahn and P. Schilpp, 155–57. La Salle, Ill.: Open Court, 1986.
———. "Reply to Smart." In *Words and Objections: Essays on the Work of W. V. Quine*, edited by D. Davidson and J. Hintikka, 292–94. Dordrecht, Holland: D. Reidel Publishing Company, 1969.
———. "Reply to Stroud." *Midwest Studies in Philosophy* 6 (1981): 473–75.
———. "Responses." In *Theories and Things*, 173–86. Cambridge: Harvard University Press, 1981.
———. *The Roots of Reference*. La Salle, Ill.: Open Court, 1974.
———. "Russell's Ontological Development." In *Theories and Things*, 73–85. Cambridge: Harvard University Press, 1981.
———. "The Sensory Support of Science." Typescript read at Washington University, St. Louis, Mo., April 22, 1986.

———. "Sticks and Stones; Or the Ins and Outs of Existence." In *On Nature*, edited by L. Rouner, 13–26. Notre Dame, Ind.: University of Notre Dame Press, 1984.
———. *Theories and Things*. Cambridge: Harvard University Press, 1981.
———. "Things and Their Place in Theories." In *Theories and Things*, 1–23. Cambridge: Harvard University Press, 1981.
———. *The Time of My Life: An Autobiography*. Cambridge: M.I.T. Press, 1985.
———. "Truth by Convention." In *The Ways of Paradox and Other Essays*, 77–106. Rev. and enlarged, paperback. Cambridge: Harvard University Press, 1979.
———. "Two Dogmas of Empiricism." In *From a Logical Point of View*, 20–46. 2d ed. rev., paperback. Cambridge: Harvard University Press, 1980.
———. "Use and Its Place in Meaning." In *Theories and Things*, 43–54. Cambridge: Harvard University Press, 1981.
———. *The Ways of Paradox and Other Essays*. 3d printing, rev. and enlarged, paperback. Cambridge: Harvard University Press, 1979.
———. "What I Believe." In *What I Believe*, edited by M. Booth, 69–75. London: Waterstone, 1984.
———. *Word and Object*. 5th reprint, paperback. Cambridge: M.I.T. Press, 1970.
———, and J. S. Ullian. *The Web of Belief*. 2d ed., paperback. New York: Random House, 1978.
Rorty, R. "Indeterminacy of Translation and of Truth." *Synthese* 23 (1972): 443–62.
———. *Philosophy and the Mirror of Nature*. Reprint with corrections, paperback. Princeton, N.J.: Princeton University Press, 1979.
Roth, P. "Theories of Nature and the Nature of Theories." *Mind* 79 (1980): 431–38.
Rouner, L. ed. *On Nature*. Notre Dame, Ind.: University of Notre Dame Press, 1984.
Shahan, R. *American Philosophy from Edwards to Quine*. Norman: University of Oklahoma Press, 1977.
Siegel, H. "Empirical Psychology, Naturalized Epistemology, and First Philosophy." *Philosophy of Science* 51 (1984): 667–76.
———. "Justification, Discovery, and the Naturalizing of Epistemology." *Philosophy of Science* 47 (1980): 297–320.
Smart, J. "Quine's Philosophy of Science." In *Words and Objections: Essays on the Work of W. V. Quine*, edited by D. Davidson and J. Hintikka, 3–13. Dordrecht, Holland: D. Reidel Publishing Company, 1969.
Stroud, B. "The Significance of Naturalized Epistemology." *Midwest Studies in Philosophy* 6 (1981): 455–71.
———. *The Significance of Philosophical Scepticism*. Oxford: Oxford University Press, 1984.
———. "The Significance of Scepticism." In *Transcendental Arguments and*

Science, edited by P. Bieri, R. Horstmann, and L. Kruger, 277–97. Dordrecht, Holland: D. Reidel Publishing Company, 1979.

White, M. "Normative Ethics, Normative Epistemology, and Quine's Holism." In *The Philosophy of W. V. Quine,* edited by L. Hahn and P. Schilpp, 649–62. La Salle, Ill.: Open Court, 1986.

INDEX

Analogical synthesis, 3–4, 6, 12, 37
Analytical hypotheses, 104–6, 132.
 See also Language learning
Analytic-synthetic distinction: and explicative definitions, 86; and holism, 37–42, 85, 96–100; and indeterminacy of translation, 95; and language learning, 101; and lexical definitions, 86; rejected by Quine, 13–14, 28, 37–42, 85–86; and stipulated definitions, 86. *See also* Grice, H. P.; Priest, Graham
Analyticity. *See* Analytic-synthetic distinction; Naturalistic-behavioristic conception of language
A priori truth, 26, 28, 31
Aune, Bruce, 103, 109–11, 125
Ayer, A. J., 20

Beatty, Harry, 103, 127–29
Behaviorism, 79, 127–31. *See* Language learning; Scientific semantics; Naturalistic-behavioristic conception of language

Bellarmine, Cardinal, 75–76
Berkeley, Bishop George, 75

Carnap, Rudolf, 27, 38, 46, 100
Carroll, Lewis, 97
Chomsky, Noam, 103–6, 108–9, 111, 116, 124–25, 180n.1
Circularity, 25, 29–31, 46–47. *See also* Reciprocal containment; Skepticism
Conservatism, in hypotheses, 17–18

Davidson, Donald, 81, 123, 142–44, 152–54
Descartes, René, 25–26, 46
Dewey, John, 8
Duhem thesis (Duhem-Quine thesis). *See* Holism

Empiricism: cardinal tenets of, 6–7, 28–29, 47–48; enlightened, 30, 56–57; as epistemology of ontology, 44–45; externalization of, 54–57, 66, 82; Quine's argument against, 25–28, 46–47. *See also*

Empiricism (*continued*)
Epistemology; Genetic approach; Naturalism; Naturalized epistemology
Epistemology: central questions of, 1–2, 5–6, 22, 54–55; contained in ontology, 44–48, 59–60, 63, 66, 138; as theory of method and evidence, 44–45, 111; traditional, 24–28, 33, 43, 45–46, 48, 53–54, 56–57, 69. *See also* Genetic approach; Naturalism; Naturalized epistemology
Essentialism, 14–15. *See also* Modal logic
Eternal sentence, 4. *See also* Language learning
Ethics: purported methodological infirmity of, 155–56, 166–67; purported methodological infirmity of, criticized by Flanagan, 167–72, 175; purported methodological infirmity of, criticized by White, 167, 172–75 passim. *See also* Meta-ethics; Morality; Values

Fact of the matter, 9, 102–25 passim, 131–40 passim, 152–53, 155–56. *See also* Translation versus physics
Fallibilism, 46–47, 63, 66
Field, Hartry, 135–38, 141–42, 152–53
Flanagan, Owen J., 167–72, 175
Føllesdal, Dagfinn, 103, 107–9, 111, 123–25, 180 nn.2, 3
Friedman, Michael, 103, 125–27

Galileo, 73, 75–76
Geisteswissenschaften, 79–80
Generality, in hypotheses, 19
Genetic approach, 7, 55–56, 65–67, 82. *See also* Empiricism
Gestalten, 31, 42, 65

Gibson, Roger F., Jr., 121, 180 n.3
Goodman, Nelson, 38
Grice, H. P., 39, 86–96, 101, 180 n.2
Grunbaum, Adolf, 34–35, 51

Hanson, Norwood, 73–74, 81
Harman, Gilbert, 88
Holism: alleged inconsistency with analytic-synthetic distinction, 93–100 passim; cognitive status of, 36–37, 51; as construed by Flanagan, 169–70; as construed by Rorty, 80, 84; differentiated from underdetermination of physical theory, 116; explained, 12–13, 32–33, 36–37, 80, 84; and fallibilism, 46; and indeterminacy of translation, 107; Quine's argument for, 33–42 passim, 51; and Quine's view of science, 16; as refutation of analyticity and reductionism, 14, 28, 34, 38–39, 85; and rules of inference, 99; as source of naturalism, 24, 31, 51; warning by Quine against overstating his, 170
Hume, David, 27, 86

Idea-idea, 26
Idealism, 25–26
Indeterminacy of translation: discussed by Beatty, 127–29; discussed by Chomsky, 103–4; discussed by Davidson, 142; discussed by Field, 136–42 passim; discussed by Føllesdal, 107–11, 180 nn.2, 3; discussed by Friedman, 125–26; discussed by Rorty, 103–11 passim, 124–25; explained, 9–10, 102, 113. *See also* Fact of the matter; Translation versus physics
Inscrutability of reference: argument for, 135; as corollary of ontological relativity, 143; discussed

by Davidson, 142; discussed by Field, 136–42 passim; discussed by Leeds, 151–52; explained, 10, 152–54. *See also* Ontological relativity; Proxy-functions
Instrumentalism, 16–17, 50–52. *See also* Naturalism; Realism
Intensions, rejected by Quine, 13

Kant, Immanuel, 64, 86
Kantian, Quine is not a, 36, 49, 52
Kripke, Saul, 103, 127, 129
Kuhn, Thomas, 73–74, 81

Language learning, 2–4, 6, 8, 12, 14, 32–33, 36–37, 44, 81–82, 101
Leeds, Stephen, 145, 149–54
Leibniz, G. W. von, 86
Levin, Michael, 145–49, 154
Locke, John, 25
Logical truth, 20

Mathematical truth, 20
Maxim of minimum mutilation, 17
Meta-ethics, 20–21, 157. *See also* Ethics; Morality; Values
Mill, John Stuart, 20
Modal logic, 14–16. *See also* Essentialism
Modesty, in hypotheses, 18
Mohanty, J. N., 139
Morality: Quine on the institution of, 157; Quine on the nature and origin of moral values, 158–61; Quine on the nature of moral conflicts, 162–66. *See also* Ethics; Meta-ethics; Values
Museum myth, 8, 137, 141, 153. *See also* Indeterminacy of translation; Inscrutability of reference; Ontological relativity; 'Refer'

Naturalism: does not repudiate epistemology, 44, 55–56; explained, 23–24, 51, 78–79; and ontology, 11; Quine's avowal of, 8, 23–24, 78; and reconciliation of instrumentalism and realism, 50–52; and skepticism, 58–60, 63; sources of, 24–31. *See also* Empiricism; Naturalized epistemology
Naturalistic-behavioristic conception of language: and analyticity, 13–14, 22; explained, 2–5; as framework of Quine's philosophy, 2, 7, 21–22; and holism, 12–13, 22; and indeterminacy of translation, 9–10, 22; and inscrutability of reference, 10, 22; and intensions, 13, 22; and meaning, 2, 4, 8; and modal logic, 14–16, 22; and ontological relativity, 10–11, 22; and philosophy of science, 16–19, 22; and radical epistemological reductionism, 14, 22; and synonymy, 13–14, 22; and underdetermination of physical theory, 12, 22
Naturalistic-behavioristic thesis, 1–2, 4–10, 96. *See also* Naturalistic-behavioristic conception of language
Naturalized epistemology: criticized by Putnam, 67–68; criticized by Rorty, 66–84 passim; criticized by Siegel, 67–69; criticized by Stroud, 56–67 passim; explained, 24, 29, 43–44, 46, 53, 55–56; has liberating effects, 84, 178; as normative, 47, 67–69; Quine's argument for, 25–31 passim; and the reciprocal containment of epistemology and ontology, 43–52 passim, 56, 59–60, 63, 138; soundness of Quine's argument for, 31–43 passim. *See also* Empiricism; Epistemology; Naturalism
Naturwissenschaften, 79–80

Neurath's boat, 24, 37, 43–44, 115. *See also* Naturalism; Naturalized epistemology

Observation, 5–6. *See also* Sensory evidence; Observation sentences
Observation sentences: defined, 4, 73–74; as evidence, 6, 55, 65–66, 81–84; as gateway to naturalized epistemology, 7, 55; and holism, 12, 32–33; how learned, 36–37, 66, 81; meanings of, 170; in place of observation, 6; relativized to speech community, 79–80; semantical role, 6–7, 55. *See also* Language learning
Occasion sentences, 4, 11. *See also* Language learning
Ontological relativity: criticized by Davidson, 142–44, 153–54; criticized by Field, 135–42 passim, 153; criticized by Leeds, 149–54; criticized by Levin, 145–49, 154; explained, 10–11; and naturalism, 11; three levels of, 132–35. *See also* Inscrutability of reference; Proxy-functions; 'Refer'; Reciprocal containment
Ontology: contained in epistemology, 44–45, 48–49, 52, 60; and inscrutability of reference, 11; as theory of what there is, 44–45, 111. *See also* Naturalism; Naturalized epistemology
Ostension, 3–4. *See also* Language learning; Observation sentences

Physicalism, 78–79
Physical objects, 16–17
Pleasure (pain), 158–61
Polanyi, Michael, 73–74, 81
Precision, in hypotheses, 19
Priest, Graham, 96–100

Proxy-functions, 11, 134–35, 142, 153. *See also* Inscrutability of reference; Ontological relativity
Putnam, Hilary, 67, 69–70, 78, 83, 100

Quantification, 133–34

Radical epistemological reductionism, 14, 28. *See also* Analytic-synthetic distinction; Empiricism
Rationalism, 25–26
Rational reconstruction, 27, 29, 46. *See also* Carnap, Rudolf; Empiricism
Realism: and Quine's philosophy of science, 16–17; reconciled with instrumentalism, 50–52. *See also* Unregenerate realism
Reciprocal containment of epistemology and ontology. *See* Naturalized epistemology
'Refer', Quine's usage of, 139, 152
Reference. *See* Inscrutability of reference; Language learning; 'Refer'
Refutability, in hypotheses, 19
Rorty, Richard: as advocate of epistemological behaviorism, 79; as advocate of naturalism, 79; as advocate of physicalism, 79; as critic of indeterminacy of translation, 103, 105–6, 108–9, 111, 124–26; as critic of naturalized epistemology, 69–84 passim; and holism, 79–84 passim; and irrelevance of psychology to epistemology, 71–82 passim; and the *Naturwissenschaften-Geistenwissenschaften* distinction, 79–80; mentioned, 64
Roth, Paul A., 36

Science: justification of, 29–30, 66, 75, 83; Quine's philosophy of,

16–19. *See also* Naturalized epistemology
Scientific semantics, 4–5
Scientism. *See* Naturalism
Sensory evidence, 48. *See also* Observation; Observation sentences
Siegel, Harvey, 36, 67–70, 83
Simplicity, in hypotheses, 18–19
Skepticism, 29–31, 42, 46, 51, 56–61, 64, 66, 69, 153–54. *See also* Circularity; Empiricism; Naturalism; Naturalized epistemology
Smart, J. J. C., 17
Socrates, 164
Standing sentence, 4. *See also* Language learning
Stevenson, Charles L., 163
Stimulus meaning, 4–5, 10. *See also* Language learning
Strawson, P. F. *See* Grice, H. P.
Stroud, Barry: argues that naturalized epistemology cannot answer the skeptic, 60–66 passim; argues that naturalized epistemology does not answer the skeptic, 56–60; argues that naturalized epistemology fails to be epistemology, 64–67; mentioned, 83, 148–49
Synonymy. *See* Analytic-synthetic distinction; Naturalistic-behavioristic conception of language

Tarski, Alfred, 38

Translation versus physics: Aune on, 109–11; Chomsky on, 104–6, 111; explained, 111–24; Føllesdale on, 107–11, 180 nn.2, 3; Rorty on, 105–6, 111. *See also* Fact of the matter; Naturalism
Truth-functions, 99

Underdetermination of physical theory: differentiated from holism, 116; explained, 11–12, 102, 116–24 passim; and instrumentalism, 50–52; Quine's vacillations regarding, 17, 113–24 passim. *See also* Fact of the matter; Indeterminacy of translation
Unregenerate realism, 24, 29, 31, 42–43, 51, 64, 79. *See also* Naturalism

Values: moral versus nonmoral, 159–61; ultimate versus derivative moral, 157–66 passim, 171–72. *See also* Ethics; Meta-ethics; Morality
Verdict functions, 99
Verificationism, 27, 94, 107, 180 n.2

Watson, J. B., 175
White, Morton, 38, 167, 172–73, 175
Wittgenstein, Ludwig, 127, 129

The author and publisher of this volume are grateful to the publishers of the following books and periodicals for permission to reprint copyrighted material:

Erkenntnis: "On Empirically Equivalent Systems of the World," by W. V. Quine, *Erkenntnis* 9, no. 3 (1975): 313–28, and "Quine on Naturalism and Epistemology," by Roger F. Gibson, Jr., *Erkenntnis* 27 (1987): 57–78; copyright © 1975 and 1987 by D. Reidel Publishing Company, reprinted by permission.

Journal of Philosophy: "How to Think about Reference," by Stephen Leeds, *Journal of Philosophy* 15 (1973): 485–503.

Journal of Thought: "A New Perspective on Quine," by Roger F. Gibson, Jr., *Journal of Thought* 18 (Summer 1983): 73–84.

Metaphilosophy: "Stroud on Naturalized Epistemology," by Roger F. Gibson, Jr. *Metaphilosophy* (forthcoming).

M.I.T. Press: *Word and Object*, by W. V. Quine, copyright © 1960 by the Massachusetts Institute of Technology; 5th printing, 1970.

Open Court Publishing Company: *The Roots of Reference*, by W. V. Quine (1974); "Reply to Roger F. Gibson, Jr.," "Reply to Hilary Putnam," and "Reply to Morton White," by W. V. Quine, "Normative Ethics, Normative Epistemology, and Quine's Holism," by Morton White, and "Translation, Physics, and Facts of the Matter," by Roger F. Gibson, Jr., in *The Philosophy of W. V. Quine*, edited by L. E. Hahn and P. A. Schilpp (1986).

Oxford University Press: "The Nature of Natural Knowledge," by W. V. Quine, in *Mind and Language,* edited by Samuel Guttenplan (1975); *The Significance of Philosophical Scepticism,* by Barry Stroud (1984).

Philosophical Quarterly: "Two Dogmas of Quineanism," by Graham Priest, *Philosophical Quarterly* 29 (1979): 289–301.

Philosophical Review: "In Defense of a Dogma," by H. P. Grice and P. F. Strawson, *Philosophical Review* 65, no. 2 (1956): 141–58.

W. V. Quine, copyright holder: "Ontological Relativity" and "Epistemology Naturalized," in *Ontological Relativity and Other Essays,* by W. V. Quine (New York: Columbia University Press, 1969), 2d printing, 1971.

Synthese: "Quine's Dilemma," by Roger F. Gibson, Jr., *Synthese* 69 (1986): 27–39.

University of Chicago Press: "Quinean Ethics," by Owen J. Flanagan, Jr., *Ethics* 93 (October 1982): 56–74; "Flanagan on Quinean Ethics," by Roger F. Gibson, Jr., forthcoming in *Ethics* 98 (April 1988); copyright © 1982 and 1988 by the University of Chicago, all rights reserved.